*Particular* **Voices**

*The MIT Press*   Cambridge, Massachusetts   London, England

*Particular* **Voices**   *Portraits of Gay and Lesbian Writers*

**Robert Giard**

This book was set in Janson by Graphic Composition, Inc. and was printed and bound in the United States of America.

Library of Congress Cataloging-in-Publication Data

Giard, Robert.
  Particular voices : portraits of gay and lesbian writers / Robert Giard.
    p.   cm.
  ISBN 0-262-07180-0 (alk. paper)
  1. Authors, American—20th century—Portraits.   2. Gays' writings, American—History and criticism—Theory, etc.
3. Homosexuality and literature—United States.   4. Lesbians—United States—Portraits.   5. Gay men—United States—Portraits.   6. Gays—Literary collections.   I. Title.
PS153.G38G515   1997
810.9'920664—dc21
  [B]                                          96-47002
                                                  CIP

# Contents

**Foreword**  *Julia VanHaaften*

WILDE YOU'LL NEVER DIE!! The tomb
of Oscar Wilde, Père Lachaise
Cemetery, Paris, 1991

When I think about Bob Giard's *Particular Voices*, his emblematic portraits of Allen Ginsberg and Joan Nestle come instantly to mind. These cultural icons are so well-known and so widely reproduced that I can no longer recall whether I had seen them before 1990 when Bob wrote to me about his project to photograph contemporary American gay and lesbian literary figures. I was immediately impressed by the key facets of this personal assignment: the elegantly restrained yet completely engaging and intimate images; the historical community of literary creators it represented; its thesis in Bob's desire to honor the centrality of literature and information, which libraries make accessible freely and confidentially, as a vitalizing and validating force in the life experience of many gay people; the ambitious scale of the project itself; and his striking progress to date. (We have Bruce Cratsley, whose photographs I admire and had begun to acquire for the permanent collection, to thank for suggesting to Bob that he contact me.)

An appointment to view *Particular Voices* soon followed, and with a single purchase The New York Public Library's collection was modestly launched. My initial choice (via the Miriam and Ira D. Wallach Fund), of one of Bob's earliest portraits, *Allen Ginsberg with His Own Portrait of William Burroughs* (1985), was guided by the existence of a significant archive (one hundred prints) of photographs by Allen Ginsberg especially printed and inscribed for the Photography Collection. What better complement to this holding than a playful portrait of its creator depicted in the act of showing another photographer one of his own. (Plus, it contained a portrait of Burroughs not in The Library's archive!—two for the price of one.) However, not content to collect just one or two of a series when a larger selection should be obtained, I naturally envisioned the acquisition of additional prints representing the most important figures from his record.

My initial desire for a few choice additions quickly grew to archive proportions as Bob continued to expand the scope and vision of his project, so that today the Wallach Division's Photography Collection is *Particular Voices*'s largest institutional collector. Each of the more than one hundred exquisite $16 \times 20$ inch black-and-white prints was chosen first for artistic reasons and then rationalized on the basis of the subject's prominence and cultural significance. Bob and I tried to be representative in terms of male to female, geographic location, and influence. Beyond a few nationally prominent figures, however, gay literature was terra incognita to me. Patiently, Bob—the former teacher—led me through its recent history, proving an impartial critic and a reliable historian. As I made my selections, Bob pursued his subjects around the nation and I came to look forward to his postcards, with economically minuscule handwriting, signaling the advent of another body of portraits and literature to learn about.

The commitment of The Library to Robert Giard's *Particular Voices* series is founded on seemingly unconnected and perhaps unlikely bits of fact. Some are personal, others institutional; still others are political in the very broadest sense, concerning visibility, knowledge, and influence. The most obvious resides in the confluence of photographic portraiture with literary achievement as a natural area of attention—most readers are eager to see the face of the author behind the words. The Library has, for example, an outstanding collection of hundreds of portraits by Carl Van Vechten held in the Berg Collection for British and American Literature, the Theatre Collection, and the Schomburg Center for Research in Black Culture. In addition, there are portrait files in the Print Room, the Schomburg Center, and the Theatre Collection at the Library for the Performing Arts that contain images of poets, novelists, journalists, editors, and playwrights. The Ginsberg archive mentioned above consists largely of snapshots and studies of Ginsberg's literary contemporaries from the 1950s to the present.

Building the archive for posterity is a major objective of all primary sources collecting in the research library community. As an institution consecrated to the free interchange of ideas and information, The New York Public Library has in the last decade, under the leadership of former Associate Director of the Center for the Humanities Rodney Phillips, committed time and resources to the social phenomenon of increasingly public and forthright expression concerning sexual orientation and all its literary manifestations. For example, in 1988, the International Gay Information Center archives came to the Rare Books and Manuscripts Division. This acquisition in turn helped lead to gifts of related collections from other gay-and lesbian-related organizations such as Fierce Pussy, ACT UP/NY, and Gay Men's Health Crisis, as well as such individuals as Howard Brown, Martin Duberman, Diana Davies, Rudy Grillo, Jonathan Ned Katz, Craig Rodwell, and Israel David Fishman, the last-named a founding leader of the American Library Association Task Force on Gay Liberation. For in the final analysis, the library community historically has been professionally hospitable to gays. In 1994 The Library drew on some of these and other collections for its historic exhibition *Becoming Visible: The Legacy of Stonewall* on the twenty-fifth anniversary of those pivotal days in September 1969, overseen by NYPL curator of Manuscripts Mimi Bowling, with Fred Wasserman and Molly McGarry.

In recent years the Photography Collection has acquired—by gift, purchase, and bequest—several other photograph collections relevant to the documentation of gay history and lifestyles. Two of the most notable are physique photographs from the 1950s by Bruce of L.A. and insider coverage of New York's annual Gay Pride Rally and Parade by Bruce Cratsley. Additional gay photograph collections have arrived by arrangement with the Coalition for the Arts's Estate Project, which connects work with a permanent institutional home upon an artist's untimely death from AIDS: Mark Hood's witty urban collages are not particularly "gay" in any visual or descriptive way, whereas Joseph Caputo's wrenching documentation of the first AIDS quilt presentation in Washington, D.C., specifically is.

Not much older than the statistical generation of baby boomers, Robert Giard set out in the mid-1980s to capture photographically the first wave of the postwar, beatnik into baby-boom generation to achieve literary prominence and general public recognition as *gays*. To his great pleasure (and credit) Bob also sought out their surviving spiritual and literary predecessors, ensuring that his visual history is honest and coherent, and that these seminal figures are thereby honored. It has been a true professional privilege to work with him to help build this archive for the future.

JULIA VANHAAFTEN is Curator of Photographs, Miriam and Ira D. Wallach Division of Art, Prints and Photographs, The New York Public Library / Center for the Humanities.

**Self-Portrait of a Gay Reader**   *Robert Giard*

—the point is to look . . .   *Dodie Bellamy*

That's all I can do, describe.   *Mark Doty*

**George Stambolian** with Dürer Self-
Portrait, Amagansett, NY, 1987

When I was ten years old, I looked up the word "homosexual" in the family dictionary. Symbolic act: I've been a gay reader ever since.

*Particular Voices* begins and ends with the picture of a book. The book is my theme. In his essay on gay writing, Christopher Bram asserts that "we need a history of readers as well as authors," and Joan Nestle implies the same throughout her own essay on lesbian writing. My project is as much about reading as it is about writing, as much about readers as it is about writers. As my friend and neighbor George Stambolian knew so well, all portraits are a form of self-portrait, and this book is very much the autobiography of one gay reader.

I have always turned to books, seeking through them to gain perspective on experience. There were of course the classics which formed a part of my general education—books by Whitman and Cather, Stein and Proust, Wilde, Colette, Forster, Gide, and Mann. But the first books which in the sixties I deliberately sought out because I knew them to be written with specifically gay content or by homosexuals were by Vidal, Baldwin, Isherwood, Mart Crowley, and Isabel Miller. These were followed in the early seventies by novels by Rita Mae Brown and Patricia Nell Warren.

This is a book of portraits of gay and lesbian writers. I made the selection from a much larger body of photographs which I began in 1985 and on which I am still at work. Be advised that what you see here is not intended to be definitive. It is a microcosm, not a pantheon, not a canon. It is, I hope, representative—of my project and of the subject of gay and lesbian writing.

I can trace the origins of this project back to several specific events.

Every June my lover Jonathan and I would participate in New York City's Lesbian and Gay Pride march. My response was characteristically one of heady immersion in the communal experience of celebrating the Stonewall Rebellion of 1969. That particular June in 1985, a friend suggested that after the march we go over to the Public Theater to see the evening performance of Larry Kramer's *The Normal Heart.* As I sat watching the play unfold in the darkened space of the arena-style theater, its walls inscribed with the names of the dead, some of which I recognized, I was moved to a sense of urgency. The general euphoria of the march earlier in the day was coming up against this dramatization of present suffering and loss, a renewed consciousness of the historical indignities which gay people have encountered, and a further reminder that my own days could prove briefer than most of us are accustomed to anticipating. By the end of the evening, I had arrived at a decision about my work: that it should be of use to other gay people by recording something of note about our experience, our history, and our culture.

A few weeks later, in July, my friend Bill took me for my birthday to a performance of William Hoffmann's play *As Is.* This occasion confirmed my intention to attach whatever skill or insight I might possess to an overtly gay/lesbian theme. There had always been a pronounced gay element in my work. Many of my portraits were of gay people. Some of the nudes—of men, usually gay men—could be described as homoerotic. Nevertheless, these gay or homoerotic elements were not the same as a sustained body of work that chronicled a significant aspect of gay life. Here were the pieces: I was gay; I was a portrait photographer; and books had helped form me. My own undergraduate degree was in English and American Literature, and I held an M.A. in Comparative Literature.

Soon after, I wrote to both Kramer and Hoffman, asking if I might do their portraits, and in August of 1985 I photographed Hoffmann, thereby inaugurating the project.

At about this same time, George Stambolian was editing the first volume of what was to become New American Library's *Men on Men* series of new gay writing. We were both deeply interested in books and pictures that spoke to us as gay men. He was reading and encountering members of the Violet Quill in New York City and the gay experimental fiction writers of San Francisco. George suggested that I, as a portrait photographer, might like to photograph some of them. In September, at the apartment of critic David Kalstone, I photographed Edmund White, over from Paris for the promotion of the recently published *Caracole*. My archive was under way.

When I first undertook this work, I did not realize just how extensive a task lay ahead of me. Nor did a lot of other people, gay or straight. When I'd inform them that I had so far photographed thirty writers for the series, they'd regard me with surprise and query, "You mean there are more?" I was learning myself that there were quite a few more. Six months from its inception, I found that I was committing every available moment to the project.

I began with men because I was familiar with their books and their experience and had some initial contacts. Within a year, having read more lesbian writing, I started to photograph women. Since I had always been a reader, there was a nucleus of authors whose work I already knew. I wrote to them. That same good friend Bill who took me to *As Is* was a member of Men of All Colors Together in New York City. He put in a word for me with poet and playwright Assotto Saint (Yves Lubin) who in turn referred me to Samuel R. Delany, Sapphire, and members of Other Countries. This pattern would repeat itself as one writer would lead me to others and I accumulated numerous scraps of paper bearing names, addresses, phone numbers, and book titles. Thus began the process of haunting the bookstores, reading the work of an author, communicating first by letter, eventually following this up with a phone call, setting a date, and finally traveling to the writer to make the portrait.

My work began close to home in New York City and gradually branched out from there. Assembling the archive entailed a literal journey. The place name which accompanies each portrait indicates where that photograph was made. In most, though not all, cases, I traveled to the writer's home base. I grew interested in the gay and lesbian culture of a particular city or region and in the writers who spoke from that place, regardless of whether their work was widely known elsewhere. Whenever I wasn't teaching and could come up with the money—and sometimes even when I couldn't—I traveled to photograph for the series. Often I felt like Mercury, bearing greetings, gossip, and opinions across time and space from one member of the writers' community to another.

I never learned to drive, for reasons that probably mingle in equal parts history, chance, economy, aesthetics, and pathology. As the narrator in Douglas Sadownick's novel *Sacred Lips of the Bronx* (1994) comments: "I liked seeing people more than I liked seeing cars." I love the whiff of romance and adventure, largely a holdover from an earlier epoch of history, that clings to public transportation, not to mention the ample opportunities it affords to read, observe, meditate, and, not least, practice the art of patience. I always travel with a snack and a book or two: food for both body and spirit.

My memories of gathering these portraits are of a distinctly physical nature, of getting me, my knapsack of film and equipment, and my tripod from one destination to another. I remember walking—whether the few blocks on upper Broadway in New York City from Joan Nestle at the Lesbian Herstory Archives to Marilyn Hacker or the few miles along Santa Monica Boulevard in Los Angeles that separated Forman Brown's El Centro Avenue house-cum-theater from Harry Hay and John Burnside's La Cresta Court bungalow, since destroyed by fire. Or bicycling in summer to playwright Joe Pintauro, in autumn to Blanche Wiesen Cook and Clare Coss, in winter to novelist James McCourt and Vincent Virga, author of the queer Gothic *Gaywyck*. Taking a ferryboat to Audre Lorde on Staten Island, Jane Rule on Galiano Island, Chrystos on Bainbridge Island. A bus and taxi combination to May Sarton. A train to Minneapolis for the *James White* and *Evergreen Reviews*. Trying to figure out which Los Angeles city bus might get me, in the days immediately following the '94 earthquake, to Joseph Hansen, who was living a block away from a collapsed section of the freeway.

I recall weather too and precise meteorological conditions. The heat, humidity, and wafting of a small fan in Holly Hughes's New York City apartment. Heavy rain and sudden deep puddles en route to poet/artist Joe Brainard. The morass of snow and slush I had to navigate to reach David Leavitt by bicycle and Lesléa Newman by train. The aftershocks I waited out in Los Angeles before tripping the shutter with my cable release. Street flooding in the Midwest during the summer of '93, visible from historian Jim Steakley's front stoop in Madison, Wisconsin.

There was a personal journey too, and a part of it was back in time. I had grown up in a working-class neighborhood in Hartford, Connecticut, in the 1940s and 1950s,

attending a parochial school of Franco-American, Irish, Italian, and Slavic kids, some of whose parents and probably all of whose grandparents had come from "the old country." I encountered these Franco-American working-class roots once again in reading David Plante's *Francoeur Trilogy*, set in Providence, Rhode Island, and in conversations with poet Steven Riel and historian Allan Bérubé, both of whom grew up in the Connecticut Valley.

When I entered public high school, I was automatically placed on the slower track, despite the fact that I had been a good student in grammar school. It was simply assumed that most kids coming out of my neighborhood, boys in particular, were not "college material" and would go on to enter the factory system, or, if they were to move up the social and economic ladder, the insurance companies. Maybe one or two of us would become a priest or a nun. During my freshman year a senior, who, I was to learn years later, was gay, took me under his wing and introduced me to books, theater, and opera. I can recall today our enormous disappointment when, on a Saturday excursion into New York City, we were unable to get tickets to see Deborah Kerr in *Tea and Sympathy*.

A budding autodidact, each week I would check out from the Hartford Public Library a novel, a play, and the libretto for that coming Saturday's matinee broadcast from the Metropolitan Opera. On the mezzanine of G. Fox and Company, one of Hartford's wonderland department stores, I could peruse the Modern Library series as well as Nancy Drew and the Hardy Boys. It was here in the mid-fifties that I came across the 1953 Vintage paperback of *In Search of Theater* by Eric Bentley and glimpsed the possibility of art and literature as an elevated vocation. I already knew from my parochial school education, along with the times tables and how to diagram a sentence, the gravity of that concept of vocation. Bentley's book—in my mind's eye it has a purple cover—inclined me in that direction, as much for its promise of life and culture beyond Hartford as for its actual words. One year into my project, I was able to photograph Eric Bentley.

I went on to study literature in college and graduate school. I've returned regularly to Hartford to see my family and on one occasion to make a portrait for this archive of early gay rights activist Foster Gunnison III. He was living in a spanking new high-rise on the site of one of those glittering movie palaces of my youth, occupying three adjacent apartments: one for his gay rights collection, one for his railroad memorabilia, and a third for his last enthusiasm, smokers' rights.

Sometimes I am asked what being gay or lesbian has to do with being a writer. I make the assumption that a book issues from the whole person. That person may include what is being relegated to the background, to an obscure corner, or even suppressed. Of course, for most of the writers whom I have photographed, being lesbian or gay or bisexual was right up there in the forefront—on the big screen. It is often the source from which the writer draws character and event, language and image. It weaves itself around the themes of family, identity, spirituality, history and politics, sex, love, gender, and death.

Some have compared being gay to being left-handed. I tend to believe that sexual orientation cuts a little more deeply into your life. It counts for something: whom you desire, whom you love, with whom you choose to live—or not to live. How can it not count to recognize at some level, no matter how submerged or close to the surface, that for many people you are somehow less—less man or less woman, less human, less serious, less significant, less

deserving? Can it really make no difference realizing that some feel subtle or downright contempt for who you are, even hate you, and are convinced that you have no history, no story worth telling or worth listening to, that you are not even out there in the world, existing? With this series I want the world to know that we *are* here, have a past, and many stories to tell.

*Particular Voices* is a self-portrait, an autobiography, a journey; it is also a collaboration. By and large, the subjects of these photographs met me halfway—more than halfway. Everyone sat with full knowledge of the nature of the project.

When I began, my intention was to photograph living, working authors. Now, ten years later, as I review not just this selection but the entire archive to date, I find myself looking at a slice of literary and social history. There are faces that are not in the larger collection and consequently do not appear in the pages of this book. Tennessee Williams and Jane Chambers died in 1983, and Truman Capote in 1984, not long before I undertook the work. Isherwood died soon after—in 1986, but before I could make my first trip to the West Coast. I had just recently sent off a letter to James Baldwin when news of his death arrived in 1987. Of course, much as I would like to have their portraits, I have no idea whether they would have been willing to sit for me.

A small percentage never responded to my initial letter or chose not to return my phone call. A certain number declined to be photographed, offering reasons both thin and thoughtful. Some individuals were brusque, others more polite and even introspective, sharing with me their hesitation. A few—Robert Duncan, Gale Wilhelm, Richard Hall, for example—felt that they were too ill or fragile or altered to be photographed. Some I simply did not reach in time:

Bruce Nugent, James Barr, May Swenson, Reinaldo Areinas, Karen Brodine, James Kirkwood, Ethyl Eichelberger. Again, I cannot predict what their responses would have been. Playwright Scott McPherson died after I made initial contact with him but before I could get to Chicago. Nor is my work finished.

As for the images and texts that *do* appear between the covers of this book, there is an organizing principle behind the selection and the sequencing. I open with the idea of the book, the word, the record, the archive, and move to some early pioneering figures, forms of oppression, Stonewall, gay liberation, and lesbian feminism. There follow sections on history, family, community, and identity—this last pervades many portions of the book—as well as clusters of poetry, fiction, and theater. The final part begins with attention paid to AIDS and illness, caring, death, and mourning, followed by portraits and writings that intersect with political, ethical, and moral issues. After a visionary crescendo, courtesy of Tim Miller, Bertha Harris, and Tony Kushner, a quiet coda returns us to the writer alone, to the book, and to a reaffirmation of language and story. It's been my ungrateful task to choose, from the more than five hundred photographs that I have taken, a smaller group that might represent others whose achievements are no less estimable. I've sought both to convey the range of writers and to suggest the variety of audiences out there eagerly awaiting their words. Most urgent for me was to pay tribute to those who made significant contributions in the earlier phases of our history. To all of those whom I have already photographed but whose portraits I was unable to include here and to those whose pictures I have yet to make, you *are* here in these pages. There is someone standing for you and for others like you.

For a while now, the entire enterprise of traditional portrait photography has been called into question. No doubt it is true that there is a problematic relationship between a picture and "real" knowledge. The photographer hovers somewhere between the effort to see clearly and the projection of his or her personality. A portrait embodies both our will to know and the limits of our knowledge.

Nevertheless, an impulse to pay attention, to point out, and to record persists. Furthermore, there continues to be, even in the face of all this uneasiness about the portrait process, a desire to be seen, to be known, to be counted. Perhaps the portrait has always been, at best, poised somewhere between withholding and disclosure. However, the portrait remains with us. It is hard, when invited, not to look.

Past, present, and future converge here.

Portraiture is all about paying attention in the present. Nevertheless, throughout the book, there is a valedictory quality, a looking back at our life in this century as we look to the possibilities ahead. Furthermore, in an age of disks and cyberspace, I am considering the book as we have known it in the past, a comforting physical object that may be held as we turn the pages, follow its patterns, and seek its meanings. Finally, I've made this record with an eye to the future. Photography is par excellence a medium expressive of our mortality, holding up, as it does, one time for the contemplation of another time. This motif infuses all portrait photography with a special poignancy. It is my wish that tomorrow, when a viewer looks into the eyes of the subjects of these pictures, he or she will say in a spirit of wonder, "These people were here; like me, they lived and breathed." So too will the portraits and the words which accompany them respond, "We were here; we existed. This is how we were."

# "I Wanted to Live Long Enough to Kiss a Woman":* The Life of Lesbian Literature    *Joan Nestle*

The ghost of Gertrude Stein visits
the Lesbian Herstory Archives,
New York, NY, 1988

Lesbian literature is both the holder and the breaker of secrets. Revelation and reticence mark its texts as it does the lives of its people, its women. This shifting need, to say the new word and to disguise it, the self-conscious effort to speak beyond the immediate audience, the immediate time, to another kind of hearing was a richly destabilizing force in the early history of lesbian literatures.

Traditionally European lesbian literature starts with the lyric odes of Sappho, a poet who had to create an original meter to fit her new songs of love. Refusing to sing the glories of war, she called out to her students to pay close attention to the pains and pleasures of the heart. In her own time, Sappho's lyrics won her mostly praise, but a more judgmental age and culture found her work obscene and burned her manuscripts. Now we have only fragments, pieced together from the excerpts inscribed on the sides of urns and the quoted lines embedded in the surviving manuscripts of other writers who seized upon her melodies to enrich their own texts. Yet out of the constrictions of histories not her own, she calls to us: "You may forget but/Let me tell you/ this: someone in/some future time/ will think of us" (trans. Mary Bernard). Fragments—that is how it all started. Shards of expression. Bones of language poking through the silences.

Over the European ages, male novelists and poets create their own versions of this fragmented figure, giving her a voice that reflects their own erotic politics. Balzac, Zola, Flaubert, Swinburne, Maupassant, D. H. Lawrence, and Henry James titillate their readers with portraits of the ob-

sessed and sterile lesbian, her eyes glowing with need, her womb barren of life. Even the painters found her a powerful symbol of the tantalizing demimonde; Toulouse-Lautrec and Degas sketch lesbian kisses and intertwined thighs as part of their flirtation with the forbidden edges of French society. Exotic, scary, powerful—the "lesbian" was created as a stock character in both novels of social realism and fantasies of passion. However, all during the years of this male literary representation of the deviant woman, another community was growing: the lesbian reader. Searching for parts of herself, she carefully examined each text that carried any clues.

Jeanette Foster, a young American college student in the 1930s, embodies this lesbian reader who needed both a text to validate her own erotic stirring and to connect her to a history of erotic survivors. Early in her college years, she had witnessed the punishment of two young women whose crime was so secret, it was never publicly labeled. Foster had heard the whispers and observed the injustice; appalled at her own ignorance about same-sex love and at the force of social judgment it had to bear, she began her lifelong work of piecing together a literary narrative that would make lesbian life possible. For over twenty years, she haunted libraries and antiquarian bookstores, carefully annotating her discoveries. Finally, in 1955, Foster transformed secrets and shame into a book called *Sex Variant Women in Literature*. Foreshadowing the work of Grier, Faderman, and Zimmerman, Foster created an anatomy of lesbian culture, a radical political act in 1950s America.

In the beginning of the European twentieth century, the lesbian writer and reader had to contend with new ideas about sexuality and psychology that would both give new freedoms and destroy old innocences. In their pursuit of docu-

---

*Words spoken by a Jewish lesbian survivor of a Nazi concentration camp, explaining how her reading of a Polish translation of Radclyffe Hall's *Well of Loneliness* as a young girl strengthened her resolve to survive the experience.

menting the sexual varieties of the human experience, Havelock Ellis, Krafft-Ebing, and Freud created descriptive clinical categorizations of sexual difference that gave the lesbian writer a two-edged sword. While this new topography of the human psyche allowed "inverts" and "deviants" to exist in a scientifically cold but tolerant world, it also made suspect the swooning friendships between women that had flourished in the nineteenth century. Previous to the public discourse of the sexologists, Lillian Faderman has asserted, friendships between women both in society and in literature were viewed as romantic attachments free of the stain of the body, but once the spotlight of public attention shone on this world, innocence and purity were no longer assumed. On one hand, female independence and autonomy became synonymous with sexual deviance, but while this endangered the sanctity of romantic friendships, it made possible a new narrative of gender experience. Thus accusations of "perversion" opened up the door to an imaginative exploration of difference.

When Radclyffe Hall sat down to write her culture-shaping novel, *The Well of Loneliness*, both edges of the sword—the possibility of public acceptance of her deviance and the medical need to pathologize a woman's passion and strength—were biting into her imagination. Knowing she was not a "traditional" woman, John as she was called by her lover and wife Lady Una Troubridge, seized the territory of the novel to explore the inner life of a "masculine" woman and so started the turbulent history of this one text in the literary and social development of several lesbian communities.

In 1928, trusting in the power of revelation, she allowed *The Well* to face its public, but while the sexologists had made scientific discussion possible, a novel that had a lesbian kiss and God and country was too much for modern England. Unlike what Oscar Wilde had faced over forty years earlier, Hall found herself in a courtroom, defending not herself but her novel. Refusing to dilute the novel's theme by endorsing her lawyer's depiction of the novel as as study of romantic friendship, Hall watched her novel fall to the censor's axe. *The Well*, however, found its audience in France, in America, and in just five years it was turning up in other novels as a cultural code word that allowed lesbians to find one another.

The 1920s were rich with lesbian voices, voices that pointed in the direction of other imaginative choices in revealing the complexities and, sometimes, fun of the lesbian perspective. Natalie Clifford Barney, who appears in Hall's novel as an avant-garde salon hostess, and her circle of friends, which included Renee Vivien and Romaine Brooks, Gertrude Stein, Magaret Anderson, Jane Heap, and Djuna Barnes, were part of the expatriate community in Paris that gave birth to literary modernism. Witty, iconoclastic, experimental, they joined with European writers like Colette and Virginia Woolf to transform both prevailing literary forms and the public language of woman's desire. Perhaps because of their stylistic density or their avoidance of public gender bending, except in Woolf's playful *Orlando*, or the indulgences allowed exiled foreigners, these lesbian writers were not hauled off to court to defend their revelations; their sense of style and self-possession would form a living legacy for lesbian writers of the early seventies.

Back on American homeground and reaching into the previous century, many lesbian writers chose not to reveal their erotic selves in their public texts. While living lives that ran the whole gamut of same-sex possibilities—from romantic friendships to Boston marriages to husband and wife unions—writers like Sarah Orne Jewett, Emily Dickinson,

Amy Lowell, Willa Cather, Edna St. Vincent Millay, Angelina Grimke, Elizabeth Bowen, Daphne du Maurier, Jane Bowles, Bryher, H. D. (Hilda Doolittle), Sara Teasdale, Elizabeth Bishop, Muriel Ruckeyser, Lorraine Hansberry, Lillian Smith, and Mary Renault created a legacy of coded and layered work that is rich with ambiguity and shifting surfaces. Caught in the tension between their lives and their art, between the need to tell a secret and to keep one, they offer texts that are reinvented with each new decade of sexual politics. Some writers, like May Swenson and May Sarton, emboldened by the gay and lesbian civil rights battle, took long journeys in working out what it means to have their work included in the gay and lesbian anthologies of the 1980s.

Starting in the 1920s with the blues lyrics of Bessie Smith and Ma Rainey, with the poetry of Mae V. Cowdery, with the cabaret acts of Gladys Bentley and Moms Mabley, the communal and private life of urban African-American lesbians began to form its own literary narrative. By the 1930s, lesbian writers had started to chronicle a growing community of women who were leaving small towns and cities throughout this country and coming to the larger cities to find both employment and one another. *Diana of a Thousand Cities*, written by Diana Fredericks and published in the 1930s, is an early example of the paperback novel, usually written under an assumed name like "Randy Salem" and sold as pornography, that made its way into neighborhood drugstores. Marked by their covers, which bore titles like *Women of the Shadows* and *Journey to Lesbos*, many of these books offered lesbian readers what they could get nowhere else: romance, erotic images, and lesbian folklore. Continuing well into the sixties, the lesbian pulp novels paradoxically formed a body of survival literature while at the

same time employing the enforced iconography of sexual deviance. Authors like Valerie Taylor (*Journey to Fulfillment*) Gale Wilhelm (*Torchlight to Valhalla*), Patricia Highsmith writing as Claire Morgan (*Price of Salt*), and Ann Bannon (*Odd Girl Out* and the *Beebo Brinker* series) created characters and situations that were recognizable and vivid. On their pages, department store clerks and secretaries made their way to all-girl bars in Greenwich Village and learned how to survive in a policed and marginalized community. Before the advent of independent lesbian publishers and during some of the most restrictive political and social decades of this country, these paperbacks, priced at thirty-five cents a copy and marked "for adult readers only," became treasured subversive narratives, lovingly passed on from one lesbian to another, often as a way to welcome a young woman "into the life."

In America, the birth of the formal lesbian and gay civil rights struggle can be dated to the late forties when a group of gay men living in California, Harry Hay among them, formed the Mattachine Society. Using their organizing skills honed in the Left and progressive movements, they began what would become this country's homophile movement. As part of its outreach campaign, Mattachine published *One Magazine*, a small journal that made its way to thousands of gay people, bringing them up to date on legal, medical, and cultural issues of importance. Scattered among the depressing news of police raids and the latest religious diatribes were short stories, poems, and essays.

In 1956, Daughters of Bilitis, the first lesbian civil rights organization, under the leadership of eight women, including Del Martin and Phyllis Lyon, launched its own journal, *The Ladder*. From 1956 until 1972, *The Ladder* published original lesbian fiction and poetry with extensive reviews of literature of lesbian interest. In 1972, Barbara Grier, who was to become the founding spirit of Naiad Press, the largest lesbian press in the world, became the editor, continuing the tradition of her bibliophile predecessor, Jeanette Foster. Here in the pages of this small journal with its early esoteric cover design, a ladder reaching up to the heavens as silhouetted young women climb its steps, appeared many of the nascent issues that were to find fuller and more varied voices in the decades to come: assimilationism versus separatism, the propriety of butch-fem, the alliance between lesbianism and feminism. Mailed out in brown paper wrappers or found in the racks of offbeat journals carried by counter culture neighborhood stores, *The Ladder* gave lesbian writers such as Rita Mae Brown and Jane Rule a forum for their work. Other writers, like Lorraine Hansberry, engaged by the cultural issues covered in it pages, wrote letters outlining their dreams of a more accepting world.

*The Ladder* and its 1940s' predecessor, *Vice-Versa*, the brave creation of "Lisa Ben," launched the history of lesbian journals in this country that made a public lesbian literature possible in the second half of the twentieth century—a literature whose production is in the hands of lesbians, whose readership is a clearly defined lesbian community, and whose writers no longer use a language of codes or subterfuge. Most of the lesbian writers who look out at you from the pages of this book had early pieces published in such journals as *The Furies, Sinister Wisdom, Chrysalis, Azalea, Quest, Conditions, Thirteenth Moon, Feminary, Focus, Common Lives/Lesbian Lives,* and *Lady Unique Inclination of the Night,* which affixed a handmade pouch of spiritual blessings on the cover of every one of its issues.

Under the impetus of the women's movement, lesbians moved to control their own cultural forums. Throughout the 1970s and 1980s lesbian presses and publishers sought out authentic and yet heterogeneous lesbian voices: Bertha Harris, Judy Grahn, Kate Millett, Martha Shelley, Karla Jay, Dorothy Allison, Michelle Cliff, Beth Brant, Kitty Tsui, Cherríe Moraga, Cheryl Clarke, Lee Lynch, Wyllyce Kim, Jewelle Gomez, Paula Gunn Allen, Gloria Anzualdúa, Becky Birtha. Building on the first wave of independent writers like Charlotte Bunch who along with Rita Mae Brown and photographer Joan Biren gave the Washington, D.C., publication *The Furies* its bite and wit, like Fran Winant who formed her own Violet Press to produce her early books of poetry, like Alma Routsong who peddled her now classic novel *A Place for Us* (*Patience and Sarah*) on the corners of Greenwich Village streets, like June Arnold and Elana Nachman/Dykewomon, who created a new gender-free language in their experimental novels *The Cook and The Carpenter* and *Riverfinger Women*, lesbian publishing ventures such as Daughters, Diana, Persephone, Naiad, Firebrand, and Kitchen Table invested themselves in making sure lesbian writers would not have to go underground again.

Inspired by the liberating struggles of other marginalized peoples, lesbian writers forged into new terrains. Playwrights and performance artists such as Jane Chambers, Maria Irene Fornes, Paula Vogel, Holly Hughes, Rebecca Ranson, Pamela Sneed, Claudia Allen, Carmelita Tropicana, Lisa Kron, Dorothy Randall Gray, and Chris Cinque; theater companies such as WOW, whose founding performers—Peggy Shaw and Louise Weaver—have always held true to the vision of a grassroots lesbian performance space, now reach audiences across the country. Sometimes, recalling the early days of this century, their words call down the wrath of government funding agencies and conservative watchdog groups, but these performers and writers have made a choice to create a challenging public narrative about gender, class, and race, issues that often make their art hot to handle.

Sparked by this avalanche of talent and vision, women's bookstores sprang up around the country, combining business with politics, celebration with conflict, and always providing the essential service to lesbian writers—making their books available while mainstream bookstores turned their backs. Places like Mama Bear, Old Wives Tale, Djuna Books, Womanbooks, Emma's, and Judith's Room became reading rooms, discussion forums, gathering places for their cities' often embattled lesbian community. Now there are over a hundred feminist bookstores in this country, and a publication, *Feminist Bookstore News*, edited by Carol Seajay, reports on the art of publishing, promoting, and selling lesbian and feminist books. The publishing surge that began in the early 1970s and continues today—Aunt Lute Books, Cleis Press, Seal Press, Clothespin Fever Press, joining the long-established Naiad Press and Firebrand Books—documents how far we have come as a writing and reading community from the days when Jeanette Foster pledged herself to a lifelong search for literary tracings of the lesbian presence.

One of the unique tenets of much of modern lesbian literature in this country has been its insistence on a moral social vision, moral in its critique of power and exclusion. Even the vagaries of style were used to question the status quo; June Arnold in *The Cook and the Carpenter*, Elana Nachman/Dykewomon in *Riverfinger Woman*, Jill Johnston's later columns in the *Village Voice* with their idiosyncratic transformations of language, while calling up the far-reaching shadow of Gertrude Stein, also insist on a new social order, where language is freed from the domination of the male gender. Anthologies like *Home Girls* (Barbara Smith, editor), *This Bridge Called My Back* (Cherríe Moraga and Gloria Anzaldúa, editors), *Nice Jewish Girls* (Evelyn Torton Beck, editor), *A Gathering of the Spirits* (Beth Brant, editor) and *Compañeras* (Juanita Diaz Ramos, editor) are constructed around erasing silences, giving African-American, Native-American, Jewish-American, and Latina lesbians a place to control fully the depiction of their own realities. Sally Gearhart and Joanna Russ use the conventions of the utopian novel and science fiction to imagine worlds where women run free, creating new histories and inhabiting worlds where gender is both fluid and superfluous.

Ann Allen Shockley, a long-time civil rights activist fighting for racially inclusive library collections, courageously brings together the Baptist Church and lesbian desire in *Say Jesus and Come to Me*. Audre Lorde, who also bore the African name Gamba Adisa, who was poet laureate of New York State and a major voice in the international struggle against racism, transformed autobiography in *Zami* into biomythography, giving her the space to travel deeply into the Caribbean and lesbian history she carried with her. Michelle Cliff in *Abeng* and Gloria Anzaldúa in *La Frontera* also reach into cultural histories, allowing their home selves to break through the surfaces of their narratives. Barbara Smith, Elly Bulkin, Judith McDaniel, Mab Segrest, Kate Rushin, Irena Klepfisz, Minnie Bruce Pratt, and Melanie Kaye/Kantrowitz devote long years to anti-racist, anti-classist and anti-anti-Semitic work, in poems, essays, short stories, and in creating presses like Kitchen Table: Women of Color press, which exists to ensure the visibility of writings by women of color. Adrienne Rich, a writer of international acclaim, has endured critical repudiation because she writes from the place where politics and poetry wear the same face, where the urge of the word is tied to dreams of hope and descriptions of despair. Not only are the secrets of the lesbian text being broken open by these writers and so many more but the power of their disclosures is being put at the service of far-reaching social revisioning.

The lesbian literatures of the 1980s and 1990s show the influence of a postmodern worldview, though in some sense lesbian literature has been transgressive from its first voicing to the present. The AIDS crisis and all it represents in terms of governmental betrayal, accumulated personal losses, increase of homophobic violence, and the complexity of desire in the face of death are intrinsic parts of the work of Sarah Schulman, Eileen Myles, Rebecca Brown, Madelyn Arnold, Lydia Swartz, and Gerry Gomez Pearlberg. Gayle Rubin, Pat Califia, Dorothy Allison, Madeline Davis, Elizabeth Kennedy, Sapphire, and Leslie Feinberg, whether they are writing theory or history, short stories or novels, confront us with edges and insights that demand rethinking and deeper confrontations with our own versions of lesbian selves.

For many years, lesbian authors have portrayed the pain of an enforced sexuality on the body and the psyche of women, but in the last ten years another text has been created, one that celebrates and explores, in concrete and frank language, the wonder of lesbian lust. Journals like *Bad Attitude* and *On Our Backs* have been joined by numerous anthologies of erotic fiction. Pat Califia, Tee Corinne, Dorothy Allison, myself, and a host of other writers have decided to answer the outsider's question, "But what is it that they do?," for the insider's enjoyment.

Because of the continued success of lesbian presses, genre fiction is thriving; lesbian detective stories fill up the shelves. Barbara Wilson, Mary Wings, Claire McNab, Nikki Baker, Ellen Hart, and Katherine V. Forrest infuse a blend of feminism and lesbianism into the tough boys' territory, creating a new social and erotic atmosphere for the whodunit. Daphne du Maurier, who wrote her renowned romances from within her closet doors, is now followed by a generation of lesbian romance writers who have nothing to hide: Sarah Aldridge, Lee Lynch, Georgia Cotrell, and Robbi Sommers are just some of the carriers of the romantic torch. Enthusiasts of the short story and the novel have the work of Ruthann Robson, Sandy Boucher, Lucy Jane Bledsoe, Jacqueline Woodson, Shay Youngblood, Blanche McCrary Boyd, Judith Schwartz, Cherry Muhanji, Vickie Sears, Dionne Brand, Carole Maso, Jenifer Levin, Terri de la Peña, and Lesléa Newman, as well as numerous anthologies to fulfill their hunger. All the themes of modern lesbian life live in these stories: abuse and its survival, love and its complexities, family life and its challenges, homophobia and its scars, gender and its reshaping.

Finally we have our poets, the lesbian poets who return to the fragment, the bare bones of language, but not this time because silence seems the only possible language. This time they choose their language under the direction of their own imaginations: Pat Parker, Audre Lorde, Judy Grahn, Marilyn Hacker, Joan Larkin, Naomi Replansky, Joy Harjo, June Jordan, Jane Miller, Maureen Seaton, Judith Barrington, Olga Broumas, Chrystos, Melinda Goodman, Susan Griffin, Irena Klepfisz, Honor Moore, Adrienne Rich, Suzanne Gardinier, and more.

Writing a text to match the scope and passion of Robert Giard's photographs is an impossible task. His camera has captured a vitality and abundance of lesbian creativity that my words can only hint at. The images that await you on the following pages, only a small selection from hundreds, will carry the documentation of the lesbian and gay imagination into the future in a way that Jeanette Foster could not have envisioned forty years ago. Like her, we cannot predict which way world culture and politics will go in the next hundred years in relation to its lesbian and gay citizens. Will our words be allowed to live? Will our children be able to find us? As long as these photographs exist, with their queer, complex, and different faces, the world will know that at one point in time, with our words and our bodies, we chose revelation.

# Mapping the Territory: Gay Men's Writing    *Christopher Bram*

Statue of Walt Whitman, Arrow Park,
NY, 1994

For the longest time, gay men and women seemed to be a community of the book, at least on weeknights when we weren't a community of the bar. With all other public forums closed to us, we searched the libraries for titles that would tell us a simple truth: You are not alone. The books were never so important as when there were so few. More often than not, the truth came disguised as sad morality tales or shelved under "Psychology, Abnormal."

The great change began roughly twenty years ago, in both the books and the people who read them. The flowering of gay and lesbian writing has been astounding, a literary explosion that is positively uncanny in an age that many critics consider post-literate. It was part of a larger explosion, of course. We are not only a people of many books now but of parades, political campaigns, PAC funds, and TV commercials. The literature has become as wide and diverse as the communities that make and use it. A remarkable variety is suggested by Robert Giard's photographs, a dense forest of American faces.

One is tempted just to stroll through the forest and point out favorite trees. Each picture represents a unique combination of experience, talent, and achievement. All that these people have in common is that they write, and they're gay, and some are extraordinary. But one can't help wanting to sktech a map of the territory in an attempt to understand where we are.

Joan Nestle and I have divided the challenge of offering an overview by gender. But we are not on separate planets. When I first began to read as a gay man, wanting to see what my life might be like, I found pieces of myself in Jane Rule and Adrienne Rich that were missing in John Rechy and Allen Ginsberg. I know several women who get the rest of their story from reading men. We complete each other's work, and gender is no more a barrier here than it is—or should be—in the world at large.

What is gay literature?

Most authors dislike the very notion, although few still bristle over being called "gay writers." The smart ones respond with jokes. "A gay play is any play that wants to sleep with another play of its gender," quipped playwright Robert Chesley. Such wisecracks come out of anxiety. Writers want to work their private visions for the largest audience possible. The idea of "literature" is narrow enough without an adjective attached. And writing within any minority group has a noisome political burden. We're expected to provide witnesses for the defense and even the prosecution, when what we really want to do is offer new words that everyone will remember and quote long after a particular trial is over.

Nevertheless, the best working definition of gay literature might be that it's the fiction, poetry, drama, history, and essays written by, about, and for gay men.

All three prepositions are slippery. Does John Cheever qualify as a gay author? Just how gay are James Purdy's characters? The last, however, *for*, is the trickiest, and perhaps the most important. It posits an audience, part community, part market, something to support a writer's gamble that readers exist who will understand him, who can be moved, disturbed, soothed, or confronted in the most meaningful ways. Other readers are welcomed and the relationship is not exclusive. But as a writer myself, I feel that my first audience are those who have been in places of heart and mind that I know firsthand. I strive to write about equals for my equals, without condescension, apology, or stale preconception. It makes me more honest.

We need a history of readers as well as authors.

The early poems and novels often look like those proverbial trees that crash silently when nobody is around to hear. Yet there was an audience even before the writers dared to admit it. John Addington Symonds thought he'd discovered a fellow soul in *Leaves of Grass*, although when he wrote to Walt Whitman, repeatedly, the Good Gray Poet lied, refusing to sacrifice his hard-earned fame to be the figurehead of a secret society. Men who were "like that" recommended *The Portrait of Dorian Gray* to one another—and even some critics understood what Oscar Wilde's novel was really about, one reviewer claiming the tale would interest only outlawed lords and depraved telegraph boys.

It was an age of coded works, some more innocent than others. Herman Melville may have been unaware of how much he was revealing, but Henry James understood the stakes. Even Proust, who produced our first full picture of a gay communal underworld, pretended not to be writing about himself but creating an allegory of the universal Fall, with inversion standing in for original sin. One could chronicle the literary use and abuse of homosexuality, from Balzac to Genet to Mishima, as not just a piece of life but an all-purpose metaphor for criminal ideas.

Proust, however, marks another important turning point: the triumph of the autobiographical. In the chaos of the twentieth century, personal experience was seized as a rare patch of solid ground. Autobiography no longer hid in the machinery of three-decker novels or the formal conventions of poetry but became a subject in itself. Women wrote about their experience as women; the writers of the Harlem Renaissance, about black life. Even straight white men—and it's odd that more isn't made of this—no longer pretended to write about everyone but focused exclusively on their experience as straight white men. More and more often, when a male author loved men, it blatantly entered his work. Somerset Maugham managed to keep it out, but not André Gide or E. M. Forster—although he stashed those stories in a drawer—or the respectably married Thomas Mann.

There was a slow but steady accumulation of titles over the following decades. In the United States alone, we had *A Better Angel* (1933) by Forman Brown, under the pseudonym of Richard Meeker, *The Young and Evil* (1933) by Parker Tyler and Charles Henri Ford, *The Gallery* (1947) by John Horne Burns, *The City and the Pillar* (1949) by Gore Vidal, *Quatrefoil* (1950) by James Barr, *Giovanni's Room* (1956) by James Baldwin, *Kaddish and Other Poems* (1961) by Allen Ginsberg, *A Single Man* (1964) by Christopher Isherwood, *Totempole* (1965) by Sanford Friedman, *City of Night* (1966) by John Rechy, *The Boys in the Band* (1968) by Mart Crowley, *Selected Poems of Frank O'Hara* (1973), and *The Story of Harold* (1974) by George Selden, under the pseudonym of Terry Andrews. To the world outside, these works were often sensational nightmares or exotic case studies, but to those in the life they were partial yet badly needed mirrors of reality.

The great change only began with the 1969 Stonewall riots. Literature is rarely in sync with current events. The ground had to be prepared. The first half of the seventies saw the rise of gay newspapers, the growth of gay and lesbian bookstores, the birth of gay literary magazines and presses. Michael Denneny, one of the founders of *Christopher Street* magazine in 1976 with Charles Ortleb and Patrick Merla, has said that they expected to be inundated with a backlog of unpublished work. No, it was not until there was an outlet for such writing that most of it was written. The first successful gay male novel of the new era was *The Front Runner* (1973), whose author was a woman.

As is often noted, 1978 was the miracle year of gay letters, with the publication of *Dancer from the Dance* by Andrew Holleran, *Faggots* by Larry Kramer, and *Nocturnes for the King of Naples* by Edmund White, as well as *Tales of the City* by Armistead Maupin, *Splendora* by Edward Swift, and *The Family* by David Plante. The map suddenly changed; it was as if a whole new country had appeared. The predecessors went from being random curiosities to ancestors, forefathers.

This new country grew slowly at first. There was an attempt to create gay fiction by pouring homosexuality into old commercial molds. None of this genre writing took except for mysteries, a form already being explored by Joseph Hansen since *Skinflick* in 1970. An important twist to the story is that commercial gay fiction, gay trash if you will, did not succeed. Gay writing in all genres has had to have some seriousness and craft if it were to find readers. When gay men want trash, they buy the same potboilers as everyone else. Even our pornography tends to be better written than its heterosexual counterpart. Editors flopped around in a hunt for the next Andrew Holleran, assuming gay fiction must be about life in ghetto fast lanes. That assumption was loosened in 1983 by the success of Robert Ferro's *The Family of Max Desir,* then broken for good in 1986 with David Leavitt's *Family Dancing.* Publishing discovered the gay midlist novel. The books would not be bestsellers, but there was a small yet solid market for good, intelligent writing. Every house suddenly seemed to want a homosexual man or two in its catalogue.

AIDS added further urgency to the work. Writers needed to write and, more important, readers needed to read about this new slow-motion cataclysm, desperate to name their fear, grief, and hope. Looking through these portraits, one cannot help being struck again by how many careers were cut short by the epidemic: George Whitmore, Charles Ludlam, Allen Barnett, Richard Hall, Roy Gonsalves, Alan Bowne, Melvin Dixon, John Preston, Manuel Ramos Otero, Stan Leventhal, Paul Monette, Essex Hemphill, and too, too many others. We cannot even guess at the careers silenced before they could begin.

Nevertheless, the literature continues to grow. It expands in new directions as more voices join in, gay men out-side or straddling the ghetto, authors who bring with them other strong identities, racial, ethnic, religious, even sexualities that aren't strictly gay. When our commentators get sociological, they expect a hierarchical unity of gay life. The reality requires something closer to William James's treatment of religion, a *Varieties of Homosexual Experience,* which our poetry and prose have begun to provide.

When we discuss authors, the natural tendency is to order them by generation: before Stonewall, after Stonewall, AIDS and beyond. Each group seems to work with and against what was produced by the preceding flight.

There's truth to that but it's not the full story. We talk about generations as if they come at ten- or even five-year intervals, ignoring the fact that it takes years to write a book, and most writers find voices and turfs long before they're published. Authors often don't know who their siblings are until after the fact. If the flurry of novels about gay men and their families in the eighties seemed like a reaction against the family-less novels of the seventies, it wasn't just the writers responding but the editors and reading public.

More important to a writer is the tradition he or she chooses to work in, the different sets of examples, styles, and strategies that run like currents through every genre. These streams are not timeless but do have surprising longevity. In mapping the territory, tradition can be used as the longitude to the latitude of generation.

Let me use literary fiction as an example. It's the area which I have thought about the most in an attempt to understand who I might be. Here's my list of contemporary traditions, illustrated with a sample of elders and peers:

a.  *The avant-garde.* Experiments and moods, prose that ranges from the shapely to the raw, with just a breath of story, often erotic, to keep the pieces aloft. William Bur-

roughs, Robert Glück, Dennis Cooper, Sam D'Allesandro. (It says something about the continuity of tradition
that what we call the avant-garde has retained much the
same identity for at least fifty years.)

b. *The Gothic.* Fiction as expressionist fever dream, a dark
unreality with its own nightmare truths. James Purdy,
Truman Capote, Paul Bowles, Alfred Chester.

c. *High art.* Fiction as beautiful, autonomous object, perfect sentences and cool control taking precedent—although emotion often slips in. Edmund White, Andrew
Holleran, Robert Ferro, Christopher Coe, Matthew
Stadler, Fenton Johnson.

d. *Emotional realism.* Good prose is still important but the
emphasis is on character and feeling. Christopher Isherwood, James Baldwin, Jonathan Strong, David Leavitt,
Allen Barnett, Melvin Dixon, Jaime Manrique, Lev Raphael, Michael Cunningham, Paul Reidinger, Philip
Gambone, Paul Russell, Norman Wong, Mark Merlis,
Scott Heim.

e. *Comic realism.* Story is more important, with a friendly
looseness to the prose. Serious topics are touched on but
the overall tone is good-humored. Armistead Maupin,
Edward Swift, Stephen McCauley, David Feinberg, John
Weir, Larry Duplechan.

f. *Fabulism.* An overload of story, character, and invention,
three-ring circuses where conventional structure and realism are ignored, although the emotion is often very
real. Larry Kramer, Allan Gurganus, Tom Spanbauer,
Randall Kenan, Peter Gadol.

Established traditions also play through poetry (the decep-
tive formality of Henri Cole or Timothy Liu, say, as
opposed to the prosy conversation of Frank O'Hara and
Walta Borawski or the fiery chants of Essex Hemphill and
Assotto Saint) and playwriting (the subversive sit-com of
Harvey Fierstein, the raw yet neatly sliced life of Joe Pintauro, the wild monologues of Luis Alfaro).

As with any game of categories, my breakdown of fiction can't help being debatable and even comic. There are
writers like Dale Peck who merge traditions (Gothic, high
art, and fabulism) and others who change over time (Edmund White has shifted toward emotional realism). As for
myself, I want to be an emotional realist but suspect I'm a
comic realist and wonder if I might not be happier trying
my hand at fabulism. Then there are writers in other
genres whose work overlaps literary fiction. Michael Nava
writes mysteries that are full of emotional realism. Lars
Eighner's erotic tales touch on high art. Samuel R. Delany's
science fantasy dances in and out all over the map.

Nevertheless, two truths emerge from this provisional
list: First, at any given time, one tradition seems to hold
sway. The Gothic dominated before Stonewall, high art in
the seventies and early eighties (political identity smuggled
into literature in a gorgeous Trojan horse) and, this year at
least, emotional realism. But the other important point the
list makes is that no tradition ever quite disappears. There's
always somebody out there practicing each one. Isherwood
wrote plainspeak realism long before Stonewall. A writer in
his twenties, Joey Manley, has returned to the Gothic to
play variations on Purdy and Capote.

Criticism tends to privilege one tradition over another,
which is what makes this categorizing potentially pernicious. Just as there's constant debate over whose homosexuality is more authentic, there is endless argument over what
qualifies as true gay literature. Is Dennis Cooper, whose
work crosses over to straight fans of the experimental, more
gay than David Feinberg? Is Allan Gurganus, because his
fiction contains such a broad range of sexualities, detrimen-
tally less gay then Felice Picano? What constitutes the true

subject of gay fiction? Coming out? Sexual adventure? Unrequited love? AIDS? All of the above?

These are cheater questions, shortcuts for judging books without having to read them. The truth is that good work can be done in any tradition, and bad work too. And just when you're about to declare a branch dead, a writer comes along and breathes new life into it.

We also need to acknowledge that none of these traditions is strictly gay. There are pansexual kinships and influences. Edmund White is frequently compared to Vladimir Nabokov, for good reason. I hear the lessons for both Faulkner and García Márquez in Randall Kenan's books. So it goes outside fiction, too. Tony Kushner's polyphonic epics draw upon Shaw, Brecht and, of course, Shakespeare. James Merrill's work is permeated with the enameled wit of Pope and Eliot. Mark Doty somehow marries Merrill with Frank O'Hara, but I also catch Galway Kinnell's love of physical anarchy in his poems. There are echoes of Rilke in Bernard Cooper's essays, and of C. Van Woodward and other literate historians in Martin Duberman's history.

More is happening here than new wine in old bottles. The bottles can be remarkably elastic. The strongest wine sometimes alters the shapes from within, so that certain traditions will never be the same.

There was once something called the literary mainstream. Its recent demise is often mourned as a Balkanization of culture, as if books were now at war. I see the change as a badly needed case of decentralization. As recently as the seventies, any novel written by a woman about women was considered "women's fiction," parochial, or, worse, feminist. Forty years ago, African-American writing was treated as backroom, defined solely by Richard Wright and Ralph Ellison, which was easy to do when so few other black authors were published. But in a world of books as diverse as the real world of men and women, boundaries begin to blur. We must recognize that, instead of a mainstream, there are many currents, a hundred tributaries that don't remain separate from one another or always flow in the same direction.

I believe that literary truth must be personal and local before it can have value for a wider audience. Working within a specific community anchors literature, gives it relevance and human scale. The best art often seems to come out of smaller city-states of culture: from Elizabethan London, to the Italian and Japanese cinemas of the fifties and sixties, to New York City's own Theater of the Ridiculous. Not coterie art, not in-crowd art, but art that looks hard through the particular to the general. As the century comes to a close, the writing of gay men, like that of women— both lesbian and straight—and racial minorities, brings a powerful electric charge of personal experience and communal need to American culture.

Gay literature is a small yet miraculously vital country, a hothouse republic of letters, a country within a country, and not as foreign as it looks. If readers can find value in writers as strange and alien as Shakespeare, Marlowe, Spenser, and other Elizabethans without being seventeenth-century Englishmen themselves, they certainly don't need to be gay to get emotion and insight from a poem by Maurice Kenny or a story by Paul Gervais or a play by Victor Bumbalo.

As gay writers have learned from others, certainly non-gay readers can learn from us. We cultivate our own corners of the forest but are free to visit each other. We owe it to ourselves to visit. Difference, combined with curiosity, respect, and empathy, can produce a living multidimensionality, like a landscape seen with a hundred different pairs of eyes.

*Portraits* **and Texts**

I once believed that the work of advocacy was the work of picket lines and protests, sit-ins and street theater, public hearings and private lobby efforts. Now I realize that the work of advocacy is also the work of the word—our talking and teaching, our writing and witnessing, our texts and testimonies. It is true that work aims at useful effect and words at intersubjective understanding. There is certainty about work, visible accomplishments to be admired, a changed world to appreciate. The word is more often gratuitous, its usefulness never certain, its effects problematic. But the word is also gesture and action. People are mobilized by its power and caught in its consequences. Through the word we incite others to act, set forth our meanings, indicate what is to be done.

JONATHAN G. SILIN
in *Sex, Death, and the Education of Children: Our Passion for Ignorance in the Age of AIDS* (1995)

**Jim Kepner,** Boston, MA, 1992
Kepner established the International Gay/Lesbian Archive: Natalie Barney/Edward Carpenter Library in Los Angeles, CA.

4

But the most searing reminder of our colonized world was the bathroom line. Now I know it stands for all the pain and glory of my time, and I carry that line and the women who endured it deep within me. Because we were labeled deviants, our bathroom habits had to be watched. Only one woman at a time was allowed into the toilet because we could not be trusted. Thus the toilet line was born, a twisting horizon of Lesbian women waiting for permission to urinate, to shit.

The line flowed past the far wall, past the bar, the front room tables, and reached into the back room. Guarding the entrance to the toilet was a short, square, handsome butch woman, the same every night, whose job it was to twist around her hand our allotted amount of toilet paper. She was us, an obscenity, doing the man's tricks so we could breathe. The line awaited all of us every night, and we developed a line act. We joked, we cruised, we commented on the length of time one of us took, we made special pleas to allow hot-and-heavy lovers in together, knowing full well that our lady would not permit it. I stood, a femme, loving the women on either side of me, loving my comrades for their style, the power of their stance, the hair hitting the collar, the thrown-out hip, the hand encircling the beer can. Our eyes played the line, subtle touches, gentle shyness weaved under the blaring jokes, the music, the surveillance. We lived on that line; restricted and judged; we took deep breaths and played.

But buried deep in our endurance was our fury. That line was practice and theory seared into one. We wove our freedoms, our culture, around their obstacles of hatred, but we also paid our price. Every time I took the fistful of toilet paper, I swore eventual liberation. It would be, however, liberation with a memory.

JOAN NESTLE
in *A Restricted Country* (1987)

**Joan Nestle,** New York, NY, 1987
With Deborah Edel and Judith Schwartz, Nestle founded the
Lesbian Herstory Archives in New York City.

**J.K.**   What was the origin of the name "Mattachine"?

**H.H.**   One of the cultural developments I had discussed and illustrated in my Labor School class on "Historical Materialist Development of Music" was the function of the medieval-Renaissance French *Sociétés Joyeux*. One was known as the *Société Mattachine*. These societies, lifelong secret fraternities of unmarried townsmen who never performed in public unmasked, were dedicated to going out into the countryside and conducting dances and rituals during the Feast of Fools, at the Vernal Equinox. Sometimes these dance rituals, or masques, were peasant protests against oppression—with the maskers, in the people's name, receiving the brunt of a given lord's vicious retaliation. So we took the name Mattachine because we felt that we 1950s Gays were also a masked people, unknown and anonymous, who might become engaged in morale building and helping ourselves and others, through struggle, to move toward *total* redress and change.

About the fall of 1951 I decided that organizing the Mattachine was a call to me deeper than the innermost reaches of spirit, a vision-quest more important than life.

HARRY HAY
in an interview in Jonathan Ned Katz's *Gay American History* (1976)

**Harry Hay** (*left*) with **John Burnside** (*right*), Los Angeles, CA, 1989
In 1950 Hay founded the Mattachine Society, an early homophile group.

Daughters of Bilitis began with eight women: four Lesbian couples, four blue-collar and four white-collar workers, among whom were one Filipina and one Chicana.

The idea originated with Marie, a short brown-skinned woman who had come from the Philippine Islands. In contrast to the United States, the Philippines have no public sanctions or discrimination against homosexuals and Marie envisioned a club for Lesbians here in the States that would give them an opportunity to meet and socialize outside of the gay bars. She also felt that women needed privacy—privacy not only from the watchful eye of the police, but from gaping tourists in the bars and from inquisitive parents and families.

So in our eagerness to meet other Lesbians, we found ourselves on the evening of September 21, 1955, laying plans for a secret Lesbian club. For four consecutive weeks we met to draw up a constitution and bylaws. At the fourth meeting there still remained the question of a name for the fledgling organization.

"How about Daughters of Bilitis?" Nancy suggested. The rest of us looked at her blankly.

"I ran across this book by Pierre Louys that has in it this long poem called 'Songs of Bilitis.'" Nancy held up the volume she'd been holding on her lap. "It's really quite beautiful love poetry, but what's even more interesting, Bilitis is supposed to have lived on Lesbos at the time of Sappho."

"We thought that 'Daughters of Bilitis' would sound like any other women's lodge—you know, like the Daughters of the Nile or the DAR," Priscilla added. "'Bilitis' would mean something to us, but not to any outsider. If anyone asked us, we could always say we belong to a poetry club."

PHYLLIS LYON AND DEL MARTIN
in *Lesbian/Woman* (1972, updated 1991)

**Del Martin** (*left*) and **Phyllis Lyon** (*right*), San Francisco, CA, 1989
In 1955 Lyon and Martin began the Daughters of Bilitis, the first
lesbian organization in the United States.

What really changed my image and gave me a much more positive feeling about homosexuality—even though I still thought it was a misfortune that needed to be changed— were the novels. In some of the so-called scientific materials I read, there were references to fiction titles, and I began to seek these out. As I remember, *The Well of Loneliness* was the first book I latched on to. It was widely mentioned in the documentary literature and was also more available than others. That really hit home, because even though there were differences between myself and the heroine, I still identified with her emotional state, with her feelings. The book has an unhappy ending, of course. It was distressing to me, I suppose, that at the end she deliberately sends away her lover, in order to allow the younger woman the chance of "normal happiness." It seemed to me that she had sacrificed needlessly.

I was living at home at the time. I had flunked out of college and gone back home in disgrace. I had taken a clerical job, and I was spending my spare time in the public library and going to secondhand bookstores. My father went into my room one day, found my copy of *The Well of Loneliness*, and wrote me a letter about it. We were living in the same house, and he couldn't bring himself to talk to me about it. He sent me a letter telling me this was an immoral book, that I had no business owning it, and that I should dispose

of it. Not by giving it away, where someone else would be contaminated by it; I had to dispose of it by burning. Well, I simply hid it better and told him that I had disposed of it. This incident reinforced my sense of taboo about the subject matter.

Then I began to find other books. I remember specifically *Extraordinary Women* by Compton Mackenzie, *Dusty Answer* by Rosamond Lehmann, and an earlier novel by Radclyffe Hall, which was not explicitly Lesbian but which did have a covert Lesbian theme, and was strongly feminist, although I didn't see it as such at the time—a book called *The Unlit Lamp*. I searched these out, I made some effort to get them, and they, in turn, led me to other titles. The fiction made a big difference, because here were human beings that were fleshed out in a dimension that simply wasn't available in the scientific materials, which were always examining us from a clinical point of view in which we were diseased case histories. I appreciated the novels, because even though most of them had unhappy endings, they did picture us as diverse people who had our happinesses.

BARBARA GITTINGS
in an interview in Jonathan Katz's *Gay American History* (1976)

**Barbara Gittings** (*left*) and **Kay Tobin Lahusen** (*right*), Philadelphia, PA, 1991
Gittings, former editor of *The Ladder,* an early lesbian publication, helped assemble "A Gay Bibliography" for the American Library Association. Tobin Lahusen, an activist, wrote and photographed for *The Ladder.* In 1972 she co-edited with Randy Wicker *The Gay Crusaders,* a book of interviews with fifteen gay and lesbian leaders, including Gittings, Lyon and Martin, and Craig Rodwell.

Afterwards I went up on the stage to speak to him. "Did you really know Whitman?" I asked in awe.

"Yes," said the patriarch. "I was very young, but he shook my hand and laid his hand on top of my head."

"Well, Mr. Garland [Hamlin Garland, author of *A Son of the Middle Border*]," I said with the rash bravado of youth, "I've shaken your hand, but may I put my hand where Whitman laid his?"

He was somewhat taken aback, but he smiled.

"I want to be linked in with Whitman," I stammered, feeling my face grow red.

"Of course," he said, and bowed his head slightly. I put my left hand on his silver mane. Someone giggled, and I escaped sweating into the auditorium.

That was the genesis of the idea. The next day I wrote to Lord Alfred Douglas, finding his address in *Who's Who*. . . . [T]hree years later, 1937, . . . I made my first trip to Europe as a literary pilgrim, to visit Gertrude Stein at her invitation, and Thomas Mann and André Gide, all of whom seemed a little curious about me. And after a little side trip to Trinity College at Cambridge University to visit Whewell's Court and Great Court B2 where A. E. Housman had lived for twenty-five years (to stand silently weeping, with chills along my spine), I wrote again to Lord Alfred and received a short note from him, asking me to come down to Hove to call on him should I find the time during my London stay.

I must honestly admit that I had no interest whatsoever in Lord Alfred Douglas as a person or as a writer, but only in the fact that he and Oscar Wilde had been lovers, and that back in those shrouded days the name of Wilde had a magic all its own for us who had to live without the benefits of liberation or exposure of our wicked lives. Besides, I was in my twenties and Lord Alfred was by then sixty-seven, and in anyone's book that's *old*. To go to bed with him was hardly the most attractive prospect in the world—it was terrifying, even repulsive. But if I wanted to link myself to Oscar Wilde more directly than I was linked to Whitman, there was no other way.

SAMUEL M. STEWARD
in *Chapters from an Autobiography* (1980)

**Samuel M. Steward** (Phil Andros), Berkeley, CA, 1988

While working in the catalog department of the Kansas City, Kansas, Public Library in the winter of 1956, I came across a reference in the Cumulative Book Index to a new book, *Sex Variant Women In Literature*, by a Jeannette H. Foster. I was then twenty-three and I had been collecting Lesbian literature for seven years. Having gathered nearly one hundred books I felt that I had achieved some sort of record and I had long since planned to write a book about this special genre. So my joy at finding this book was mixed, momentarily, with sadness. Calling a local bookstore to order a copy, I had the good fortune to be told that they had "heard" that the author was right in the Kansas City area, connected with the University of Kansas City (now University of Missouri at Kansas City). I called the university library and found that, indeed, Dr. Jeannette H. Foster was on their staff, away for the day, but right in my area.

With the brashness that only a twenty-three-year-old might have, I found her telephone number and called her up. Thus began my lifelong friendship with the author, and my love affair with the book. Beside me as I write this is my first copy of it, and its inscription reads "For Barbara Grier, This Volume's First Fan. Jeannette H. Foster". The world of Lesbian literature has changed a great deal in these past twenty years, but, as those of you who are reading this afterword in its proper place know, there is no replacement for this book, and no substitute for its in-depth analysis of the genre.

BARBARA GRIER
in the Afterword to the 1975 Diana Press and 1985 Naiad Press reissues of Jeannette H. Foster's *Sex Variant Women in Literature* (1956)

**Barbara Grier** (*right*) and **Donna McBride** (*left*), New York, NY, 1989
In 1972 Grier and McBride, along with Sarah Aldridge and Muriel Crawford, co-founded The Naiad press, one of the first lesbian publishing houses. Grier was also editor of *The Ladder* from 1968 to 1972. In 1967, under the pseudonym "Gene Damon," she published (with Lee Stuart) *The Lesbian in Literature,* a bibliography.

**Craig Rodwell,** New York, NY, 1992
In 1967 Rodwell opened the earliest gay and lesbian bookstore—
the Oscar Wilde Memorial Bookshop in Greenwich Village.

**Carol Seajay,** San Francisco, CA, 1994
Since 1976 Seajay has published and edited *Feminist Bookstore News*. In addition, she co-founded Old Wives' Tales Bookstore in San Francisco.

**The Bloodroot Collective,** Bridgeport, CT, 1995
*From left to right:* Noel Furie, Selma Miriam, and Betsey Beaven. The Collective founded this restaurant/bookstore in 1977 and has published three cookbooks that intersperse excerpts from women's writings with vegetarian recipes.

In the half-century between 1890 and the beginning of the Second World War, a highly visible, remarkably complex, and continually changing gay male world took shape in New York City. That world included several gay neighborhood enclaves, widely publicized dances and other social events, and a host of commercial establishments where gay men gathered, ranging from saloons, speakeasies, and bars to cheap cafeterias and elegant restaurants. The men who participated in that world forged a distinctive culture with its own language and customs, its own traditions and folk histories, its own heroes and heroines. They organized male beauty contests at Coney Island and drag balls in Harlem; they performed at gay clubs in the Village and at tourist traps in Times Square. Gay writers and performers produced a flurry of gay literature and theater in the 1920s and early 1930s; gay impresarios organized cultural events that sustained and enhanced gay men's communal ties and group identity. Some gay men were involved in long-term monogamous relationships they called marriages; others participated in an extensive sexual underground that by the beginning of the century included well-known cruising areas in the city's parks and streets, gay bathhouses, and saloons with back rooms where men met for sex.

The gay world that flourished before World War II has been almost entirely forgotten in popular memory and overlooked by professional historians; it is not supposed to have existed. This book seeks to restore that world to history, to chart its geography, and to recapture its culture and politics. In doing so, it challenges three widespread myths about the history of gay life before the rise of the gay movement, which I call the myths of isolation, invisibility, and internalization.

GEORGE CHAUNCEY
in *Gay New York: Gender, Urban Culture, and the Making of the Gay Male World, 1890–1940* (1994)

**George Chauncey,** New York, NY, 1991

the street was so long and *narrow* . . . so long and narrow
. . . and blue . . . in the distance it reached the stars . . . and
if he walked long enough . . . far enough . . . he could reach
the stars too . . . the narrow blue was so empty . . . quiet . . .
Alex walked music . . . it was nice to walk in the blue after a
party . . . Zora had shone again . . . her stories . . . she always shone . . . and Monty was glad . . . every one was glad
when Zora shone . . . he was glad he had gone to Monty's
party . . . Monty had a nice place in the village . . . nice
lights . . . and friends and wine . . . mother would be scan-
dalized that he could think of going to a party . . . without a
copper to his name . . . but then mother had never been to
Monty's . . . and mother had never seen the street seem
long and narrow and blue . . . Alex walked music . . . the
click of his heels kept time with a tune in his mind . . . he
glanced into a lighted cafe window . . . inside were people
sipping coffee . . . men . . . why did they sit there in the
loud light . . . didn't they know that outside the street . . .
the narrow blue street met the stars . . . that if they walked
long enough . . . far enough . . . Alex walked and the click
of his heels sounded . . . and had an echo . . . sound being
tossed back and forth . . . back and forth . . . some one was
approaching . . . and their echoes mingled . . . and gave the
sound of castenets . . . Alex liked the sound of the approaching man's footsteps . . . he walked music also . . . he
knew the beauty of the narrow blue . . . Alex knew that by
the way their echoes mingled . . . he wished he would speak
. . . but strangers don't speak at four o'clock in the morning
. . . at least if they did he couldn't imagine what would be
said. . . . maybe . . . pardon me but are you walking toward
the stars . . . yes, sir, and if you walk long enough . . . then
may I walk with you I want to reach the stars too . . . per-
done me senor tiene vd. fosforo . . . Alex was glad he had
been addressed in Spanish . . . to have been asked for a

match in English . . . or to have been addressed in English
at all . . . would have been blasphemy just then . . . Alex
handed him a match . . . he glanced at this companion ap-
prehensively in the match glow . . . he was afraid that his ap-
pearance would shatter the blue thoughts . . . and stars . . .
ah . . . his face was a perfect complement to his voice . . .
and the echo of their steps mingled . . . they walked in silence . . . the castanets of their heels clicking accompani-
ment . . . the stranger inhaled deeply and with a nod of
content and a smile . . . blew a cloud of smoke . . . Alex felt
like singing . . . the stranger knew the magic of blue smoke
also . . . they continued in silence . . . the castanets of their
heels clicking rhythmically . . . Alex turned in his doorway
. . . up the stairs and the stranger waited for him to light
the room . . . no need for words . . . they had always known
each other. . . . . . . . as they undressed by the blue dawn . . .
Alex knew he had never seen a more perfect being . . . his
body was all symmetry and music . . . and Alex called him
Beauty. . . . long they lay . . . blowing smoke and exchanging thoughts . . . and Alex swallowed with difficulty . . . he
felt a glow of tremor . . . and they talked and . . . slept . . .

RICHARD BRUCE (Bruce Nugent)
in "Smoke, Lilies and Jade" (1926)

One of the earliest published works of fiction by a black writer to deal
with the theme of homosexuality, this short story appeared in the first
and only issue of *FIRE!! A Quarterly Devoted to the Younger Negro Writer*,
edited by Wallace Thurman.

Tribute to **Bruce Nugent,** 1994
The art work is by Nugent; the portrait of Nugent is by Tom Wirth.

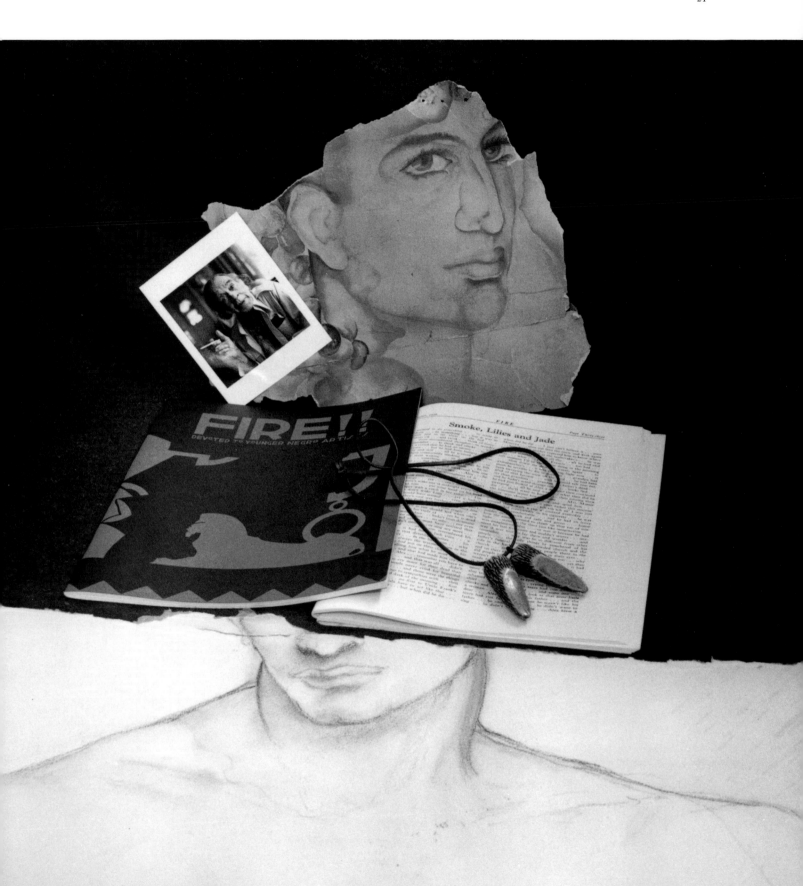

Gabriel and Louis had gotten a room in the same building with Karel. Karel's room was next door to theirs. He told them he was sleepy and left them.

In his own room after a while he thought he knew. He thought he knew he didn't quite know. But he knew. He would imagine he knew; that was just as good.

Instead of undressing and getting into bed he walked into the hall and knocked on their door. That was quite possible for him to do he thought; it was possible because they knew it was just possible. So there he was; in it; in the room.

Louis and Gabriel were stretched half-clothed on top of the bed. Some garments, very dirty, were flung about with a recklessness which Karel marked, the recklessness that was truly artistic.

Karel was on his guard with them; he felt a bit self-conscious because he had not been kind to them. Louis' trousers, drawn up by short suspenders, attracted him as his skin had attracted him at Julian's. Louis' face above a black sweater with a white mooncurved wide stripe draped over the chest was alive. Now, as mostly, as always almost, Louis conveyed thoughtfulness to him, thoughtfulness now behind a bruised mouth, and behind eyes. He permitted himself to look at Louis as he had thought of seeing him when on the other side of the wall. Yes he thought.

Louis' activity was in his favor. In repose his face was dark, even morbid. When smiling it attracted because it was evil and young. Moreover, Karel saw that his smile gave his jaw the correct proportion, the without which not beauty, in spite of the swollen spot on his cheek. He sat down by Louis' outstretched form and was gratified to have him move closer to him.

CHARLES HENRI FORD AND PARKER TYLER
in *The Young and Evil* (1933)

Forman Brown (*right*) with his cousin **Harry Burnett,** Los Angeles, CA, 1989

His hand, fumbling for the envelope, upset something which clattered to the floor. He stooped and felt for it under his chair. It was the "David." He held it upright in the palm of his hand, facing the window. Behind it the distilled yellow light of the winter afternoon, thin and fine and lucent, as honey, threw the tiny figure into tender silhouette. Kurt set it on the deep ledge of the window, and kneeling, turned it slowly about, smiling at the impertinent angle of the hat; the slim arm holding the broad sword as a boy might hold a baseball bat; the attenuated thigh; the round knee-joints; the slight swell of the belly; the small round buttocks.

He turned, almost with reluctance, to the telegram. "PLEASE TRUST ME" it said, "CAN EXPLAIN EVERYTHING ARRIVING BROOKWAY NINE FORTY SEVEN TONIGHT DAVID."

Kurt let the yellow square of paper slip to the floor, and a calmness flooded over him that he had never, he thought, known before. Kurt and David. You and I. It's got to be. Tonight David would be here with him, in this room, and the plan he had for the future, the house, the books, the music, the quiet, the whole precious dream, he would share with David. The certainty of his love for David, of David's love for him, was as absolute and as right and as restful as this pale and now fading light of the March afternoon. From the shelf nearby he took a book of poems he had bought in New York, opening it at random, leaned forward, and tilted the book to the dimming light. "Herakles and the Preliminary Fleece," he read.

*"And as he crashed through bush and chaining vine,*
*damning them all, and shouting out for Hylas—"*

for Hylas. And suddenly, unaccountably, he was a little boy again, and back in the ugly oak chair beside the front window in the house at home, straining his eyes over the Tanglewood Tales, or Bullfinch, or Gayley.

*"Hylas, the pale Praxitilean boy,*
*Dropped slowly through a world of wavering green,*
*Like a slow-motion picture on a screen, ·*
*Unreal, white, haloed with the alloy*
*Water had made of his metallic hair,*
*A floating sea-frond, gold and verdigris,*
*To the cool dim and pendulous languor he*
*had only seen in those perverse dreams where*
*Perfectest bodies by his narrow bed*
*Wove a white ravishment in his sleeping head."*

Across the page fell the shadow of the "David," reversed and distorted. He closed the book quietly and lay back in the chair, smiling and content, the years commingled and integrated in an enchantment he was unwilling to break. This poet, somewhere, understanding. Herakles and his Hylas, David and his Jonathan, Kurt and his David, Clayton and his dancing disciple. Strange that so suddenly, from such a swirl and seething, life should smooth to the calm of a summer pool—a pool so pregnant with quiet strength that all the fears and distrusts sank into it and out of sight. Strength here against laughter and derision, strength here for the spectral years ahead, strength, and joy in strength.

A knock at the door.

"Come," said Kurt, and almost added "Mother."

It was Herbert, the porter, with a bundle of firewood.

"Bless me, Mr. Gray! Didn't see you at all there in the dark, sir. Reading? In that light? You'll strain your eyes, sir. Better let me put on the lights."

Kurt smiled in the darkness.

"All right, Herbert. Put them on."

RICHARD MEEKER (Forman Brown)
in *Better Angel* (1933)

Laura finished her drink without answering. She put it down on the bar and looked for the bartender. She wouldn't care what Beebo said, she wouldn't look at her, she wouldn't answer her. She didn't dare.

"You don't need to tell me about it," Beebo went on. "Because I already know. I've lived through it, too. You fall in love. You're young, inexperienced. What the hell, maybe you're a virgin, even. You fall, up to your ears, and there's nobody to talk to, nobody to lean on. You're all alone with that great big miserable feeling and she's driving you out of your mind. Every time you look at her, every time you're near her. Finally you give in to it—and she's straight." She said the last word with such acid sharpness that Laura jumped. "End of story," Beebo added. "End of soap opera. Beginning of soap opera. That's all the Village is, honey, just one crazy little soap opera after another, like Jack says. All tangled up with each other, one piled on top of the next, ad infinitum. Mary loves Jane loves Joan loves Jean loves Beebo loves Laura." She stopped and grinned at Laura.

"Doesn't mean a thing," she said. "It goes on forever. Where one stops another begins." She looked around The Cellar with Laura following her gaze. "I know most of the girls in here," she said. "I've probably slept with half of them. I've lived with half of the half I've slept with. I've loved half of the half I've lived with. What does it all come to?"

She turned to Laura who was caught with her fascinated face very close to Beebo's. She started to back away but Beebo's arm around her waist tightened and kept her close. "You know something, baby? It doesn't matter. Nothing matters. You don't like me, and that doesn't matter. Someday maybe you'll love me, and that won't matter either. Because it won't last. Not down here. Not anywhere in the world, if you're gay. You'll never find peace, you'll never find Love. With a capital L."

She took a drag on her cigarette and let it flow out of her nostrils. "L for Love," she said, looking into space. "L for Laura." She turned and smiled at her, a little sadly. "L for Lust and L for the L of it. L for Lesbian. L for Let's— let's," she said, and blew smoke softly into Laura's ear. Laura was startled to feel the strength of the feeling inside her.

ANN BANNON
in *I Am a Woman* (1959)

## A Supermarket in California

What thoughts I have of you tonight, Walt Whitman, for I walked down the sidestreets under the trees with a headache self-conscious looking at the full moon.

In my hungry fatigue, and shopping for images, I went into the neon fruit supermarket, dreaming of your enumerations!

What peaches and what penumbras! Whole families shopping at night! Aisles full of husbands! Wives in the avocados, babies in the tomatoes!—and you, Garcia Lorca, what were you doing down by the watermelons?

I saw you, Walt Whitman, childless, lonely old grubber, poking among the meats in the refrigerator and eyeing the grocery boys.

I heard you asking questions of each: Who killed the pork chops? What price bananas? Are you my Angel?

I wandered in and out of the brilliant stacks of cans following you, and followed in my imagination by the store detective.

We strode down the open corridors together in our solitary fancy tasting artichokes, possessing every frozen delicacy, and never passing the cashier.

Where are you going, Walt Whitman? The doors close in an hour. Which way does your beard point tonight?

(I touched your book and dream of our odyssey in the supermarket and feel absurd.)

Will we walk all night through solitary streets? The trees add shade to shade, lights out in the houses, we'll both be lonely.

Will we stroll dreaming of the lost America of love past blue automobiles in driveways, home to our silent cottage?

Ah, dear father, graybeard, lonely old courage-teacher, what America did you have when Charon quit poling his ferry and you got out on a smoking bank and stood watching the boat disappear on the black waters of Lethe?

ALLEN GINSBERG
in *Howl and Other Poems* (1956)

As Ann bent down toward her, Evelyn took hold of the soft, damp hair at the back of Ann's neck and held her away. But, as Evelyn looked at the face held back from her own, the rain-gray eyes, the fine bones, the mouth, she felt the weight and length of Ann's body measuring her own. Her hand relaxed its hold, all her flesh welcoming the long embrace. But simple physical desire could not silence her recovering brain. Slowly, carefully, almost painfully, she turned Ann's weight in her arms until she could withdraw.

"I live in the desert of the heart," Evelyn said quietly. "I can't love the whole damned world."

"Love me, Evelyn."

"I do."

"But you don't want me?"

Evelyn looked at Ann, the child she had always wanted, the friend she had once had, the lover she had never considered. Of course she wanted Ann. Pride, morality, and inexperience had kept her from admitting it frankly to herself from the first moment she had seen Ann. Guilt and goodness must now keep her from admitting it to Ann.

"No relationship is without erotic feeling," Evelyn said. She had heard it somewhere at a cocktail party, an academic cocktail party. Someone else had added, as she added now, "But that doesn't necessarily mean it has to be acted upon." Ann looked away. "I'm sorry, Ann."

Evelyn wanted to say something else, to explain, to justify. "I'm married, Ann," she wanted to say. "I mustn't. I can't." But George could hardly save her now. He was not even a conventional excuse. "I don't know anything about this sort of thing," she wanted to say, but it was not true. If she had never actually made love to another woman, she was intellectually emancipated in all perversions of flesh, mind, and spirit. Her academic training had seen to that. "Forgive me, Ann," she might say; but Evelyn did not really want to be forgiven.

JANE RULE
in *Desert of the Heart* (1964)

**Jane Rule,** Galiano Island, British Columbia, 1994

Stephen's cabin-counselor, to whom he took an immediate liking, was new at Potawatomi. His name was Uncle Hank. When Stephen asked Uncle Hank what activity he was in charge of, he was surprised by his counselor's answer. "Totempole."

"Totempole? What's that?"

"Haven't you ever seen a totempole, Steve?"

"Sure, I have. In the Natural History Museum. But I never knew it was an activity."

"Oh," Uncle Hank reconsidered. "I guess I'm really in charge of arts and crafts."

"Where's Uncle Dave?"

"Who?"

"The *old* arts and crafts counselor."

"He isn't back this summer."

Uncle Hank's simple statement sent a tingle down Stephen's spine and saddened him, but only for a moment. After all Uncle Dave was pretty old and pretty ugly. As nice as he was, he had never been a favorite—not like Uncle Alf or Uncle Tony, both of whom were back! But even *they* were pretty ugly, pretty skinny compared to Uncle Hank.

For a moment Stephen stopped making his bed to observe Uncle Hank. He had such a big nose, big eyes, big hands; his thighs and calves looked very, very powerful exposed, as they were, below his khaki shorts. He was almost as tall as Daddy and just as good-looking, but altogether different— much, much younger, stockier, not bald. There was something untamed about Uncle Hank; something about his trout-colored curls, his intense black eyes, his prominent cheekbones and wiry body-hair that made him seem savage. And yet, he wasn't. He was easygoing, soft-spoken, sensitive. Stephen knew intuitively that Uncle Hank would never have to raise his voice or slam things down the way Daddy did. Somehow you could sense his strength without his giving any demonstration of it . . . "Uncle Hank," Stephen confided, "I'm awful glad you're in the bunk next to mine."

"Thanks, Steve. So am I."

SANFORD FRIEDMAN
in *Totempole* (1965)

So we climbed the gangplank. Sarah was afraid, her eyes big like a child's, but she kept up with me. The boilers were building pressure, getting ready, making a noise like nothing I'd ever heard. Like a dragon, perhaps. A herd of dragons. The deck pulsed under our feet like a panting dog, and it was hot though the wind off the harbor was cold.

"I've heard these things do blow up," Sarah said.

"And carriages overturn, and horses throw their riders, and walkers fall into pits, and oxen gore, and if we tried I'm sure we could smother in our beds." ("Bed," I amended in a whisper.) "Trees fall, lightning strikes. Let her blow!" (I whispered, "I don't care, while we're together.")

"Maybe you better hold my hand, so we won't get blowed apart," she whispered.

I took her hand. It was natural to feel timid and hold together. All the ladies were doing it. If I hadn't taken her hand someone else would have. She looked so darling, tall and worried there.

And late in the morning the tide came up the bay and up the river and our pilot nudged us out into it and the people on the deck waved and called, "Goodbye, goodbye," to the people on the dock who were shouting something our engines drowned out, but I read their lips and it was "goodbye" too. The way west was first north, up the Hudson. Not many of us would ever come back.

Midstream, the boat set to in earnest, so *fast*. A horse can gallop that fast, or seem to. It can make the wind whistle past your ears that way, for a little while. But a horse gets tired, and our wonderful big paddle wheels never did, and the tide behind us gave us the whole weight of the sea

as a shove. I held Sarah's hand and felt the ancient sea and the new wheels carry us to a life we had no pattern for, that no one we knew of had ever lived, that we must invent for ourselves on a razor's edge, and I tipped my head back and sang three hallelujahs. . . .

Sarah finished the bedstead, a shaggy rectangular frame on shaggy cornerposts. A cabinetmaker would have frowned. The thought of his frown made us laugh. We made a web of ropes stretched tight. On went the lumpy tick. On went the bridal sheets of fine linen from my hope chest, the Tree of Life quilt that was my grandmother's. Our bed was made. We stood holding hands admiring it. "O beautiful! O beautiful!" we said.

We lay down to test it and to begin our feast of love. I kissed her and enfolded her, fully trusting our hearts to flood us and our toes to curl. It was time for our feast, to have all we wanted, to be wild and careless and noisy and free. I would shout my triumph when Sarah groaned. I would groan for her. We would make the bed gallop. The floor would ring like a drum.

ISABEL MILLER
in *Patience and Sarah*, originally entitled *A Place for Us* (1969)

In 1971 this novel was the first recipient of the American Library Association's Gay/Lesbian Award.

**Isabel Miller,** Poughkeepsie, NY, 1992

The taxi driver in Rosebery Avenue, either from caution or moral indignation, had no intention of making a gesture in my favor. He stood in the road and continued to demand that I get out. This I did not immediately do. One of the boys started to drag me out. It was foolish of me to allow this to happen as, by resisting, I became part of the battle. As soon as I was in the street once more, the whole gang started to hit me from all sides. Almost immediately I fell on to my hands and knees in the gutter. For a second, I wondered whether I could stay there forever, but, fearing that I might be kicked, I staggered to my feet and was at once knocked across the pavement by a single, more carefully aimed blow. As I leaned against the front of Finsbury Town Hall covering my own equally ornate façade with my hands to try to prevent rivers of mascara from running down my cheeks, I said, "I seem to have annoyed you gentlemen in some way."

At this there was a sound of genuine amusement quite unlike the barking noise emitted by a lynching party. I knew that this was the moment to try to move away, though I could hardly see where I was going. As I lurched along the wall, voices shouted after me but no one followed. Apparently whatever point my enemies had wished to make had been established.

The mysterious thing in all such occurrences was not that strangers, sometimes without a word being uttered on either side, attacked me. It was that they never killed me. Certainly fear did not restrain them. I never made even a pretense of defending myself (not because my behavior was modeled on Christian ethics but because to try would only have provoked redoubled ferocity from my aggressors), and no one ever came to my aid. Also, these young men must have known that whatever they did to me, there would have been only the most perfunctory police inquiry into the incident, yet though on two occasions I have lain for a few seconds unconscious on the pavement, I was never damaged beyond repair. My assailants did not apparently require my death nor even my disfigurement. This was why I concluded that a large part of their motive for attacking me was to release their sexual curiosity in a manner consistent with their heavily guarded idea of manliness. They were only slightly concerned with forcing me to accept their superiority. If this latter was their whole aim, then all those street brawls were a waste of time. I regarded all heterosexuals, however low, as superior to any homosexual, however noble.

QUENTIN CRISP
in *The Naked Civil Servant* (1968)

**Quentin Crisp,** New York, NY, 1986

I remember how being young and Black and gay and lonely felt. A lot of it was fine, feeling I had the truth and the light and the key, but a lot of it was purely hell.

There were no mothers, no sisters, no heroes. We had to do it alone, like our sister Amazons, the riders on the loneliest outposts of the kingdom of Dahomey. We, young and Black and fine and gay, sweated out our first heartbreaks with no school nor office chums to share that confidence over lunch hour. Just as there were no rings to make tangible the reason for our happy secret smiles, there were no names nor reason given or shared for the tears that messed up the lab reports or the library bills.

We were good listeners, and never asked for double dates, *but didn't we know the rules?* Why did we always seem to think friendships between women were important enough to *care* about? Always we moved in a necessary remoteness that made "What did you do this weekend?" seem like an impertinent question. We discovered and explored our attention to women alone, sometimes in secret, sometimes in defiance, sometimes in little pockets that almost touched ("Why are those little Black girls always either whispering together or fighting?") but always alone, against a greater aloneness. We did it cold turkey, and although it resulted in some pretty imaginative tough women when we survived, too many of us did not survive at all.

AUDRE LORDE
in *Zami: A New Spelling of My Name* (1982)

## From Book Four

"What about writing to Mark?"
This suggestion bewildered me, "Where?
Do you have an address, in Morocco
or Paris or Switzerland?" Sooner
or later (but either too soon
or too late) we would write a joint letter
announcing our intimacy
indiscreetly, for like all clandestine
but foolhardy lovers, we had
to tell someone. This innocent, but
not innocuous bombshell pursued
him round Europe from pillar box to
*poste restante* for some months, till at last
it caught up with its target, both Hyacinth's
playmate and mine, who did what
one should do with a hand grenade, tossing
it back, without comment and under
anonymous cover to Dr.
Immanuel Star the next summer.
That pious psychiatrist, forced
to acknowledge the ongoing hetero-
dox abnormalities happening
virtually under his bed,
had no option but packing us off
to be treated by separate colleagues
of his, in a show of parental
authority somehow extended
to me. My first fling on the couch
was a flop. As in further encounters
with shrinks, my refusal in fact
to be shrunk was accounted resistance.
A single recalcitrant session
comprised my didactic analysis,
teaching me how in obscurantist,

authoritarian hands
the so-called talking cure could become
both pernicious and frankly nonsensical.
Hyacinth's psyche one might
have supposed to be sanforized, following
years of exposure to Freudian
steam, but he went like a lamb
to the cleaners. His cure was complete
in six months, when he learned to relate
to the opposite gender exclusively.
"Dr. Popescu," he murmured
the last time he laid his insomniac
head on my sceptical arm,
"says bisexuals suffer from penis-
fixation, and just have to make
up their minds!" This he did, with disastrous
results: the conformity seized
as a mode of survival would cost
him his life. We lost touch on my taking
French leave from McGill and absconding
to Paris. He married, and fathered
four children before he was 30,
while going through medical school.
Having qualified as a psychiatrist,
Hyacinth's illness eluded
the notice of colleagues and patients
and family, even his father.
He removed himself, leaving no note
but a stack of prescriptions made out
to himself for barbiturates, June
'67. His mother attempted
to follow him, falling downstairs,
and succeeded in breaking her hip.
Four years later she died in a madhouse.
His father complained at her funeral,
so I am told, as at Hyacinth's,
"Nobody listens to me!"

DARYL HINE
in *In and Out: A Confessional Poem* (1975/1989)

**Daryl Hine,** Evanston, IL, 1993

Everybody else had a childhood, for one thing—where they were coaxed and coached and taught all the shorthand. Or that's how it always seemed to me, eavesdropping my way through twenty-five years, filling in the stories of straight men's lives. First they had their shining boyhood, which made them strong and psyched them up for the leap across the chasm to adolescence, where the real rites of manhood began. I grilled them about it whenever I could, slipping the casual question in while I did their Latin homework for them, sprawled on the lawn at Andover under the reeling elms.

And every year they leaped further ahead, leaving me in the dust with all my doors closed, and each with a new and better deadbolt. Until I was twenty-five, I was the only man I knew who had no story at all. I'd long since accepted the fact that nothing had ever happened to me and nothing ever would. That's how the closet feels, once you've made your nest in it and learned to call it home. Self-pity becomes your oxygen.

I speak for no one else here, if only because I don't want to saddle the women and men of my tribe with the lead weight of my self-hatred, the particular doorless room of my internal exile. Yet I've come to learn that all our stories add up to the same imprisonment. The self-delusion of uniqueness. The festering pretense that we are the same as they are. The gutting of all our passions till we are a bunch of eunuchs, our zones of pleasure in enemy hands. Most of all, the ventriloquism, the learning how to pass for straight. Such obedient slaves we make, with such very tidy rooms.

Forty-six now and dying by inches, I finally see how our lives align at the core, if not in the sorry details. I still shiver with a kind of astonished delight when a gay brother or sister tells of that narrow escape from the coffin world of the closet. *Yes yes yes*, goes a voice in my head, *it was just like that for me.* When we laugh together then and dance in the giddy circle of freedom, we are children for real at last, because we have finally grown up. And every time we dance, our enemies writhe like the Witch in *Oz*, melting, melting—the Nazi Popes and all their brocaded minions, the rat-brain politicians, the wacko fundamentalists and their Book of Lies.

We may not win in the end, of course. Genocide is still the national sport of straight men, especially in this century of nightmares. And death by AIDS is everywhere around me, seething through the streets of this broken land. Last September I buried another lover, Stephen Kolzak—died of homophobia, murdered by barbaric priests and petty bureaucrats. So whether or not I was ever a child is a matter of very small moment. But every memoir now is a kind of manifesto, as we piece together the tale of the tribe. Our stories have died with us long enough. We mean to leave behind some map, some key, for the gay and lesbian people who follow—that they may not drown in the lies, in the hate that pools and foams like pus on the carcass of America.

PAUL MONETTE
in *Becoming a Man* (1992)

**Paul Monette,** Los Angeles, CA, 1988

A few moments later at a table in the rear of the bar, Kate said to Audie, "I need you to answer just a few questions. Then, as soon as you feel strong enough, we'll go to the station—"

"No." Audie shook her head and took a deep breath, exhaled it in a sigh that took several moments to complete. "I can't," she said.

"Audie, try and relax. Just tell me exactly what happened. I promise I'll take good care of you, I'll—"

"You don't understand," Raney said. "She can't press charges and she can't testify."

"I'm a kindergarten teacher," Audie whispered. Tears welled, spilled down her cheeks.

"This is a lesbian bar," said Raney. She gestured toward the rear of the Nightwood Bar, the parking lot. "What happened out there happened at a dyke bar."

Studying Raney's intelligent dark eyes, the handsome, chiseled face framed by the Grace Jones haircut, then Audie's round, motherly face, Kate remembered five novels she had read in college, books by Ann Bannon which Julie had loaned her while they were lovers. Those stories had been set in Greenwich Village in the fifties, when the great fear had been of police who periodically swooped down on gay bars to round up patrons, to permanently scar many of the lives of those patrons. . . .

"She can't press charges," Raney said, and reached to Audie to tenderly brush strands of gray-threaded dark hair at her temple.

KATHERINE V. FORREST
in *Murder at the Nightwood Bar* (1987)

**Katherine V. Forrest,** Los Angeles, CA, 1989

Keller, upon stepping into the park, whispered, "Odd," the first word any of us had spoken since leaving the house. Mother and I jumped. Then there they were, on the corner, waiting at the light:

"FAGGOTS HOMOS FUCKING COCKSUCKER PUSSYBOY BASTARDS—" A bottle burst and spread at our feet. "QUEER PANSIES FRUITCAKES FAGGOTS HOMOS FAGGOTS FAGGOTS FAGGOTS." Then they were gone: a jacked-up Mustang with racing stripes, fuzzy rearview mirror dice, no license plate.

Keller bent, to sift the glass through ten fanned and shaky fingers. "Look," he said. "A love poem." He said, "Diamonds."

Mother held her elbows in her hands, as if she were cold. "Wonderland."

I told her to shut up. She was getting tedious, I said. I bit my hand, the soft pulpy web between stretched thumb and forefinger. I said, from the pain, "Shit." I wasn't even upset. I turned into myself, examined every place in my body where emotion usually shows: heart and hands and head. Nothing. How funny. I said, rising on each syllable, "Keller, let's just get out of here."

"Oh pish. They won't be back."

All three of us breathed, as if Keller—his magic—had settled the issue.

He took Mother's arm in his. He pulled me to his other side.

"Besides—never let them see you run. It's an invitation."

He strode us stiffly down into the park.

"We'll have to go through to the other side, cut behind the Post Office. We don't want them to see where we came from. Follow us home. Now, do we? Not that they would, of course. Not that they're coming back. No, sir. No, ma'am. Never, never."

And there they were, we heard them, we turned. They stopped in front of the church.

Keller pulled us in, toward the fountain. He sat us on the wet, rumbling rim. He said, "Be calm. Be silent. Stay." He paced before us, hands in his pockets, head back, eyes shut. He mumbled something: magic spells? A prayer? Our backs got wet. We sat there.

Keller said, brightly, "Cigarette?" Then put them back in his pocket. "Never mind."

Slam of a car door. Somebody stood silhouette, sluggishly, in the headlights. "Faggots!" he screamed, as if to himself. "I just hate faggots."

Keller said, "Juicy Fruit?" He held a stick of it in my face. I jumped.

I said, "Thanks."

The redneck, impossibly far from us, banged his fist on the hood. Several fisted hands out the windows, assent: how many, though?

It was almost as if it didn't matter. We chewed our gum.

Then the voice was swooping, hateful falsetto: "Faggots? Ooh, faggots? Pretty pretty pretty?" Like calling a dog who knows it needs to be spanked.

I said to Mother, "So now you see. This is how we live." But this was a joke. She didn't laugh. It wasn't a joke anymore. I said to Keller, an accusation, "Tell her." But I didn't give him a chance. "Welcome to the world," I said. "Welcome to the fucking magic kingdom."

JOEY MANLEY
in *The Death of Donna-May Dean* (1991)

When Clive Barnes called *The Boys in the Band* a homosexual play, he was right. It was a homosexual period piece just as *Green Pastures* was a Negro period piece. But blacks are visible and gays are not, and Hollywood was not moved to change a whit by all this hysteria in the gay drawing rooms of Manhattan. Yet *Boys* moved homosexuals throughout the country. The internalized guilt and self-hatred of eight gay men at a Manhattan birthday party formed the best and most potent argument for gay liberation ever offered in a popular art form. It supplied concrete and personalized examples of the negative effects of what homosexuals learn about themselves from the distortions of the media. And the film caused the first public reaction by a burgeoning gay rights movement to the accepted stereotypes in Crowley's play.

Protests by gays did not dispute the existence of such stereotypes, but they were quick to point out that the view was one-sided and that the exclusive depiction or representation of any group of people by a minority stereotype is called bigotry. *The Boys in the Band* was a play about homosexuals and a homosexual play. It was a work that sprang from the subculture itself and represented bitter reflection. Society treated it as though it were a scientific expedition, but in fact it was an inner journey for countless gays who snapped to attention when confronted with the pathos of Michael's sickening routines. Many of the stereotypes put forth by

Crowley were myths that gays had accepted and even fit themselves into because there appeared to be no alternative. At the beginning of the 1960s, two British films about the life of Oscar Wilde could not even be shown in the United States because the Code had not yet been revised. The audience for *The Boys in the Band* included gay people who had grown up thinking that they were the only homosexuals in the world. The film explored passing and not being able to pass, loving and not being able to love, and above all else, surviving in a world that denied one's very existence. But it did so before an American public that was at the stage of barely being able to mention homosexuality at all. It was a gay movie for gay people, and it immediately became both a period piece and a reconfirmation of the stereotypes.

The film industry showed no sign of seeing *The Boys in the Band* as anything but a diversion in a business that was always on the lookout for a novel angle. During the Seventies Hollywood did not relinquish the stereotypes of the Crowley play but moved steadily toward solidifying them. It was the gays in the audiences of 1970 who would eventually form a rebuttal to the homosexual party guests, and their voices would grow louder with each passing year.

VITO RUSSO
in *The Celluloid Closet: Homosexuality in the Movies* (1981)

When Harry Hay, Chuck Rowland, and a few other leftist homosexuals formed the Mattachine Society in 1950, they defined their primary task as the creation of an "ethical homosexual culture." The founders of the gay emancipation movement in the United States discarded the conventional view of homosexuals and lesbians as flawed individuals. In its place, they posited that gay men and women were an oppressed minority and that, like other minorities, they possessed a culture of their own. The dominant ideology made it difficult for gays to see this. Instead, it instilled a shame and self-hatred that often produced distorted, unhappy lives. Hay and his fellows sought to transform the consciousness of homosexuals and lesbians, to replace an isolated, secret existence with a cohesive community that would then be able to take its place proudly in American society. For almost twenty years that vision was lost, until a new generation of gay radicals built a liberation movement motivated by similar goals of pride, openness, and community.

Gay liberation was able to give substance to the dreams of the Mattachine founders because of the work of homophile activists in the intervening years. However little the homophile movement seemed to have achieved in the way of specific goals, the pioneering activists of the 1950s and 1960s had managed to disseminate throughout American culture information about homosexuality that reshaped the consciousness of gay men and women. The idea that homosexuals and lesbians were a minority no longer remained confined to the living rooms of a few gays meeting secretly but was there to be taken from the pages of newspapers, books, and magazines. Gay liberation propelled hundreds of thousands of men and women to act upon that belief, but two decades of work by homophile activists had made the individuals who were ready to respond. At the time of the Stonewall riot in 1969, homosexuality had already ceased being an invisible phenomenon, and gay men and lesbians more easily participated in the collective life of the gay subculture. In attempting to build a politics based on sexual preference, the homophile movement in effect helped create the community that, later, was able to sustain a liberation effort.

JOHN D'EMILIO
in *Sexual Politics, Sexual Communities: The Making of a Homosexual Minority in the United States, 1940–1970* (1983)

**John D'Emilio,** Washington, DC, 1993

"Stonewall" is *the* emblematic event in modern lesbian and gay history. The site of a series of riots in late June–early July 1969 that resulted from a police raid on a Greenwich Village gay bar, "Stonewall" has become synonymous over the years with gay resistance to oppression. Today, the word resonates with images of insurgency and self-realization and occupies a central place in the iconography of lesbian and gay awareness. The 1969 riots are now generally taken to mark the birth of the modern gay and lesbian political movement—that moment in time when gays and lesbians recognized all at once their mistreatment and their solidarity. As such, "Stonewall" has become an empowering symbol of global proportions.

Yet remarkably—since 1994 marks the twenty-fifth anniversary of the Stonewall riots—the actual story of the upheaval has never been told completely, or been well understood. We have, since 1969, been trading the same few tales about the riots from the same few accounts—trading them for so long that they have transmogrified into simplistic myth. The decades preceding Stonewall, moreover, continue to be regarded by most gays and lesbians as some vast neolithic wasteland—and this, despite the efforts of pioneering historians like Allan Bérubé, John D'Emilio and Lillian Faderman to fill in the landscape of those years with vivid, politically astute personalities.

The time is overdue for grounding the symbolic Stonewall in empirical reality and placing the events of 1969 in historical context. In attempting to do this, I felt it was important *not* to homogenize experience to the point where individual voices are lost sight of. My intention was to embrace precisely what most contemporary historians have discarded: the ancient, essential enterprise of *telling human stories*. Too often, in my view, professional historians have yielded to a "sociologizing" tendency that reduces three-dimensional lives to statistical cardboard—and then further distances the reader with a specialized jargon that *claims* to provide greater cognitive precision but serves more often to seal off and silence familiar human sounds.

I have therefore adopted an unconventional narrative strategy in the opening sections of this book: the recreation of half a dozen lives with a particularity that conforms to no interpretative category but only to their own idiosyncratic rhythms. To focus on particular stories does not foreclose speculation about patterns of behavior but does, I believe, help to ensure that the speculation will reflect the actual disparities of individual experience. My belief in the irreducible specialness of each life combines with a paradoxical belief in the possibility that lives, however special, can be shared. It is, if you like, a belief in democracy: the importance of the individual, the commonality of life. . . .

My hope is that the focus on individuals and on narrative will increase the ability of readers to identify—some with one story, some with another—with experiences different from, but comparable to, their own. I know of no other way to make the past *really* speak to the present. And gay men and lesbians—so long denied any history—have a special need and claim on historical writing that is at once accurate *and* accessible.

MARTIN DUBERMAN
in *Stonewall* (1993)

**Martin Duberman,** New York, NY, 1987

In the Stonewall the dance floor had been taken over by Latins . . .

Then the music went off, and the bar was full of cops, the bright lights came on, and we were all ordered out onto the street, everyone except the police working there. I suppose the police expected us to run away into the night, as we'd always done before, but we stood across the street on the sidewalk of the small triangular park. Inside the metal palisades rose the dignified, smaller-than-lifesize statue of the Civil War officer General Sheridan.

Our group drew a still larger crowd. The cops hustled half of the bartenders into a squad car and drove off, leaving several policemen behind, barricaded inside the Stonewall with the remaining staff. Everyone booed the cops, just as though they were committing a shameful act. We kept exchanging peripheral glances, excited and afraid. I had an urge to be responsible and disperse the crowd peacefully, send everyone home. After all, what were we protesting? Our right to our "pathetic malady"?

But in spite of myself a wild exhilaration swept over me . . .

. . . Someone beside me called out, "Gay is good," in imitation of the new slogan, "Black is beautiful," and we all laughed and pressed closer toward the door. The traffic on Christopher had come to a standstill.

Lou, a black grease mark on his T-shirt, was standing beside me, holding my hand, chanting, "Gay is good." We were all chanting it, knowing how ridiculous we were being in this parody of a real demonstration but feeling giddily confident anyway. Now someone said, "We're the Pink Panthers," and that made us laugh again. Then I caught myself foolishly imagining that gays might someday constitute a community rather than a diagnosis.

"This could be the first funny revolution," Lou said. "Aren't these guys great, Bunny? Lily Law should never had messed with us on the day Judy died. Look, they've turned the parking meter into a battering ram." . . .

Down the street, some of our men turned over a parked Volkswagen. The cops rushed down to it while behind them another car was overturned. Its windows shattered and fell out. Now everyone was singing the civil rights song, "We Shall Overcome."

The riot squad was called in. It marched like a Roman army behind shields down Christopher from the women's prison, which was loud with catcalls and the clatter of metal drinking cups against steel bars. The squad, clubs flying, drove the gay men down Christopher, but everyone doubled back through Gay Street and emerged behind the squad in a chorus line, dancing the can-can. "Yoo-hoo, yoo-hoo," they called.

Lou and I stayed out all night, whooping like kids, huddling in groups to plan tomorrow's strategy, heckling the army of cops who were closing off all of Sheridan Square as a riot zone and refusing to let cars or pedestrians pass through it.

I stayed over at Lou's. We hugged each other in bed like brothers, but we were too excited to sleep. We rushed down to buy the morning papers to see how the Stonewall Uprising had been described. "It's really our Bastille Day," Lou said. But we couldn't find a single mention in the press of the turning point of our lives.

EDMUND WHITE
in *The Beautiful Room is Empty* (1988)

**Edmund White,** New York, NY, 1985

(Flashing red lights illuminate the stage accompanied by a rise and fall of sirens. A triumphant BOOM BOOM enters, followed by a gleeful TIMOTHY and a protective JACK.)

**Boom Boom (Brandishing handcuffed hands above her head)**   Look, everyone, I'm engaged!

**C.B.**   How'd you get away?

**Boom Boom**   While they were shoving us in the back of the paddy wagon, Miss Marsha was sneaking us out the front by the driver's door.

**Murfino**   Where was the driver?

**Jack (Unlocking BOOM BOOM's handcuffs)**   Watching the fun.

**Timothy**   The crowd's getting bigger by the minute—

**Boom Boom**   —they're tossing pennies at the cops—

**Timothy**   —they upended a VW—

**Jack**   —they emptied the gas all over the front of the Stonewall—

**Boom Boom**   —they're lighting matches and flicking them at the—

**Murfino (Hurriedly exiting stage left.)**   —oh, my God, my bar!!

**Ceil (Entering stage right, carrying a box of Sarah Lee.)**   Boom Boom!

**Boom Boom**   Ceil!

**(BOOM BOOM and CEIL fall into each other's arms.)**

**Ceil**   They told me you were incarcerated.

**Boom Boom**   I was sprung.

**Ceil**   I was coming to visit you in jail. **(Giving the box of cake to BOOM BOOM.)** I swiped you this cake just in case.

**Boom Boom (Opening the cake box.)**   Sarah Lee? How . . . (Nonplus.) . . . thoughtful.

**Ceil**   Look inside . . . look inside . . .

**Boom Boom (Removing a nail file from the cake.)**   A nail file?

**Ceil**   I wanted you should be well groomed.

DORIC WILSON
in *Street Theater* (1982)

**Howard Cruse,** Queens, NY, 1989

This twentieth anniversary commemorative edition of *Out of the Closets: Voices of Gay Liberation* evokes in us, as its editors, a feeling of great pride mixed with a tinge of sadness. We are gratified indeed that this collection, hailed by many of its reviewers and fans as a "classic," has now become one. As the first positive collection of writing by, about, and for gay people, it helped to herald the way for what has become a wealth of lesbian and gay bookstores, publishers, and lines of books from mainstream, university, and gay-owned presses. Younger readers may find it hard to believe that both of the editors grew up without access to any positive gay or lesbian books or other material. One of the most important goals of books like this one has, therefore, been accomplished: No one need grow up again thinking that he or she is the only gay person in the world, an experience all too common only two decades ago.

This anthology played a significant role in that transformation, going through five printings and two editions. After Pyramid Books released a mass market paperback in 1974, the book could be found at the front of supermarkets and on book racks in bus and train station newsstands. It signaled to nongay consumers that we are indeed everywhere, and it gave lesbians and gay men who lived outside major metropolitan areas access to this book. A few other important lesbian and gay male books were available by 1974, including *Lesbian/Woman* by Del Martin and Phyllis Lyon, *Sappho Was a Right-on Woman* by Sidney Abbott and Barbara Love, and *The Gay Militants* by Donn Teal. However, *Out of the Closets*, because of its mass market distribution, was often the first contact gay people had with the ideas and lives of other gay people. . . .

Rereading *Out of the Closets*, we are struck by two central facts.

- The initial thrust of the post-Stonewall gay liberation movement was shaped by the 1960s counterculture, the black civil rights movement, the New Left, and radical feminism.
- Radical gay liberationists—and those are the men and women whose voices were carefully selected and presented in this book—had a vision of revolutionary change both for society at large and for the way gay men and women should live their lives.

KARLA JAY AND ALLEN YOUNG, editors
in the Introduction to the 1992 edition of *Out of the Closets: Voices of Gay Liberation*, an anthology first published in 1972

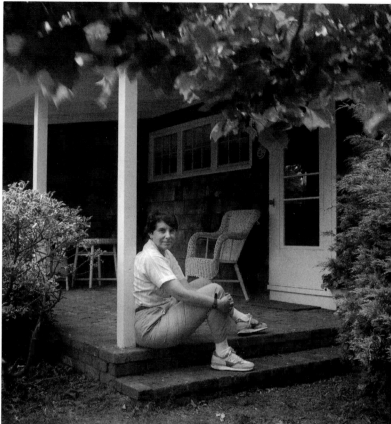

**Allen Young,** Orange, MA, 1992                    **Karla Jay,** Sagaponack, NY, 1991

Before the paper was even complete, it was decided that the one perfect way to introduce it would be at the second Congress to Unite Women in 1970. The Lesbians would return to the scene of earlier oppressive action against them with their paper entitled *The Woman-Identified Woman*, which today remains the best statement on the Lesbian in a sexist culture. The Lesbians, angered after pervasive and persistent oppression from other women, would not just take a literature table; they would take over the congress, and force the issue into open discussion.

Plans were carefully made.

On Friday night, as soon as the last drumbeat from Burning City theater's presentation ceased, the lights went out. When they went on again, there were twenty Lesbians at the front of the auditorium who wore T-shirts proclaiming them the Lavender Menace. They demanded the microphone, which was handed down from the stage, and a gay woman spoke, charging the women's movement with sexism, with discrimination against Lesbian sisters. Some of the 400 women in the audience had worked with the gay women on Women's Liberation actions but had not known until this minute that they were Lesbians. One or two Menaces talked effectively about their oppression, making it real, helping the sisters to see what they were doing. A call was made for women who agreed or sympathized to join

them at the front of the room. At least thirty more women arose from their seats and went to the front. Most Lesbians in the audience were really torn. Some came slowly forward. Others never budged. The microphone was declared "open," and women lined up to use it.

One of the last women who talked had been a scheduled speaker for the program that never took place. She was a professor at Columbia, a founding member of Columbia Women's Liberation, and Chairman of the Education Committee of New York N.O.W. She was shy but she struggled to speak. "I know what these women are talking about. I was there. In some ways I still am there." The tension, the pain, were in her voice. Those women who had not yet risen to leave leaned forward to hear her words over the commotion. They could not know that this woman's personal life would become the focus of a nationwide movement hassle. This was the first time that Professor Kate Millett—a few months later to become a celebrated author and international Women's Liberation theorist—had spoken about her sexuality.

SIDNEY ABBOTT AND BARBARA LOVE
in *Sappho Was a Right-On Woman: A Liberated View of Lesbianism* (1972)

*Top:* **Barbara Love,** Danbury, CT, 1994

*Bottom:* **Sidney Abbott,** Poughkeepsie, NY, 1992

*Top left:* **Robin Morgan,** author and former editor-in-chief of *Ms.* magazine, New York, NY, 1992

*Top right:* **Andrea Dworkin,** author, Brooklyn, NY, 1992

*Bottom left:* **Charlotte Bunch,** author and theorist, Brooklyn, NY, 1990

*Bottom right:* **Jill Johnston,** author of *Lesbian Nation: The Feminist Solution* (1973), New York, NY, 1993

*Opposite:* **Kate Millett,** author of *Sexual Politics* (1970), New York, NY, 1987

Looking wary, Siena accompanied her across the street and into the narrow, glass-paned doorway of Sisterhood Bookstore. Veronica led her among browsing customers, past the revolving racks of feminist-titled paperbacks, past the display table of current hardcover releases, past women-themed greeting cards, records and music cassettes, past the well-stocked display cases of feminist jewelry and pottery, past the growing numbers of books on Third World women.

Near the rear of the store, she paused and gestured towards the south wall. Her eyes shone as she pointed out well-remembered titles—novels by Katherine V. Forrest, Jane Rule and Ann Allen Shockley; poetry by Judy Grahn, Audre Lorde and Adrienne Rich; non-fiction by Gloria Anzaldúa and Cherríe Moraga.

Siena gazed at the rows of lesbian publications. "I never imagined there'd be this many."

"Starting in the late sixties, the silence was broken. If it hadn't been for the women's movement, lesbian literature would still be hidden." Veronica's eyes never left that book-lined wall. "Whenever I feel discouraged, alienated, I stand here and look at all these books, remember these writers—and my spirits rise. I want to be part of this."

Siena did not look at her. "You're not afraid to go public?"

"I'm terrified. But hiding, keeping silent, won't solve anything. I'm a writer—and I have to write what I know. That's what I'm trying to do, and I hope to do it for the rest of my life. Someday, I have to take the risk of being public. I want you to be aware of that. Being with me means being out—maybe not right at this moment, but definitely in the future."

TERRI DE LA PEÑA
in *Margins* (1992)

**Terri de la Peña,** Santa Monica, CA, six days after the January 1994 Northridge earthquake

BUT I PERSEVERED, IN MY OWN QUIET WAY. THE BOOKSTORE YIELDED ANOTHER HELPFUL VOLUME.

TOO NERVOUS TO READ SOMETHING SO BLATANT IN PUBLIC, I **BOUGHT** IT.

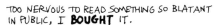

PULSE WELL ABOVE MAXIMUM RECOMMENDED RATE.

I READ THE WHOLE BOOK VORACIOUSLY. IT WAS VERY ENCOURAGING. WHEN I WAS DONE, I TORE THE COVER OFF, STUFFED THE REST OF IT IN A BROWN PAPER BAG, AND HID IT UNDER MY MATTRESS.

NEXT, I TOOK TO READING THE LESBIAN CHAPTER OF MY ROOMMATE'S **HITE REPORT** WHILE SHE WAS OUT.

HI!

HI... UH... I WAS JUST LOOKING FOR YOUR DICTIONARY.

ONE THING LED TO ANOTHER, AND BEFORE THE SEMESTER WAS OVER I HAD DEVOURED **DESERT OF THE HEART, RUBYFRUIT JUNGLE,** AND **THE WELL OF LONELINESS.**

WHERE'S TH' SEXY PARTS?

FLIP

THE WALL OF LONELINESS
RADCLYFFE HALL

CHRISTMAS BREAK WAS INTERMINABLE. MY PARENTS FAILED TO NOTICE THAT I HAD BECOME A THREAT TO THE NUCLEAR FAMILY.

A CHENILLE ROBE! THANKS.

... MY FULL ACADEMIC PASSION WAS RESERVED FOR A **DIFFERENT** ODYSSEY... THE QUEST FOR MY **PEOPLE.**

OUT OF THE CLOSETS AND INTO THE STREETS
SAPPHO WAS A RIGHT-ON WOMAN
HOMOSEXUALITIES MASTERS & JOHNSON
LESBIAN NATION
THE GAY REPORT

OUR RIGHT TO LOVE

ALISON BECHDEL

in *Gay Comics #19* (1993)

**Alison Bechdel,** Grand Isle, VT, 1995

## A History of Lesbianism

How they came into the world,
the women-loving-women
came in three by three
and four by four
the women-loving-women
came in ten by ten
and ten by ten again
until there were more
than you could count

    they took care of each other
    the best they knew how
    and of each other's children,
    if they had any.

How they lived in the world,
the women-loving-women
learned as much as they were allowed
and walked and wore their clothes
the way they liked
whenever they could. They did whatever
they knew to be happy or free
and worked and worked and worked.
The women-loving-women
in America were called dykes
and some liked it
and some did not.

they made love to each other
the best they knew how
and for the best reasons

How they went out of the world,
the women-loving-women
went out one by one
having withstood greater and lesser
trials, and much hatred
from other people, they went out
one by one, each having tried
in her own way to overthrow
the rule of men over women,
they tried it one by one
and hundred by hundred,
until each came in her own way
to the end of her life
and died.

    The subject of lesbianism
    is very ordinary; it's the question
    of male domination that makes everybody
    angry.

JUDY GRAHN
in *The Work of a Common Woman* (1978)

The Earring: **Judy Grahn** (*left*), Oakland, CA, 1988

For a century, research on the history of homosexuality has been constrained by the intolerance of governments and academics alike. John Addington Symonds, the nineteenth-century British classicist and arguably the first modern historian of homosexuality, in 1883 dared print only ten copies of his study of Greek homosexuality, *A Problem in Greek Ethics*. In 1897, four years after his death, his executor bought out the first edition of Havelock Ellis's *Sexual Inversion* because Symonds' essay had been appended, and forbade any reference to Symonds in the second edition (which the British government, in any case, promptly suppressed). In Berlin, Magnus Hirschfeld and other German homosexual intellectuals founded the Institute for Sex Research in 1919, only to see its research collection destroyed in 1933 in the first major book-burning organized by the Nazis (the photograph of the fire consuming the Institute's library is famous, but captions rarely indicate the subject matter of the burning books). In this country, the courageous men and women who launched the ONE Institute for Homophile Studies in Los Angeles in the mid-1950s were ignored by Cold War–era scholars. Even the prestigious Kinsey Institute for Sex Research lost most of its funding in 1954 when conservatives denounced its research findings, particularly regarding the high incidence of homosexual behavior in the United States, as a threat to the moral fiber of the country. As recently as 1982, foreign scholars attending an international gay history conference in Toronto had to misrepresent their purpose to Canadian immigration officials for fear of being refused admittance. Repression and marginalization have often been the lot of historians of homosexuality as well as of homosexuals themselves.

But two developments, one in the political arena and one in the world of history itself, have resulted in an unprecedented outpouring of scholarship in lesbian and gay history in the last decade. Most important has been the success of the lesbian and gay movement in creating a more tolerant climate in which such work could be undertaken and in challenging certain orthodoxies, particularly psychological theories of pathology, which had hindered creative thinking about sexuality for decades. Indeed, much of the first wave of historical research was undertaken by people with backgrounds in the movement rather than the academy,

**Dorr Legg** at the ONE Institute in Los Angeles, CA, 1994
Founded in 1952, this homosexual rights and educational organization published the *ONE Institute Quarterly*. Legg edited *Homophile Studies in Theory and Practice* (1994).

most notably Jonathan Katz, whose pioneering collection of documents and commentaries, *Gay American History* (1976), signalled the new era of scholarship. Grass-roots gay archives and history projects sprang up in several American cities in the late 1970s, including New York's Lesbian Herstory Archives, founded by Joan Nestle, Judith Schwartz, and Deborah Edel, and San Francisco's Lesbian and Gay History Project, which has supported, among other studies, the work of Allan Bérubé on World War II, Estelle Freedman, Liz Stevens, and Allan Bérubé on cross-dressing women, and Eric Garber on the Harlem Renaissance (all three studies are represented in this volume).

Professional historians have generally been slower to take up the subject. Some have been reluctant to published in the field due to fear of the possible consequences for their careers; sympathetic faculty still caution graduate students to avoid linking themselves to so "controversial" a topic. Many scholars still consider the history of homosexuality a marginal field, if not an embarrassing or distasteful subject of study. But the doors of the academy have begun to open. Gay and lesbian activists on campus have helped pry them ajar, but so too have changing ideas about what constitutes acceptable historical inquiry, particularly the recent ascendancy of social history within the discipline. The interest that gay and lesbian historians take in ordinary people, the structure of everyday life, and the "private" sphere is consistent with—and a logical extension of—the concerns of the new social historians. The dramatic growth of women's history, in particular, has played a groundbreaking role by sensitizing historians to issues of gender and sexuality and by providing institutional support for a variety of new perspectives. Some of the most widely discussed essays and books in women's history, such as Carroll Smith-Rosenberg's essay on "The Female World of Love and Ritual," have highlighted questions of concern to historians of lesbianism. As historians have paid more attention to the questions addressed by women's history and social history, their openness to gay and lesbian history has grown.

MARTIN DUBERMAN, MARTHA VICINUS, AND GEORGE CHAUNCEY, JR., editors
in the Introduction to *Hidden from History: Reclaiming the Gay and Lesbian Past* (1989)

**Deborah Edel,** Brooklyn, NY, 1992

Edel, a co-founder of the Lesbian Herstory Archives, is seen here
with a collage of covers from classic lesbian pulp novels of the
1950s and 1960s, among them Ann Bannon's *I Am a Woman*.

**Juanita (Diaz) Ramos,** New York, NY, 1988

Ramos was founder, with Mariana Romo-Carmona and Elizabeth
Crespo, of the Latina Lesbian History Project and editor of
*Compañeras: Latina Lesbians (An Anthology)* in 1987.

We have been the silent minority, the silenced minority—invisible women, invisible men. Early on, the alleged enormity of our "sin" justified the denial of our existence, even our physical destruction. Our "crime" was not merely against society, not only against humanity, but "against nature"—we were outlaws against the universe. Long did we remain literally and metaphorically unspeakable, "among Christians not to be named"—nameless. To speak our name, to roll that word over the tongue, was to make our existence tangible, physical; it came too close to some mystical union with us, some carnal knowledge of that "abominable" ghost, that lurking possibility within. For long, like women conceived only in relation to men, we were allowed only relative intellectual existence, conceived only in relation to, as deviants from, a minority of—an "abnormal" and embarrassing poor relation. For long we were a people perceived out of time and out of place—socially unsituated, without a history—the mutant progeny of some heterosexual union, freaks. Our existence as a long-oppressed, long-resistant social group was not explored. We remained an unknown people, our character defamed. The heterosexual dictatorship has tried to keep us out of sight and out of mind; its homosexuality taboo has kept us in the dark. That time is over. The people of the shadows have seen the light; Gay people are coming out—and moving on—to organized action against an oppressive society.

In recent years the liberation movements of Lesbians and Gay men have politicized, given historical dimension to, and radically altered the traditional concept of homosexuality, as well as the social situation, relations, ideas, and emotions of some homosexuals. Those of us affected by this movement have experienced a basic change in our sense of self. As we acted upon our society we acted upon ourselves; as we changed the world we changed our minds; sexual subversives, we overturned our psychic states. From a sense of our homosexuality as a personal and devastating fate, a private, secret shame, we moved with often dizzying speed to the consciousness of ourselves as members of an oppressed social group. As the personal and political came together in our lives, so it merged in our heads, and we came to see the previously hidden connections between our private lives and public selves; we were politicized, body and soul. In one quick, bright flash we experienced a secular revelation: we too were among America's mistreated. We moved in a brief span of time from a sense that there was something deeply wrong with us to the realization that there was something radically wrong with that society which had done its best to destroy us. We moved from various forms of self-negation to newfound outrage and action against those lethal conditions. From hiding our sexual and affectional natures, we moved to publicly affirm a deep and good part of our being. Starting with a sense of ourselves as characters in a closet drama, the passive victims of a family tragedy, we experienced ourselves as initiators and assertive actors in a movement for social change. We experienced the present as history, ourselves as historymakers. In our lives and in our hearts, we experienced the change from one historical form of homosexuality to another. We experienced homosexuality as historical.

JONATHAN NED KATZ
in *Gay American History* (1976)

**Jonathan Ned Katz** on the day after Gay Pride Weekend, New York, NY, 1988

In 1992, when the patriots among us will be celebrating the five-hundredth anniversary of the discovery of America by Christopher Columbus, our cultural historians may wish to mark the centenary of an intellectual landfall of almost equal importance for the conceptual geography of the human sciences: the invention of homosexuality by Charles Gilbert Chaddock. Though he may never rank with Columbus in the annals of individual achievement, Chaddock would hardly seem to merit the obscurity which has surrounded him throughout the past hundred years. An early translator of Krafft-Ebing's classical medical handbook of sexual deviance, the *Psychopathia sexualis*, Chaddock is credited by the *Oxford English Dictionary* with having introduced "homo-sexuality" into the English language in 1892, in order to render a German cognate twenty years its senior. Homosexuality, for better or for worse, has been with us ever since. . . .

It is not exactly my intention to argue that homosexuality, as we commonly understand it today, didn't exist before 1892. How, indeed, could it have failed to exist? The very word displays a most workmanlike and scientific indiffer-ence to cultural and environmental factors, looking only to the sexes of the persons engaged in the sexual act. More-over, if homosexuality didn't exist before 1892, heterosexuality couldn't have existed either (it came into being, in fact, like Eve from Adam's rib, eight years later), and without heterosexuality, where would all of us be right now?

The comparatively recent genesis of heterosexuality—strictly speaking, a twentieth-century affair—should provide a clue to the profundity of the cultural issues over which, hitherto, I have been so lightly skating. How is it possible that until the year 1900 there was not a precise, value-free, scientific term available to speakers of the English language for designating what we would now regard, in retrospect, as the mode of sexual behavior favored by the vast majority of people in our culture? Any answer to that question must direct our attention to the inescapable historicity of even the most innocent, unassuming, and seemingly objective of cultural representations.

DAVID M. HALPERIN
in *One Hundred Years of Homosexuality* (1990)

In 1843 the American author William Cullen Bryant wrote an essay for the *Evening Post* in which he glowingly described a trip to Vermont, where, among nature's beauties, he had the opportunity to observe a beautiful "female friendship" between two revered "maiden ladies." Bryant was not alone in his boundless admiration for the pair and the peaceful and loving relationship they established together, as he said when he gave their history:

In their youthful days, they took each other as companions for life, and this union, no less sacred to them than the tie of marriage, has subsisted, in uninterrupted harmony, for 40 years, during which they have shared each others' occupations and pleasures and works of charity while in health, and watched over each other tenderly in sickness. . . . They slept on the same pillow and had a common purse, and adopted each others relations, and . . . I would tell you of their dwelling, encircled with roses, . . . and I would speak of the friendly attentions which their neighbors, people of kind hearts and simple manners, seem to take pleasure in bestowing upon them.

If such a description of love between two women had been published in an American newspaper a century later, surely the editor's desk would have been piled high with correspondence about immorality in Vermont (slept on the same pillow!) and the two women in question would have felt constrained to sue Bryant for defamation of character in order to clear their good names. In 1843, however, the two ladies were flattered and the newspaper's readers were charmed.

What is apparent through this example and hundreds of others that have now been well documented by social historians is that women's intimate relationships were universally encouraged in centuries outside of our own. There were, of course, some limitations placed on those relationships as far as society was concerned. For instance, if an eligible male came along, the women were not to feel that they could send him on his way in favor of their romantic friendship; they were not to hope that they could find gainful employment to support such a same-sex love relationship permanently or that they could usurp any other male privileges in support of that relationship; and they were not to intimate in any way that an erotic element might possibly exist in their love for each other. Outside of those strictures, female same-sex love—or "romantic friendship," as it was long called—was a respected social institution in America. . . . While some outrageous, lawless women might have stooped to unspeakable activity with other females, there was no such thing as a "lesbian" as the twentieth century recognizes the term; there was only the rare woman who behaved immorally, who was thought to live far outside the pale of decent womanhood. It was not until the second half of the nineteenth century that the *category* of the lesbian— or the female sexual invert—was formulated. Once she was widely recognized as an entity, however, relationships such as the one Bryant described took on an entirely different meaning—not only as viewed by society, but also as viewed by the two women who were involved. They now had a set of concepts and questions (which were uncomfortable to many of them) by which they had to scrutinize feelings that would have been seen as natural and even admirable in earlier days.

LILLIAN FADERMAN
in *Odd Girls and Twilight Lovers* (1991)

The great "success story" of romantic friendship is that of Sarah Ponsonby and Eleanor Butler, "the Ladies of Llangollen." Sarah and Eleanor were two upper-class Irishwomen who managed to run off together and share thereafter every waking and sleeping moment (until one of them died fifty-three years later), just as countless women prayed (fruitlessly, in most cases) in their letters to their romantic friends that they might be able to do. In 1778, Sarah and Eleanor, both of wealthy, titled families, eloped. They dressed in men's clothes for the elopement, hoping thereby to be less conspicuous on the road. When they were pursued and foiled in their escape by their families the first time, they ran away a second time. Finally their relatives were convinced that nothing would change their minds, and they let the two women be. Eventually Sarah and Eleanor were even given small stipends, and in 1787 Sarah received a pension from the king. They settled in Wales, and in 1780 procured a cottage in Llangollen Vale. In no time at all they established a marvelous garden. With very little money but wonderful taste and imagination, they redecorated the cottage (which they christened Plas Newydd), and their home became a shrine to romantic friendship in their generation and in later generations.

LILLIAN FADERMAN
in *Surpassing the Love of Men* (1981)

Soon after the visitation Sarah took over the management of the household, and Eleanor retired to her studies and her books. They began to read more widely, Tasso, Ariosto, and other medieval Italian writers, the Latin classics in English translations, Ossian, William Cowper, Dr. Johnson. They enjoyed travel books and collections of French letters, books about formal gardens, animal husbandry, the novels of Jean-Jacques Rousseau, Samuel Richardson, and Henry Fielding. In everything they read, they searched for literary confirmation of their own natures, evidence of existence of women like themselves. Their desire was not so much to find allies as to identify themselves as belonging properly in some corner, at the point of some acute angle in the geometry of the human race. In the evenings, with all the windows closed and the shutters secured against the ambiguities and terrors of the night outside, a clutch of candles lit close to their book, they scoured the pages for some mention of an existence like their own.

DORIS GRUMBACH
in *The Ladies* (1984), a fiction about the Ladies of Llangollen

Since friendship and love are rarely about straight teeth or bony clavicles, one must pause to ask how it has served history to caricature Lorena Hickok, and why she was for so long disregarded. Like the disappearance of ER's correspondence with Earl Miller, the answer in retrospect seems evident: Today, our generation continues to cringe and turn away from cross-class, cross-generational, or same-sex relationships. In this instance, however, both Eleanor Roosevelt and Lorena Hickok saved their correspondence, although Hickok typed, edited, and then burned the originals of ER's letters between 1932 and 1933 and many more of her own letters over the years. For all the deletions and restraint, the thousands of letters that remain are amorous and specific.

ER repeatedly ended her ten-, twelve-, fifteen-page daily letters with expressions of love and longing. There are few ambiguities in this correspondence, and a letter that was defined as "particularly susceptible to misinterpretation" reads: "I wish I could lie down beside you tonight & take you in my arms."

After a long separation, during which both ER and Hick counted the days until their reunion, Hick noted: "Only eight more days . . . Funny how even the dearest face will fade away in time. Most clearly I remember your eyes, with a kind of teasing smile in them, and the feeling of that soft spot just north-east of the corner of your mouth against my lips. . . ."

The fact is that ER and Hick were not involved in a schoolgirl "smash." They did not meet in a nineteenth-century storybook, or swoon unrequitedly upon a nineteenth-century campus. They were neither saints nor adolescents. Nor were they virgins or mermaids. They were two adult women, in the prime of their lives, committed to working out a relationship under very difficult circumstances. They had each already lived several other lives. They knew the score. They appreciated the risks and the dangers. They had both experienced pain in loving. They never thought it would be easy or smooth. They gave each other pleasure and comfort, trust and love. They touched each other deeply, loved profoundly, and moved on. They sought to avoid gossip. And, for the most part, they succeeded. They wrote to each other exactly what they meant to write. Sigmund Freud notwithstanding: A cigar may not always be a cigar, but the "north-east corner of your mouth against my lips" is always the northeast corner.

BLANCHE WIESEN COOK
in *Eleanor Roosevelt, Volume I* (1992)

**Blanche Wiesen Cook,** East Hampton, NY, 1993

**Allen Ellenzweig,** Amagansett, NY, 1988

Ellenzweig is the author of *The Homoerotic Photograph: Male Images from Durieu/Delacroix to Mapplethorpe* (1992).

**James Saslow,** New York, NY, 1986

Saslow is the author of *Ganymede in the Renaissance:*
*Homosexuality in Art and Siociety* (1986).

. . . in combat missions another art of illusion—camouflage—could save lives. These two arts required similar skills. Robert Fleischer remembered "going out on a training mission and after a while, after forced marches and bivouacs and night campaigns, we had to do an overnight kind of dig-in and camouflaged the area with simulated antiaircraft equipment. And I went with who I was assigned with and I kind of got involved in doing the camouflage. I thought it was kind of fun to put the trees and everything around. I said, 'My goodness, this is just like stage sets, what the hell!' And I was very good at it. And the guys that were in charge were astounded because they figured that [it would be] a real drag with a sissy along. [But] I turned [out] to be the one that really accomplished [something]."

The easy transition from costume and set design to camouflage design for combat was not overlooked by classification officers. Many GIs who were classified as camoufleurs had as civilians worked in the decorative arts as window dressers, display artists, fashion designers or set and costume designers—professions that were stereotyped as homosexual. These men were equally capable of outfitting female impersonators and disguising matériel. At March Field, California, the 4th Air Force Engineer Camouflage School, which included some of the cast and crew from *This Is the Army*, produced a GI show called *You Bet Your Life*, with which the Air Force taught the men "the art and science of deceiving the enemy and saving the soldier's own life." At the end of the show, the song the camoufleurs sang about their craft had parallel meanings that described other artists of illusion as well—including the GI female impersonator and the gay GI who passed as heterosexual. "It's so confusing," the camoufleurs sang to their soldier audiences,

*But so amusing,*
*The ruses*
*One uses*
*Are nature's own scheme. . . .*
*Though we're like mirages,*
*We're all camouflages—*
*Things Are Not What They Seem. . . .*
*No,*
*Things are never quite what they seem!*

Both camouflage and female impersonation could serve gay GIs as metaphors for the fine art of "blending in"—their everyday use of protective "ruses" to keep from being exposed.

ALLAN BÉRUBÉ
in *Coming Out Under Fire: The History of Gay Men and Women in World War Two* (1990)

**Allan Bérubé,** San Francisco, CA, 1994

**Ken**   When we were in school here we used to sleep over and diddle with each other.

**John**   We were twelve years old.

**Sally**   The two of you?

**June**   The three of us.

**Shirley**   Oh, that's—

**Sally**   It certainly is.

**Ken**   I'd been in love with you for years.

**John**   You were not. That was just diddling.

**Ken**   Oh yeah, remember the double date when you couldn't get Margy Majors to go all the way—

**John**   One time. And I was drunk.

**Ken**   Well, I wasn't. I had planned it all week. I knew damn well you weren't going to get anywhere with Margy.

**Gwen**   Oh, God. Remember going all the way!

**Ken**   I must have been in love with you at least two years before we ran off to Berkeley. He was never out of this V-neck, sky-blue cashmere sweater, full of holes.

**John**   Mostly from you poking your finger in them.

**Gwen**   He's ticklish.

**June**   Very.

**Ken**   Well, then you discovered the Copper Queen.

**Gwen**   That would be me.

**June**   Nobody said John didn't know a good thing when he saw it.

**Gwen**   Damn straight. (*Jed returns with milk and Ken's cane.*)

**Ken**   And they all lived happily ever after.

**Gwen**   Oh, I loved us then. I remember once we bought twenty dollars' worth of daffodils and your mother and I ran up and down on the Nimitz Freeway giving them to all the stalled drivers.

**Weston**   Why?

**Gwen**   Why? June had decided they were wonderful.

**June**   Unfortunately, they hated us. The traffic started moving; we nearly got run down.

**Ken**   You were decidedly before your time.

**Gwen**   That fuckin' war! Damn, it fucked us. It broke my heart when we weren't together. If only you'd come with us to Europe everything would have been so different. The whole idea was going off to escape from your draft thing.

I'll never forgive you for chickening out on that.

**Ken**   I didn't chicken out; you were just afraid of the competition.

**Gwen**   You would never have been in Nam, you wouldn't have been injured; June wouldn't have gotten militant and estranged from us.

**Weston**   I read this book. Like about war experiences in Nam? It said shock and dope were like common. In the god-damned reading room; Fairleigh Dickinson University.

**Ken**   (*To Shirley.*) I defy anyone to diagram that sentence.

**Weston**   Really heavy.

**Ken**   The reading room at Fairleigh Dickinson was heavy? Vietnam was heavy or the book was heavy.

**Weston**   You were there, man, I can't tell you.

**Ken**   Nothing was common except the American troops, and we were very common indeed.

**Weston**   Like you're trying to be cool, but you still carry it around.

**Ken**   However awkwardly.

**Sally**   Your mother was very proud that you went. I could have killed her.

**Ken**   Wasn't that interesting? I thought so, too. And ashamed that I came back.

**Shirley**   Oh, that isn't true.

**June**   The hell it ain't.

**Sally**   Don't kid yourself.

**Weston**   You still think about it.

**Ken**   I don't wake up screaming any more from visions of my buddies floating through the blue sky in pieces, if that's what you mean . . .

**Weston**   Oh, shit.

**Ken**   Exactly that. The dream is more likely of some god-damned general moving down the row of beds in the hospital, handing out medals like aspirin. That's the first thing I saw when I regained consciousness.

**June**   Beating the bushes for heroes.

**Shirley**   Uncle Ken has five medals.

**Ken**   You may not be proud of that.

LANFORD WILSON
in *The Fifth of July* (1978)

**Lanford Wilson,** Sag Harbor, NY, 1986

The Grove was a resort, a place where people flocked in their leisure time if they could afford it, but it was also much, much more. Resorts like Provincetown, Massachusetts, Key West, Florida, and the Grove were (and to a large degree still are) the *only* public places gays could socialize and assemble without constant fear of hostile straight society. Of these resorts the Grove was the only one with such a substantial gay majority, and so it was the safest. Other beach or mountain retreats, like those of the Catskill Mountains "borscht belt," served minority populations, too, but they were never the *only* places their residents or visitors could openly associate. Few other minorities have so depended on being hidden for survival as have gays.

Even today, most gay people hide—"stay in the closet"—to save their skins, jobs, peace of mind. Staying invisible is also in itself an edict of what Gore Vidal called the heterosexual dictatorship. Many straight people know that this one or that one is gay and can "deal with it" as long as it isn't "brought up." That was the typical lifelong arrangement between Grovers and their families. "Thou shalt not be 'obvious' or 'flagrant'" is the first line of the social contract gays have been handed, even by liberals. And because of the unequal power between the parties, actions straights take for granted, like dancing or holding hands, are considered flagrant between homosexuals.

In Cherry Grove, gay people escape from straight domination to become for a space of time what so many long to be—themselves. The magic begins on the ferry ride out from Sayville, Long Island. Nobody has said it better than Natalia Murray when she described finding the Grove in 1936: "This place, so close to New York—you can breathe the fresh air. When we found it, it seemed so secret, wonderful. You see people—just leaving Sayville they breathe freer."

During that tranquil twenty minutes in the belly of an old and grimy ferry in the company of other lesbians and gay men with their groceries, belongings, and pets, "America"—not only the land of traffic and shopping malls, but also the land where the "general population" seems content for AIDS to kill the "homos," where "Death to Queers" is spraypainted on the white walls of the Sayville train station and Senator Jesse Helms easily defeats any legislation associated with our well-being—that "America" is left behind, sinks down in the wake of the ferry, and for an afternoon or weekend or season, we live as others do as if in a dream. Even during my first summer I began to wonder how this little sandspit came to be, as far as we now know, the world's *only* geography controlled by gay men and women.

ESTHER NEWTON
in *Cherry Grove, Fire Island: Sixty Years in America's First Gay and Lesbian Town* (1993)

He was just a face I saw in a discotheque one winter, but it was I who ended up going back to Fire Island to pick up his things. Now my father used to say, and I agree: There is nothing so unhappy as going through the clothes of a friend who has died, to see what may be used and what should be given to charity.

But Malone was hardly even a friend—something much more, and much less, perhaps—and so it felt odd to be traveling out there yesterday afternoon. It was a fine autumn day, the last week of October, and as the taxi drove from the train station in Sayville to the docks, that village had never looked more attractive. There was an unspoken celebration in the very silence, of the end of that long summer season, when a hundred taxis a day like ours crisscrossed the streets between the train station and the docks, taking the inhabitants of Manhattan across that shallow bay to their revelries on the beach of Fire Island. It was a journey between islands, after all: from Manhattan, to Long Island, to Fire Island, and the last island of the three was nothing but a sandbar, as slim as a parenthesis, enclosing the Atlantic, the very last fringe of soil on which a man might put up his house, and leave behind him all—absolutely all—of that huge continent to the west. There are New Yorkers who boast they've never been west of the Hudson, but the exhausted souls who went each weekend of summer to their houses on that long sandbar known among certain crowds as the Dangerous Island (dangerous because you could lose your heart, your reputation, your contact lenses), they put an even more disdainful distance between themselves and America: free, free at last.

ANDREW HOLLERAN
in *Dancer from the Dance* (1978)

Once again, he ended up in the Castro. True, he bad-mouthed the gay ghetto at *least* twice a day, but there was a lot to be said for sheer numbers when you were looking for company.

Toad Hall and the Midnight Sun were wall-to-wall flannel, as usual. He passed them up for the Twin Peaks, where his crew-neck sweater and corduroy trousers would seem less alien to the environment.

Cruising, he had long ago decided, was a lot like hitchhiking.

It was best to dress like the people you wanted to pick you up. . . .

"Crowded, huh?" The man at the bar was wearing Levi's, a rugby shirt and red-white-and-blue Tigers. He had a pleasant, square-jawed face that reminded Michael of people he had once known in the Campus Crusade for Christ.

"What is it?" asked Michael. "A full moon or something?"

"Got me. I don't keep up with that crap."

Point One in his favor. Despite Mona's proselytizing, Michael was not big on astrology freaks. He grinned. "Don't tell anybody, but the moon's in Uranus."

The man stared dumbly, then got it. "The moon's in your anus. That's a riot!"

Go ahead, Michael told himself. Ply him with cheap jokes. Have no shame.

The man obviously liked him. "What are you drinking?"

"Calistoga water."

"I figured that."

"Why"

"I don't know. You're . . . healthy-looking."

"Thanks"

The man extended his hand. "I'm Chuck."

"Michael."

"Hi, Mike."

"Oh . . . You know what, man? I gotta tell you the truth. I scoped you out when you walked in here . . . and I said, 'That's the one, Chuck.' I swear to God!"

What *was* it with this butch number? "Keep it up," Michael grinned. "I can use the strokes."

"You know what it was, man?"

"No."

The man smiled self-assuredly, then pointed to Michael's shoes. "Them."

"My shoes?"

He nodded. "Weejuns."

"Yeah?"

"And white socks."

"I see."

"They new?"

"No. I just had them half-soled."

The man shook his head reverentially, still staring at the loafers. "Half-soled. Far fucking out!"

"Excuse me, are you . . . ?"

"How many pairs you got?"

"Just these."

"I have six pairs. Black, brown, scotch grain . . ."

"You like 'em, huh?"

"You seen my ad in *The Advocate?*"

"No."

"It says . . . He held his hand up to make it graphic for Michael. "'Bass Weejuns.' Big capital letters, like."

"Catchy wording."

"I got a lotta calls. Collegiate types. Lotta guys get sick of the glitter fairies in this town."

"I can imagine."

The man moved closer, lowering his voice. "You ever . . . done it in 'em."

"Not to my recollection. Look . . . if you've got six pairs, how come you're not wearing any tonight?"

The man was aghast at his *faux pas.* "I always wear my Tigers with my rugby shirt!"

"Right."

He held his foot up for examination. "They're just like Billy Sive's. In *The Front Runner.*"

ARMISTEAD MAUPIN
in *Tales of the City* (1978)

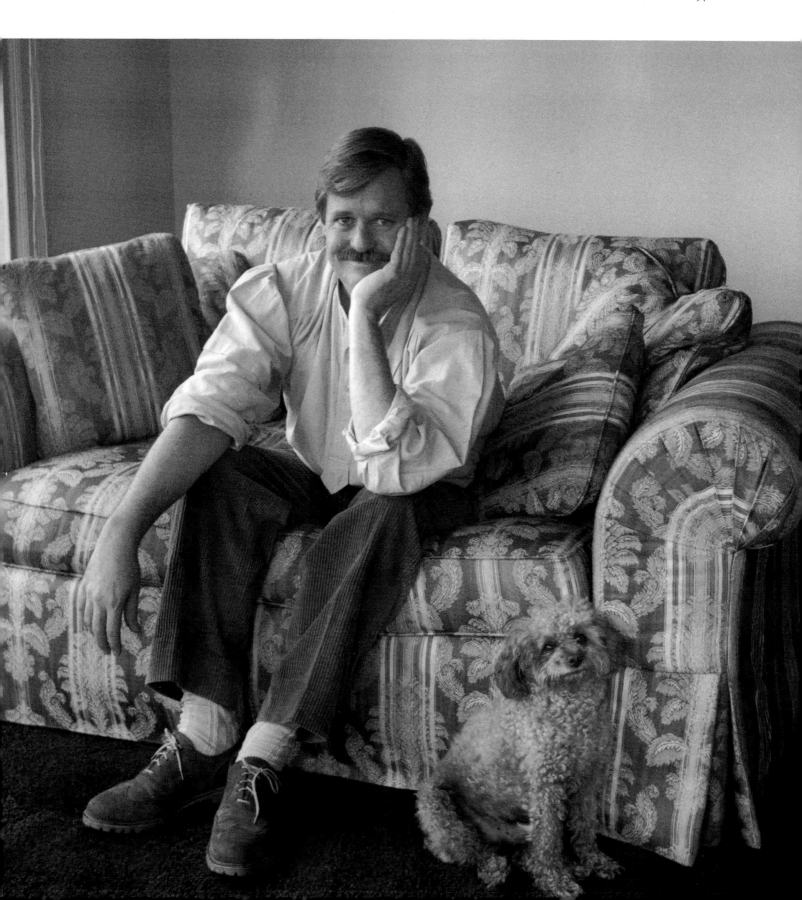

After loading Bronco and the backpack in the jeep, she pulled onto the freeway, then changed her mind and took the next exit to Babe's. The late-summer sun hung low in the west, sending long shadows across the street as Kelly dodged traffic and headed toward the bar. As she pulled the door wide, dank coolness surrounded her, the trademark of every bar she'd ever known. Air thick with the smell of stale cigarettes and whiskey with beer chasers greeted her: familiar, forbidden smells, like those that spilled out across the sidewalks of her childhood when she hurried to the grocery store for Aunt Nelda or to her best friend Sarah's house. Dark, cool smells of secrets.

"*Kelly Marie! Get away from that barroom door!*" Her mother's voice charged out of her memories. Even now, a lifetime later, she could still hear her mother's shrill whine punctuating the afternoon. And Kelly was nine years old again. "*You're asking for trouble, Missy, and that's exactly what you'll get if I ever catch you inside that den of iniquity. Do you hear me? Now, hurry along. Stop dragging your feet, I just spent twelve dollars on those shoes. Do you want them to be scuffed even before school starts? Kelly Marie, I said come on! I swear, you act just like your father's people. Kelly Marie!*"

That bar had burned the summer of her sophomore year in high school, but sometimes she could still hear the peals of laughter, the funny tinny music and sounds that seeped onto the sidewalk. Sometimes, breaths of frosty air spilled out through the half-opened doors onto the steaming sidewalks of the little Arkansas town where she was born. Through the gloom, she could see shadows moving, and sometimes a pair of eyes looking out into the white heat of the day.

"*But Mama, that's Maybelle Cain there by the window. You see her, don't you Mama? You know Maybelle, she's in my class at school. She's real nice, Mama. Can't I stop and have a Coke with her? Well, why not, I got the dime Aunt Nelda give me. Mama, she's all by herself, just settin' there a-waiting for her mama to get done workin'. Ow! That hurts! Mama, you're a-squeezin my wrist!*"

"*How many times do I have to tell you she's nothing but trash? Her mother is nothing but a common barmaid and I will not have you taking up with the likes of them . . .*" Her mother's voice faded into the past as the door to Babe's bar closed behind Kelly. A grin washed her face warm. "*Welcome to Babe's, Mama,*" her imagination called back across the miles and years, "*I'm sure you'd be the first to recognize a den of iniquity full of lezzies, queers, and all manner of undesirables. And I like being with them a whole lot better than I ever liked being with you.*"

NISA DONNELLY
in *The Bar Stories* (1989)

**Nisa Donnelly,** San Francisco, CA, 1994

It was a dark, crummy place. Red and blue lights flashed on a dance floor the size of a dining room table. Women jammed it, making a high-pitched *woo-woo* sound. No one seemed to be dancing with anyone in particular. She liked that. One group of four passed a small brown bottle from nose to nose and it caused them to dance more wildly. She made a note to try it.

She still wasn't sure that she was a lesbian. Screwing Case hadn't been bad. She supposed she could do it for the rest of her life if she had to. The couple beside her kissed. She couldn't look. The woman on the other side of her said, "Hi."

"Hi," Melissa said, her heart skipping rope in her chest.

"I'm Fancy." Fancy held out her hand.

"I'm Melissa." She pretended not to see the hand. Her palms were sweaty and she couldn't touch another woman's hand, not in this place. She still wanted to go to college.

Fancy was wearing a flannel shirt. Her hair had been dyed within an inch of its life and was orangey blond. It looked toxic. She had, dear God, a faint moustache. Melissa licked her upper lip, which was still mercifully bare. Maybe the small brown bottle was liquid male hormones. She didn't know if she had a type yet, but Fancy would never be it.

"I've never seen you here before," Fancy said.

"No," Melissa said, an answer which she felt summed up her whole life. She was disheartened that Fancy's come-on hadn't been any more original than your average dumb jock's. These lesbians were a disappointing lot.

"You want to dance?" Fancy asked.

"I can't," Melissa said.

"Ooohhh . . ." she said, "you got a girlfriend."

"Actually, I have scoliosis." She didn't know what scoliosis was, but she hoped it sounded contagious to Fancy.

"Oh, man, so many women are sick these days. Want another beer?"

"No thanks," Melissa said, setting her empty bottle on the bar. "I have to get going. I'm getting married."

"Oh," Fancy said, "a tourist."

WESLEY GIBSON
in *Shelter* (1992)

**Wesley Gibson,** Richmond, VA, 1991

And now I'm here on my own, in training to be a rugged, independent Oregonian. Living, but for Girlfriend next door, alone in the woods like a back-to-the-women's-land collectivist with all the conveniences. Nights, I walk down a pitch-black fog-shrouded country road where werewolves, for goodness sake, could get me, according to the late night movies I was raised on in New York City. Hauling wet wood, mending the barn roof (from the inside—it was raining), growing all seven tomatoes in my first-ever garden—it's all so new and hard.

But, I tell Taz in letters, it's not at all weird. It feels so natural and I'm so changed with the change in lands.

I've learned how to burn wet wood. I've blazed my own trail up to Mother Kali's Bookstore in Eugene and found as fine a feminist bookstore as any in Connecticut. Ashland is about as far from me as New York City was, but the freeway is a joy to drive compared to Bruckner Boulevard and Bloomsbury Books, in Ashland, carries lesbian novels. You can go to good—and bad—theatre year round, including Tennessee Williams' apparently lesbian play "Something Unspoken," in a recent fantastic production. Then there's the Southern Oregon Women's Writers Group, Gourmet Eating Society and Chorus. Despite Taz' fear that my writing style would change radically out here, I found this group, so unique to Southern Oregon, was just what I needed.

And look at them! At Hannah Blue Heron whose musical fantasy "From the Other Side of Madness" was performed at the Northwest Women's Cultural Festival in Olympia, Washington last year. At Tangren Pearl Time's Child who self-published a fascinating book called *The Auto Biography of Deborah Carr*. At Tee Corinne, her art, her books. At Ruth Mountaingrove, who created with Jean *Womanspirit Magazine* and is still a fountain of poetry and songs and photography. I look at these core group members and thank the mountains for welcoming me so grandly.

It's the Amazon Trail, then, I'm traveling and writing about. Every dyke has found at least a bit of it. For some it leads only as far as the nearest gay bar. Others have crisscrossed the country, the world, connecting with other lesbians along the way. For me, today, it's the I-5 corridor from L.A. to Vancouver. Tomorrow—who knows?

LEE LYNCH
in *The Amazon Trail* (1988)

**Lee Lynch,** Grants Pass, OR, 1994

**Jean Mountaingrove** at Rootworks, Sunny Valley, OR, 1994
With Ruth Mountaingrove and other women, Jean published
*WomanSpirit* magazine from 1974 to 1984.

**RFD** Managing Editors, Short Mountain, TN, 1991
*RFD* is a journal for gay men that focuses on country living. It has
been published by various gay communes since its founding in
1974. *From left to right:* Jim, Kulaya, David, Sr. Missionary P.
Delight, Vera, Martin, and Stevie. Not present: Gabby Haze.

There is nothing more important to me than home. . . .

I learned about Black feminism from the women in my family—not just from their strengths, but from their failings, from witnessing daily how they were humiliated and crushed because they had made the "mistake" of being born Black and female in a white man's country. I inherited fear and shame from them as well as hope. These conflicting feelings about being a Black woman still do battle inside of me. It is this conflict, my constantly ". . . seeing and touching/Both sides of things"* that makes my commitment real.

In the fall of 1981 before most of this book was compiled, I was searching for a title. I'd come up with one that I knew was not quite right. At the time I was also working on the story which later became "Home" and thought that I'd like to get some of the feeling of that piece into the book. One day while doing something else entirely, and playing with words in my head, "home girls" came to me. Home Girls. The girls from the neighborhood and from the block, the girls we grew up with. I knew I was onto something, particularly when I considered that so many Black people who are threatened by feminism have argued that by being a Black feminist (particularly if you are also a Lesbian) you have left the race, are no longer a part of the Black community, in short no longer have a home. . . .

I hope that *Home Girls* will inspire each of you to think deeply and to read more about Third World women than this book can contain. I sincerely hope that *Home Girls* is upsetting, because being upset is often the first step toward change. I pray that people both laugh and cry while reading it, and that it touches something familiar in you all. I hope that for you, as for me, *Home Girls* provides a means to know yourself and to be known, that between its pages you start to feel at home. Because in the end, there is nothing more important to us than home.

BARBARA SMITH

in *Home Girls: A Black Feminist Anthology* (1983)

This book contained the work of such writers as Audre Lorde, Ann Allen Shockley, Michelle Cliff, Jewelle Gomez, Becky Birtha, Cheryl Clarke, Pat Parker, June Jordan, Alice Walker, Bernice Johnson Reagon, and Kate Rushin.

*Kate Rushin, "The Bridge Poem."

**Barbara Smith,** Albany, NY, 1987
Smith was a co-founder and publisher of Kitchen Table: Women of Color Press.

# The Bridge Poem

I've had enough
I'm sick of seeing and touching
Both sides of things
Sick of being the damn bridge for everybody

Nobody can talk to anybody without me  Right

I explain my mother to my father my father to my little sister my little sister to my brother my brother to the White
Feminists the White Feminists to the Black Church Folks
the Black Church Folks to the ex-Hippies the ex-Hippies to
the Black Separatists the Black Separatists to the Artists and
the Artists to the parents of my friends . . .

Then
I've got to explain myself
To everybody

I do more translating than the U.N.

Forget it
I'm sick of filling in your gaps
Sick of being your insurance against
The isolation of your self-imposed limitations
Sick of being the crazy at your Holiday Dinners
The odd one at your Sunday Brunches
I am sick of being the sole Black friend to
Thirty-four Individual White Folks

Find another connection to the rest of the world
Something else to make you legitimate
Some other way to be political and hip
I will not be the bridge to your womanhood
Your manhood
Your human-ness

I'm sick of reminding you not to
Close off too tight for too long

Sick of mediating with your worst self
On behalf of your better selves

Sick
Of having
To remind you
To breathe
Before you
Suffocate
Your own
Fool self

Forget it
Stretch or drown
Evolve or die

You see  it's like this
The bridge I must be
Is the bridge to my own power
I must translate
My own fears
Mediate
My own weaknesses

I must be the bridge to nowhere
But my own true self
It's only then
I can be
Useful

KATE RUSHIN
in *The Black Back-Ups* (1993)

An earlier version of this poem served as the opening piece to *This
Bridge Called My Back: Writings by Radical Women of Color*, an anthology
edited by Cherríe Moraga and Gloria Anzaldúa. Originally published
by Persephone Press in 1981, it was reissued in 1983 by Kitchen Table:
Women of Color Press of New York. Included in this collection was
work by Audre Lorde, Barbara Cameron, Merle Woo, Chrystos, and
Pat Parker among others.

**Kate Rushin,** Cambridge, MA, 1987

The actual physical borderland that I'm dealing with in this book is the Texas-U.S. Southwest/Mexican border. The psychological borderlands, the sexual borderlands and the spiritual borderlands are not particular to the Southwest. In fact, the Borderlands are physically present wherever two or more cultures edge each other, where people of different races occupy the same territory, where under, lower, middle and upper classes touch, where the space between two individuals shrinks with intimacy.

I am a border woman. I grew up between two cultures, the Mexican (with a heavy Indian influence) and the Anglo (as a member of a colonized people in our own territory). I have been straddling that *tejas*-Mexican border, and others, all my life. It's not a comfortable territory to live in, this place of contradictions. Hatred, anger and exploitation are the prominent features of this landscape.

However, there have been compensations for this *mestiza*, and certain joys. Living on borders and in margins, keeping intact one's shifting and multiple identity and integrity, is like trying to swim in a new element, an "alien" element. There is an exhilaration in being a participant in the further evolution of humankind, in being "worked" on. I have the sense that certain "faculties"—not just in me but in every border resident, colored or non-colored—and dormant areas of consciousness are being activated, awakened. Strange, huh? And yes, the "alien" element has become familiar—never comfortable, not with society's clamor to uphold the old, to rejoin the flock, to go with the herd. No, not comfortable but home.

This book, then, speaks of my existence. My preoccupations with the inner life of the Self, and with the struggle of that Self amidst adversity and violation; with the confluence of primordial images; with the unique positionings consciousness takes at these confluent streams; and with my almost instinctive urge to communicate, to speak, to write about life on the borders, life in the shadows.

Books saved my sanity, knowledge opened the locked places in me and taught me first how to survive and then how to soar. *La madre naturaleza* succored me, allowed me to grow roots that anchored me to the earth. My love of images—mesquite flowering, the wind, *Ehécatl*, whispering its secret knowledge, the fleeting images of the soul in fantasy—and words, my passion for the daily struggle to render them concrete in the world and on paper, to render them flesh, keeps me alive.

GLORIA ANZALDÚA
in *Borderlands/La Frontera: The New Mestiza* (1987)

**Gloria Anzaldúa**, Oakland, CA, 1988

El otro día me encontré a García Lorca | The Other Day I Ran into García Lorca

lo reconocí

por el moño

los labios

los ojos

olivos


lloraban

guitarras

y bailaba

flamenco

la tarde

de pronto

se paró

vino

directo

a mi mesa


y me plantó

un beso

como sol

andaluz

en la boca


I recognized him

by the slim bow tie

his lips

his eyes

olive-colored


guitars

wept and

the afternoon

danced

flamenco

suddenly

he stood

walked

directly

to my table


and planted

a kiss

like an Andalusian

sun

on my lips


FRANCISCO X. ALARCÓN

in *Body in Flames/Cuerpo en llamas* (1990)


Translation by Francisco Aragon


Francisco X. Alarcón, Davis, CA, 1994

Through the viewfinder of the camera, Michael looked at the rice fields. Still only one lonely farmer. He looked up from beneath his hat but was still too far away for Michael to see his face, to discover his age. He could have been eighteen or as old as his father.

"Go out there and pick up that farmer," Michael ordered Alex. "You *bok gwei*, bringing your evil ways to China, ruining simple people's lives."

"What are you talking about? Homosexuality exists in every culture. It's not exclusively white."

"But you think you're our savior. The great white hope, aren't you?" Michael retorted. "We Chinese all want white men, no? Because we want to be like you . . ."

"Here, give me the camera and let me get a picture of you and your father in front of the ancestral Chinese home."

"I don't want to be like you."

"I told you my story, now give me back my camera and get in the picture, Emperor." Alex grabbed hold of Michael's arm.

"No." Michael pulled away from Alex and the camera fell onto the ground. The back flipped open, exposing all the film to daylight.

"I don't believe you," Alex said. "You're a real fuckin' baby."

"Go away, *bok gwei*," Michael said. "It's been fun. I'll be seeing you around."

Alex stared at Michael, shocked. For a moment Michael feared that he would say something to his father and the two old women. But would they even understand? The three of them stood, smiling and nodding. His father fidgeted back and forth. He still had not gone to the bathroom.

Alex bent down to retrieve his camera. "What's your fuckin' problem?" he said to Michael.

"Go away."

Alex began to walk alongside the field alone, the lonely tourist. As he walked, he kept watch over the farmer in the field. Michael imagined Alex having sex with the farmer and then saw himself with the farmer. The farmer's body would be skinny like his own. With each movement, their elbows, knees, bones would knock painfully together.

His father continued to pace. Hurry, hurry, Michael thought. Did his father suspect how differently his son had turned out from what he had wanted? His father had told his mother, "If I don't take him to China now, he'll forget that he was ever Chinese once he gets to Chicago." His father should never have left China: would he have turned out straight then? *I am different from you, Dad. I'm not Chinese. This is* your *homeland. Not mine.*

NORMAN WONG
in *Cultural Revolution* (1994)

"Mom? . . . Mom?"

Ginger slowly turned her head to look at Mary Ann. "What now?"

"Could I ask you one more thing, Mom?"

"All right, but this is all I can take for one night. If you want more answers, when you're sixteen you go read the divorce records. You hear?"

Mary Ann said, "Sure, Mom." She cleared her throat. "Well, if Dad had a good heart and was an O.K. person, why isn't it all right for me to do regular things with his family? Why did you take me completely away from them? Can't I be with them and you both?"

Ginger looked confused. She said, "That's too many questions to sort out. I don't want to talk about these things."

She began to rise from the chair. Looked down at Mary Ann. Her face suddenly softened. She put her hand under Mary Ann's chin and shook her head. Sat back in the chair.

"I'm only going to ever say this to you once, Mary Ann. I don't know if I can make you understand. There are so many things in the world that are cruel. People mostly, I guess. Ideas, too. But those come out of people. I suppose I don't really know. But there's badness in the world. You and John are different from lots of children. I can't do anything about him now. He will grow up with a lot of strange ideas which will separate him and won't help him get along in the world. But you, you'll be fine. You'll go to a Catholic church, schools just like other kids, and be normal. When you were born I promised you that. I looked in your crib and said, 'You're only half-Indian, but I'll make it all right.' You're going to be O.K. You'll see. You'll be just like all the other kids. I promise you, Mary Ann. No one will ever say terrible things to you. I promised."

Ginger got up and hugged Mary Ann close to her. Mary Ann could feel Ginger crying. She felt her own tears slide down her cheeks. She spoke to herself inside her head, "Oh, Mom, I'm already different. It was O.K. the way it was. It's never going to be how you think it is, and you're never going to know, are you?" She closed her eyes and saw Mother Coyote.

VICKIE SEARS
in *Simple Songs* (1990)

**Vickie Sears,** New York, NY, 1990

Neil was twelve the first time he recognized in himself something like sexuality. He was lying outside, on the grass, when Rasputin—the dog, long dead, of his childhood—began licking his face. He felt a tingle he did not recognize, pulled off his shirt to give the dog access to more of him. Rasputin's tongue tickled coolly. A wet nose started to sniff down his body, toward his bathing suit. What he felt frightened him, but he couldn't bring himself to push the dog away. Then his mother called out, "Dinner," and Rasputin was gone, more interested in food than in him.

It was the day after Rasputin was put to sleep, years later, that Neil finally stood in the kitchen, his back turned to his parents, and said, with unexpected ease, "I'm a homosexual." The words seemed insufficient, reductive. For years, he had believed his sexuality to be detachable from the essential him, but now he realized that it was part of him. He had the sudden, despairing sensation that though the words had been easy to say, the fact of their having been aired was incurably damning. Only then, for the first time, did he admit that they were true, and he shook and wept in regret for what he would not be for his mother, for having failed her. His father hung back, silent; he was absent for that moment as he was mostly absent—a strong absence. Neil always thought of him sitting on the edge of the bed in his underwear, captivated by something on television. He said, "It's O.K., Neil." But his mother was resolute; her lower lip didn't quaver. She had enormous reserves of strength to which she only gained access at moments like this one. She hugged him from behind, wrapped him in the childhood smells of perfume and brownies, and whispered, "It's O.K., honey." For once, her words seemed as inadequate as his. Neil felt himself shrunk to an embarrassed adolescent, hating her sympathy, not wanting her to touch him. It was the way he would feel from then on whenever he was in her presence—even now, at twenty-three, bringing home his lover to meet her.

DAVID LEAVITT
in *Family Dancing* (1983)

**David Leavitt,** East Hampton, NY, 1987

Jesse came out this time determined not to mention this last visit. She actually expected that, because of it, her mother would be on her best behavior. It looks like that's not going to be the case.

"We have a committee at church," she says now, assigning responsibility for her not being able to accept Kit to a higher authority. "S.O.S. Save Our Sinners. We write letters to the shows, the networks. We ask them to take off characters like hers and put on families that reflect Christian values."

Jesse tries for a serious nod, but her mother can smell her amusement, and makes a small, angry sound, a tiny click deep in her throat, and turns away to wash out a couple of glasses with a complicated looking soap-dispenser brush.

"She's not the person she plays on the show," Jesse says, because she can't not defend Kit against any attack, even one as nutty as this.

"Well, I'm sure, but she gives people ideas," her mother says, not letting go now that she has purchase. "Sets a bad example. How'd you even meet a show business person like that, anyway?" she asks now, fixing Jesse with a whammy.

"I teach with her uncle," Jesse says, then wonders if this sounds warm and family-oriented, or like Humbert Humbert recalling how he met Lolita. She watches her mother turn back to the sink and sweep into the soapy water a spatula and spoon rest that says "Spoon" on it.

"Look . . ." Jesse starts, feeling a flash of being up to this. By directly coming out to her mother, she can at least go on the offensive in this conversation, rattle her mother's cage by speaking the unspeakable, break the regional code of polite conversation: that when something is unpleasant or difficult to talk about, it is simply placed on a lower shelf of fact by not mentioning it.

"You don't have to tell me," her mother says. "It's on all the shows. Donahue. Oprah." And that's that. Her mother reaches over and tugs the quilted cozy over the toaster and shuts down the subject.

CAROL ANSHAW
in *Aquamarine* (1992)

**Carol Anshaw,** Chicago, IL, 1993

My grandmother, Lydia, and my mother, Dolores, were both talking to me from their bathroom stalls in the Times Square movie theater. I was washing the popcorn butter from my hands at the sink and didn't think it at all odd. The people in my family are always talking; conversation is a life force in our world. My great-grandmother, Grace, would narrate her life story from 7:00 A.M. until we went to bed at night. The only breaks were when we were reading, or the reverential periods when we sat looking out of our tenement windows observing the neighborhood—whose sights we naturally talked about later.

So it was not odd that Lydia and Dolores were talking nonstop from their stalls, oblivious to everyone except the three of us. I hadn't expected it to happen there. I hadn't really expected an "it" to happen at all. To be a lesbian is part of who I am, like being left-handed. It seemed a fact that needed no articulation. My first encounter with the word *bulldagger* was not charged with emotional conflict. When I was a teenager in the 1960s, my grandmother told me a story about a particular building in our Boston neighborhood that had gone to seed. She described the building's glorious past through the experience of a party she'd attended there twenty years before. The best part of the evening had been a woman she'd met and danced with . . .

My mother had started reading the graffiti written on the wall of the bathroom cubicle. We hooted at each of her dramatic renderings. Then she said (not breaking rhythm, since we all know timing is everything), "Here's one I haven't seen before—DYKES UNITE." There was that profound silence again, as if the frames of my life had ground to a halt in a projector. We were in a freeze-frame, and options played themselves out in my head in a rapid succession: Say nothing? Say something? Say what?

I laughed and said, "Yeah, but have you seen the rubber stamp on my desk at home?"

"No," said my mother, with a slight bit of puzzlement. "What's it say?"

"I saw it," my grandmother called out from her stall. "It says Lesbian Money."

"What?"

"LESBIAN MONEY," Lydia repeated loudly over the water running in the row of sinks.

"I just stamp it on my big bills," I said tentatively, and we all screamed with laughter. The other women in the restroom had only been a shadow for me in these moments, but they came into focus as I felt each one press more closely to her sink, trying to pretend that the conversation was not happening.

Since that night there has been little said on the subject. Yet. There have been some awkward moments, usually in social situations where Lydia or Dolores felt uncertain.

A couple of years after our Times Square encounter I visited my grandmother for the weekend with my lover. One of the neighbors in her building dropped by, and when she left, my grandmother spoke to me in low tones while my lover was in another room. She said we should be careful about being so open in front of other people because they weren't necessarily as fair-minded as she. I was flooded, momentarily, with shock and disappointment. But before I could respond, she heard the words and their incongruity with who she was. She grabbed my arm and demanded, "Forget I said that. Nobody pays rent around this apartment but me."

JEWELLE GOMEZ
in *Forty-Three Septembers* (1993)

**Jewelle Gomez,** Jersey City, NJ, 1987

# A Chinese Banquet

*for the one who was not invited*

it was not a very formal affair but
all the women over twelve
wore long gowns and a corsage,
except for me.

it was not a very formal affair, just
the family getting together,
*poa poa, kuw fu* without *kuw mow**
(her excuse this year is a headache).

aunts and uncles and cousins,
the grandson who is a dentist,
the one who drives a mercedes benz,
sitting down for shark's fin soup.

they talk about buying a house and
taking a two week vacation in beijing.
i suck on shrimp and squab,
dreaming of the cloudscape in your eyes.

my mother, her voice beaded with sarcasm:
you're twenty six and not getting younger.
it's about time you got a decent job.
she no longer asks when i'm getting married.

you're twenty six and not getting younger.
what are you doing with your life?
you've got to make a living.
why don't you study computer programming?

she no longer asks when i'm getting married.
one day, wanting desperately to
bridge the boundaries that separate us,
wanting desperately to touch her,

tell her: mother, i'm gay,
mother i'm gay and so happy with her.
but she will not listen,
she shakes her head.

she sits across from me,
emotions invading her face.
her eyes are wet but
she will not let tears fall.

mother, i say,
you love a man.
i love a woman.
it is not what she wants to hear.

aunts and uncles and cousins,
very much a family affair.
but you are not invited,
being neither my husband nor my wife.

aunts and uncles and cousins
eating longevity noodles
fragrant with ham inquire:
sold that old car of yours yet?

i want to tell them: my back is healing,
i dream of dragons and water.
my home is in her arms,
our bedroom ceiling the wide open sky.

KITTY TSUI

*Grandmother; uncle; aunt.
in *Words of a Woman Who Breathes Fire* (1983)

**Kitty Tsui,** Oakland, CA, 1989

How can I explain to my mother that despite all her pleading with me to grow beyond my homosexuality, I've remained intractable, true to myself? Shall I show her the irony, confirm her suspicions that, yes, her behavior may have caused my own? Shall I tell her how her love was sacred, how her goodnight kiss and whispered "there now" consummated my day? How a woman's breath in my ear is still a kind of balm in my brain? Or should I recite that, like Popeye, I am, simply, what I am? Can I admit, without her thrilling to false hopes, that, having loved a man, having mated with a man, I know I could still?

I still find men attractive, and I still recall, with sexual excitement, my escapades into heterosexual sex. I especially enjoyed the encyclopedic range of sexual imagery to draw from—the gamut, from Bible to porno. Not to mention the hundred cinematic kisses that left me breathless in the dark. Like Kim Novak and William Holden dancing to "Moonglow" in a July swelter.

Yet when a woman approaches I feel something older, less articulate. Something as absolutely hoped for as "there now." This is my polemic, justification for my nature. We all inevitably feel the pull toward some creature made luminous in the act of love. Is it toward the archetypal Momma? Or the, if you're so inclined, Daddy? If all the world's faiths sing the virtues of the Great Mother and Father, can these sex-inspired hallucinations be so pathological? Aren't all humans linked together by a need that predates adult development, when surrender was the mirror image of survival? When, at our most vulnerable, we were literally lifted up into the air toward the salvation of an adult body? Likewise, aren't our sucking lovers briefly infants, their need for us as primal as milk? Is it childish to employ our imaginations in the service of our pleasures? Is our development arrested, or are our natures finally realized?

Besides, look again: What once seemed pathological is now sleek and predacious, like you snaking through the ivy as childhood reopens. You, the stealthy hero behind enemy lines, liberating French villages, wrestling with your playmate to save the Free World. You will always find fascination in the flesh around the nipple, the back of the neck. Like my mother did in her hunger for my father. Not for the sake of procreation, not for some higher purpose or polemic. You, me, my mother, us all, our fingers branching, unabashed.

BIA LOWE
in *Wild Ride* (1995)

**Bia Lowe,** Los Angeles, CA, 1989

The trip from the construction site to our father's office required a lot less skill than trailing the lunch truck. The Pontiac rode the flow of traffic, meandered long city blocks. Typical of September weather, clouds thickened as the day wore on, and only the thinnest light strained through. Sometimes my brother would slow the car, absorbed by a billboard or a poster in a travel agency without regard for the honking behind us. One theater displayed the titles of a double feature on its marquee—both filmed in Blush Color—and my brother laughed to hear me reading: "*It Happened in a Nature Camp* and *Torrid Teasers*." I asked him what *torrid* meant. "It's when your blood boils for a girl. When she makes you pant like an animal." Bob's definition reminded me of a wolf I'd seen on a Saturday-morning cartoon; at the sight of a woman in a side-slit dress, the wolf's eyes popped out of their sockets, the ribbon of his tongue unfurled, jets of steam shrieked from his ears, and his polka-dot bow tie spun like a propeller. "What're you smiling at?" asked my brother. "You're not keeping something from me, are you? Don't tell me you've flipped over some doll in the sixth grade." Silence seemed like the perfect reply to a question charged with pride and innuendo; I let Bob believe his younger brother was a ladies' man in the making.

As we pulled into the parking lot of our father's office, I felt, I admit, a certain satisfaction in having deceived my brother. Though Bob's physical strength was superior—a phantom grip still burned my wrists—he could be made to believe about me what I wanted him to believe. Something as simple as a grin and well-timed silence could placate him, assure him I was a typical boy, freeing me for my private desires. And despite my continued fear of exposure, despite my understanding, however dim, that these desires would set me apart forever, every clandestine urge—to feel Brad's lips as he mimicked kisses, to lay my head on Jeff Chandler's chest, to touch the arms of Chief Altoon—infused me with a lust that was, I knew, as powerful as the lust of adults. In secret, I was equal.

BERNARD COOPER
in *A Year of Rhymes* (1993)

**Bernard Cooper,** Los Angeles, CA, 1989

"What's the rest of it, Chick?"

"Of what?"

"Your heritage."

"Oh. Being gay, I guess."

"You really think so?"

"I do. I really think so. Without that, I just wouldn't be the same person—I'd have a completely different point of view about almost everything—I'd have a completely different life. Some of which would be easier, I guess. But some of it would be much, much harder."

"How so?"

Because, I told her, *not* being different in America can lull you, can cripple you—even though it seems desirable to everyone, even though everything in the society pressures you into sameness—it is a handicap in the end. A handicap to live without knowing the struggle of difference—in all of its pain, its fear, its celebration, its compassion.

She thought this through. Gave a skeptical look. Saying Well, maybe, but if that's true it's something she herself has never experienced.

"That's because you don't have gay friends."

"I've never really felt the need."

"But I think the need's there, sweetie, whether you acknowledge it or not. When you don't have that—a small group or a community of friends—not even *friends*, exactly but people who *reflect* you, who share in or at least identify with your most intimate reality—you tend to feel utterly isolated, almost as if you're the last of your species, ill at ease in the world. As if you *belong* less than anyone else. As if you are *worth* less than anyone else, than all the straight people walking around proclaiming their self-righteous view of normality without even *knowing* that that's what they're doing—because that kind of careless insensitivity,

it's so deeply, habitually ingrained, that in a way you learn not to expect anything better from them."

She listened, skepticism still in her eyes. Somehow, though, I am hitting home, and know it. Hallelujah, I thought—and I didn't stop talking.

"But when you more or less surround yourself by a community of queers"—I watch her silently wince at the word, and I smile—"you create a different universe within that seemingly larger whole, a universe in which *you* are the norm, in which *you* are accepted and acceptable. You relax. You laugh, you love, you can suffer loss and openly grieve. Your passions stop embarrassing you so badly! And you begin to see that, in a very profound way, you can be sustained and have a good life with*out* all those straight people! Because the fact of the matter is that *we really don't need them.*"

"You sound pretty separatist," she teased. "Like all those phony feminists."

"Screw the feminists. I'm talking about *lesbians.*"

She laughed. "Good."

"Yes—see? We don't need the straights! Not *any* of them."

"I don't know, Chick. The world's pretty big. I think maybe we all need each other." She ran fingers over my shoulder, my neck. There was a tenderness to her, now, that I'd never directly experienced before; and, for a moment, I got the sense that our customary roles had reversed. She seemed much, much older than me. Kinder. Wiser.

"Another thing," she said quietly. "Not that I want to impede the progress of truth, beauty, or justice, mind you." She smiled. "But when you talk about creating a world in which you are the norm, you forget that norms can be deadening. Most notable accomplishment—I mean in sport, but also in the rest of life—is highly *ab*normal. Winning, for in-

stance—it can never be the norm. *Not* winning, *not* exceeding, *not* being special—those are the norms. And do you really want that?"

She'd scored a point. I told her fine, and accurate, and perceptive—but her world view avoided the whole issue of pride, of self-worth.

"And listen, Bren—don't you want to be proud of what you are? Don't you feel you deserve to be?"

"Maybe. But, you know, I'm not that interested in storming around being *proud* all the time. I know about that, I see it in the kids on my team a lot—when you're that proud of yourself you're arrogant, and when you're arrogant it's because you're afraid—you're afraid because you feel like you have something to lose, and whatever that something is, it's always on the line. You're always defending it, always more or less defensive. Personally, I say, give me the swimmer with nothing to lose. Pride doesn't impede her. And she can experience fear, or pain, but it doesn't stop her—she just throws her guts all out on the table and gets on with things—"

"Win or lose?"

"Win or win. I mean, pride is like talent, Chick—right? It only gets you so far. The rest is work. And acceptance—"

"Of the work?"

"Sure. And of your own little self, doing the work."

She was right. We both were. But, saying all these things, she had looked quite beautiful. I stopped being proud then, and stopped being afraid. Accepted what I wanted. Accepted *that* I wanted. I pushed her down by the shoulders—firmly, but gently, because the joints were aging now, required surgery, would never be the same, and I treasured every ruined inch of them the way I treasured her, and how she'd accepted the pain of them, and of work, and Kay, and me.

JENIFER LEVIN
in *The Sea of Light* (1993)

For women . . . poetry is not a luxury. It is a vital necessity of our existence. It forms the quality of the light within which we predicate our hopes and dreams toward survival and change, first made into language, then into idea, then into more tangible action. Poetry is the way we help give name to the nameless so it can be thought. The farthest horizons of our hopes and fears are cobbled by our poems, carved from the rock experiences of our daily lives.

AUDRE LORDE
in *Sister Outsider: Essays and Speeches* (1984)

**CM** When did it really start?

**JL** Well, the best account of this is Elly Bulkin's essay in *Lesbian Poetry*. Actually, the first all-women's press—The Women's Press Collective—was founded in Oakland, California, in 1970. My own passion for lesbian writing began in the early 70s. One night I heard Martha Shelley's "Lesbian Nation" program on WBAI, and I've never been the same since. It was probably in 1973 that I found Fran Winant's "Poem To My New Jacket." Later, she retitled it "Dyke Jacket." It was brave. Then I discovered *Amazon Quarterly*. It came in a plain brown wrapper—thank God! I then heard Audre Lorde, Alta, Judy Grahn, and Susan Griffin read in person. I was electrified. Their poems spoke directly to my hidden life, my real life. In '74, I met Irena Klepfisz and other lesbian poets at Alison Colbert's Focus II coffeehouse series. Together with three other women, Irena, Alison, Jan Clausen, and I formed a lesbian poets' support group. Then, in 1975, Elly Bulkin suggested that she and I collaborate on *Amazon Poetry*. We didn't use the word *lesbian* on the cover; but we printed it on the title page. As far as I know, that was the first place Adrienne Rich, May Swenson, and a lot of other women published in a lesbian context.

**CM** At the same time gay men's poetry was mushrooming. The best summary of it all is Rudy Kikel's essay, *Gay Sunshine* magazine's tenth-anniversary issue. In 1969, Paul Mariah founded ManRoot Magazine and ManRoot Press, which continues to this day to offer a fine list of gay men's writing. Winston Leyland began publishing *Gay Sunshine* magazine in 1970, and then his Gay Sunshine Press published the two best anthologies of gay men's poetry—*Angels of the Lyre* in 1975 and *Orgasms of Light* in 1977. Another important anthology had appeared even earlier, in 1973—Ian Young's *The Male Muse*. The Boston Gay Liberation Front generated both the radical magazine *Fag Rag* (1971–)—"the most loathsome publication in the English language," according to William Loeb, the virulent New Hampshire newspaper mogul—and a publishing operation, Good Gay Poets, which, since 1972, has issued an important series of poetry books by lesbian and gay men. In 1974, *RFD: A Country Journal for Gay Men Everywhere* got started in Iowa, and—now based in North Carolina [presently based in Tennessee]—is still going strong. And that same year, Andrew Bifrost created his elegantly edited and produced *Mouth of the Dragon: A Poetry Journal of Male Love*. Founded by Charles Ortleb, with Paul Baron and Michael Denneny, *Christopher Street*—still the most prestigious gay male literary magazine—made its debut in May 1976. And then Felice Picano founded The Sea Horse Press in 1977 and, in 1980, issued the landmark collection *A True Likeness: Lesbian & Gay Writing Today*.

CARL MORSE AND JOAN LARKIN, editors,
in the Introduction to *Gay and Lesbian Poetry in Our Time* (1988)

**Carl Morse,** poet and playwright, New York, NY, 1987

**Joan Larkin,** poet, Brooklyn, NY, 1987

## Living as a Lesbian Underground, ii

A faggot historian friend—once noted
now hunted—smuggled me the latest
in dyke fiction from Fiji.
I had to eat the manuscript
before I could finish it.

I was on my way underground when
uniformed children blondish forcing
my door nearly seized my journal.
I bribed them with adult books.
In a park a mustachioed gent in
trench coat no hat balding flashing
chased me for it.
(He recognized me from a photo in some old
literary review. It was a stunning photo.)
I outran him
and he yelled at me shaking his fists:

"Hey, *poeta*, hope you have a good memory.
Memory is your only redemption."

Hell I'm lucky.
I could be hiding some place
where I'm kidnapped
tortured on metal tables
fingers broken.
As it is my reveries have been confiscated
but my obsessions do me just as well.
Harder to manage and sexier.

An off-the-shelf mercenary counsels me:

"Detention is like solitude, and
don't poets need that? They'll let you
have a western classic or two,
a Norton anthology."

"Hell, what about a Portuguese-English
dictionary?"

I ask as he pulls a leisure suit over his bush
fatigues.

Around the time little Stevie Wonder's songs
were banned in the bantustans, a harried editor looked
up at me from my grazed manuscript,
shaking his head, said:

"Maybe in thirty years we can anthologize
an excerpt."

(Hell, I mimeographed the thing myself and
gave it out in the
quarantine we used to call Park Slope.)

But hell I still don't know what it's like
to be blocked by bayonets and frisked for
*The Color Purple* or be forced to dance
around a bonfire while my favorite passage
from Pushkin burns before my eyes.

A whore who'd been detained and raped
every day
for a month escaped to the red hills where
she encountered me and showed me a word
from a book
not my own:

"This word can get you violated,"

she said.

I'd never written the word.
But it was a good word.
It called me.
I had to write it or it would write me.
The pages of my journal were all written up
with words censored years before
they stopped selling blank paper,
pens, pencils, diskettes
(a few defectors had monitors).
I sneaked back into an old safe house
raided during the bombing of Tripoli.
I loosened a brick and pulled out
a suppressed manuscript
a tasty little piece
of interracial erotica
I'd written in the early days
of the emergency.
I wrote the word over and over
large and small on the back of every sheet
in cursive and in roman, in bold and fine.

I wrote it with my left hand
as well as my right.
I recited it every time I wrote it.
Played with my sex
as I wrote it
over and over.
And said it as I came
over and over

"Hey, *poeta*, memory is your only
redemption."

CHERYL CLARKE
in *Experimental Love* (1993)

**Cheryl Clarke,** Jersey City, NJ, 1987

Again for Hephaistos, the Last Time
October 1, 1973

*. . . translate for me till I*
*accomplish my corpse at last.*     W. H. AUDEN

What do we share with the past?
Assurance we are unique,
even in shipwreck. The dead
take away the world they made
certain was theirs—they die
knowing we never can have it.

As each of *us* knows, for even
a nap is enough to confirm
suspicions that when we are not
on the scene, nothing else is.
Call it the comfort of dying:
you *can* take it all with you.

"The ship is sinking": Cocteau managed to stage his
    whisper
while a camera was "well trained" (according to Stravinsky)
on the televised deathbed in Paris some dozen years ago;

his sparrow had fallen one day before this master forger
(who was hardly your *miglior fabbro*, although you had
    translated
his tangle of true and false Ginifers into you own
    Tintagel)—

finding Piaf had "gone on", as she always did, ahead
of time and tonsillitis, how could *he* help finding, too,
the vessel on the rocks, the wreck within easy reach?
Predeceased, your gaudy predecessor in death gave up
the ship—high season for sinking: Harlequin Jean, escorted
or just flanked by MacNeice and Roethke, alien
    psychopomps.

Yours though were quite as unlikely, every bit as outlandish.

This weekend, waves of applause (prerogative of popes!)
broke in the wake of a coffin leaving Santa Maria

sopra Minerva—Magnani, with Pablo Neruda your peer
on Sunday's appalling front page, though scarcely your pal:
Verga you loved, but had you stayed up late enough to see

"Mamma Roma" in his *Lupa?* Even heard of her? Like
    most
performers—like Piaf—she was, I suspect, as absent
from your now immortal reckonings as Rod McKuen et al.

You were not very fond of volcanoes—in verse or voice
    either,
and to violent Anna preferred a predictable Donna Elvira
who could always repeat her crises on key, on cue, encore!

Cocteau, you conceded, though stagy, had the *lacrimae*
    *rerum* note,
but did *you?* The *Times*, this morning, declared you had
    failed to make,
or even make your way inside, "a world of emotion".

I wonder. Given your case, or given at last your
    encasement,
who knows? Only the poems, and to me at least they speak
    volumes:
your death makes a leap-day this fall, this autumn you
    would say.

But my *personal* knowledge is odd, my evidence suspect
    even:
on a club-car up to Cambridge, two freshmen scribbled a
    note—
"Are you Carl Sandburg?" "You've ruined," you wrote back,
    "mother's day."

Was that emotion? Was this—the time backstage at the Y
when impatient to read to the rustling thousands out front,
    you asked
(possessing no small talk—and with you I possessed no
    large)

**Richard Howard,** New York, NY, 1986

why it was I no longer endured a difficult mutual friend.
"Because he calls everyone *else* either a kike or a
    cocksucker,
and since, Wystan, both he and I are . . . well, both of
    them . . ."

"My *dear*," you broke in, and I think you were genuinely
    excited,
"I never knew you were Jewish!" No, not a world of
    emotion—
say, for the time being, as you said, the emotion of a world.

    Only those poets can leave us
    whom we have never possessed.

What did you leave me? The unsaid,
mourning, hangs around me,
desperate, not catastrophic,
like a dog having a bad time.

The difference, then, between
your death and all those others
is this: you did not take
a certain world away, after
all. After you, because of you,
all songs are possible.

RICHARD HOWARD
in *Fellow Feelings* (1976)

# The Concepts Of Integrity And Closure in Poetry as I Believe They Relate To Sappho

1

There's always the question
*what else?* or *what more?*
A fragment of papyrus,
a frame from a film.
Wholeness but no closure.
Just what you'd glimpse—
two women suddenly arm in arm
crossing the beach-front walk,
the waves running like mares
behind them.

2

What is a month, for example?
Tear it out of a year like an eye
and what do you see?
Unimaginable to expect a year
could be missing an eye, or is it harder
to think of it
having one? Questions of parts
of what,
this is how I've felt
trying to look out of my self.
Just quick takes,
motor-driven and waiting for the day
it all makes sense.

3

Sappho is the lesson of parts.
Libraries you must do without
because you are the book.

4

This is what happens at parties
where women dance with one another.

Everyone kisses. Old lovers.
Tribes assume this.
Kiss and kiss. Just that much of that.
Book and book and book. I have been learned
by heart. Lovely Sappho taking in
a glance at a lovely thigh, flower
arranging someone's hair.
Like that.

Across the patio
in a canvas chair, you know
the living danger sitting there.
A fragmentary glance. An hour
in her arms, disarray
you carry for another hour
or a year, years from that day
you keep like a piece of mica or a negative.

I have held to my lips
for a moment things like smoke. Smoke
from a burning book.

5

The waves ran away like mares
and the silver sat in its soft cloth
and the shells of the sea rolled
and dragged lovingly up and back.
And some of those women simply saw
each other and some of them saw
the sea.

But Sappho, she saw everything.

ELOISE KLEIN HEALY
in *Artemis in Echo Park* (1991)

**Eloise Klein Healy,** Los Angeles, CA, 1994

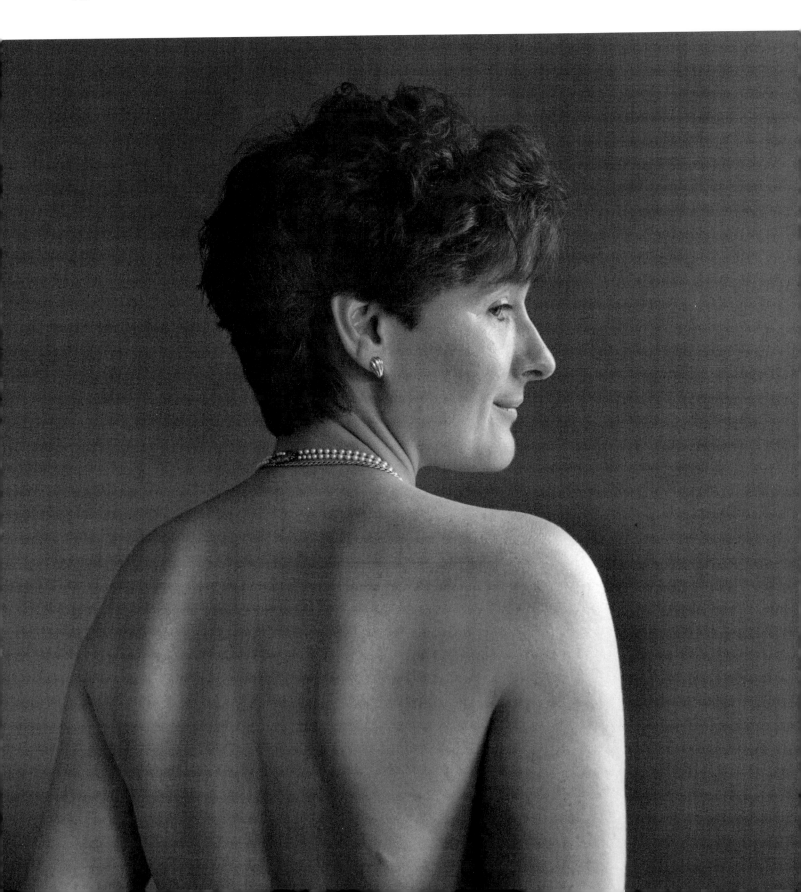

## Sleeping Beauty

I sleep, I sleep
too long, sheer hours
hound me, out
of bed and into clothes, I wake
still later, breathless, heart
racing, sleep
peeling off like a hairless
glutton, momentarily
slaked. Cold
water shocks me
back from the dream. I see
lovebites like fossils: *something*
*that did exist*

dreamlike, though
dreams have the perfect alibi, no
fingerprints, evidence
that a mirror could float
back in your own face, gleaming
its silver eye. Lovebites like fossils. Evidence.
Strewn

round my neck like a ceremonial
necklace, suddenly
snapped apart.

o

Blood. Tears. The vital
salt of our body. Each
other's mouth.
Dreamlike

the taste of you
sharpens my tongue like a thousand shells,
bitter, metallic. I know

as I sleep
that my blood runs clear
as salt
in your mouth, my eyes.

o

City-center, mid-
traffic, I
wake to your public kiss. Your name
is Judith, your kiss a sign

to the shocked pedestrians, gathered
beneath the light that means
stop
in our culture
where red is a warning, and men
threaten each other with final violence: *I will drink*
*your blood.* Your kiss
is for them

a sign of betrayal, your red
lips suspect, unspeakable
liberties as
we cross the street, kissing
against the light, singing, *This*
*is the woman I woke from sleep, the woman that woke*
*me sleeping.*

OLGA BROUMAS
in *Beginning with O* (1977)

**Olga Broumas,** Provincetown, MA, 1987

## His Body Like Christ Passed In and Out of My Life

A woman selling Bibles at the Greyhound station.
Me waiting. I was not indifferent, only hardened.
A German violin instead of her voice. Headphones
in my ears. The smell of that place, diesel and Brahms.
Me waiting as others wait. Me turning the cassette,
she turning pages in that purgatory without deliverance.
Later my lover smiling as Jesus, always late, never
his fault. Me looking back at a woman praising God.
Her devotion. My envy. A desire for permanence.
For a world without betrayal. I think of that winter,
the tracks outside my window erased from a field
of snow, me ironing sheets as if no one had slept
there. A bus heading South without me. My car
not starting, dead batteries, an empty walkman
discarded under the bed. How the world slides away.
Me diminished by the thought of him. Of spring.
What are birds returning, singing, compared to this,
the lives that I have forsaken to honor a god.

TIMOTHY LIU
in *Vox Angelica* (1992)

## Love Poem

On the narrow bed. Patterns of light
and shadow across your body. I hold

your face in my hands. Tell me, before
I kiss you, what is it like to be

so beautiful? I want to know how other
hands have touched you. What other

eyes, beneath your clothes, imagine.
And how do you imagine me? Do you

feel my calloused skin? See my twisted
bones? When you take off my clothes

will you kiss me all over? Touch me as
if my body were yours. Make me beautiful.

KENNY FRIES
in *Anesthesia* (1996)

**Kenny Fries,** Provincetown, MA, 1994

**Judith Barrington** (*left*) and **Ruth Gundle** (*right*), Portland, OR, 1994
Barrington is a poet, and Gundle is the founder of Eighth Mountain
Press.

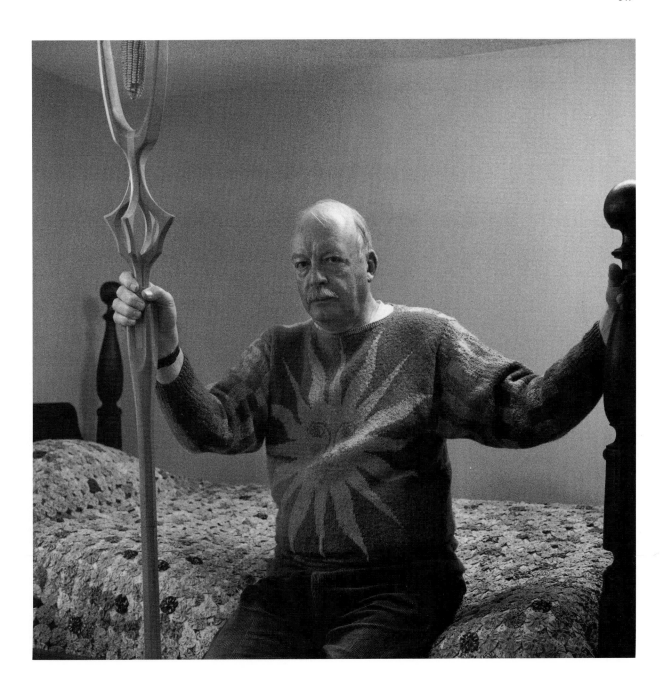

**Jonathan Williams,** Highlands, NC, 1991
Williams is a poet and, under the imprint of The Jargon Society, a
publisher. He lives with poet Tom Meyer.

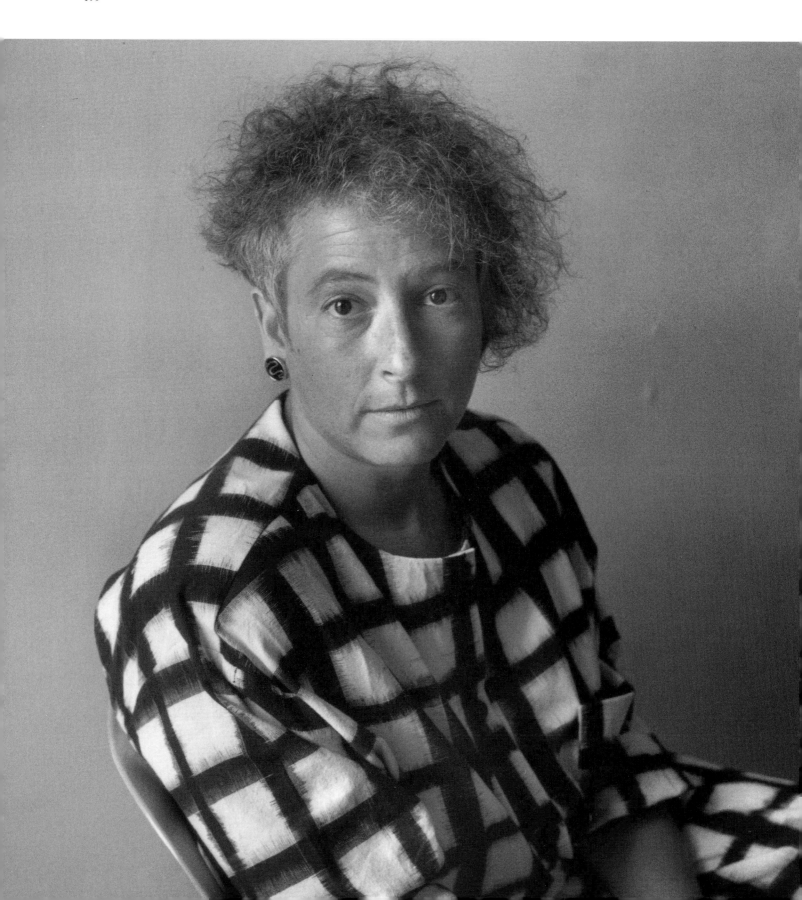

## The Subject of Our Lives

The storm has started and they say it won't stop.
Not for you, hanging on in the office after everyone has
    left.
Not for the ponies in my friend's paddock, huddled and
    still
and turning white. I know from your voice that you like
this moment—a Friday afternoon, the city between us, a
    few hours
of paperwork before you can think of dinner or a movie

or sex. I have been thinking about the snowstorm, and
    about a woman
from Chicago who put me on skis and ordered me to
    follow her
into the woods. That was years ago, and I've stopped
    thinking
about her, except during blizzards, everybody powerless
    and stuck
without milk or cream. Now I see that love is really
the subject of our lives: the authority with which you
    opened

your jacket and placed my hand, rigid, near frostbite,
against your breast, waiting for the heat to make its
    miraculous

leap; the gentle rabbi leading my parents from my sister's
    grave.
The ponies stir at the sound of grain hitting a metal
    bucket,
carried by a woman who regulates their hungers. How
    many times
have I confused hunger and love, love and power? My head
    ached

for years, it seemed, following someone's beautiful back.
My sister wouldn't sleep or wake beside one person long
    enough to
learn something. *Trust me*, you say, and I'm struck by the
    force
of your voice, the imperative form of any verb spoken in
    bed. Come home.
No, stay where you are. Longing will serve us while snow
    thickens
the sidewalks, delays the subways, tightens every street in
    town.

ROBIN BECKER
in *Giacometti's Dog* (1990)

**Robin Becker,** Provincetown, MA, 1990

# Tom

*They told me, Heraclitus, they told me you were dead.*

A key. The door. Open
shut. "Hi, Jim." "Hi,
Tom." "How didja sleep?"
"I didn't. And you?" "A
log." Blond glory, streaked,
finger-combed, curling
in kiss curls at the nape.
A kiss, like bumping fore-
heads. A god, archaic Greek
Apollo in a blue down
jacket. Fifteen degrees
no snow. Tom hates that;
me too. "French toast?"
"Of course." With apple-
sauce. The *Times,* the
obits, a great blues singer
has been taken from us
and a businessman. OJ,
coffee with milk, lecithin
to control mouth movements,
a side effect of Thorazine.
At the stove Tom sings the
release of his rock song,
"Manhattan Movie." His voice
is rich, true, his diction
perfect. I'm so in love
I want to die and take
my happiness to heaven!
No. To be with Tom
three hours
a day four days a week.
(Tom likes "assistant"
I
prefer "secretary."
No sweat: "Ain't no

flies on the lamb
of God." Ahem. Phlegm.)
Tom's eyes are "twin
compendious blue oceans in
which white sails and
gulls wildly fly." We'll
never make it. Tom's
twenty-eight, I'm fifty-
six: he isn't Proust's
"young man born to love
elderly men." He loves E.,
an eighteen-year-old
poet, whose mother feels
concern at Tom's two-
year pursuit (they only
lately made it). I'm
going to tell her how
lucky her son is, if he
is to have a homosexual
episode (or be one, as
I think he is, pretty
boy), to have a lover so
kind, so loving, so
witty—that thrash-about
laugh—I've said it
and I will. At Number
One Fifth Avenue I tell
E., "You should un-
reservedly make love
to Tom and be cosy and
tender." "I'm sorry, I
don't feel that way
about him." Later
he tells Tom,
"We had a man-

to-man talk." Sad.
I care only about Tom's
happiness. "He's not
very sexually oriented.
Here." The French toast
and applesauce are
delicious. We settle down
to read: he, a Ross
Macdonald, me *Phineas
Redux.* How superb is
Mme Goesler when she
repudiates the Duke of
Omnium's bequest of
pearls and diamonds and
a fortune (she already
has one) so they will
go to Lady Glencora, the
rightful heir, and no one
can ever say her three years'
tenderness to the dying
man was motivated. In
Tom's book a corpse is
found in corrupt upper-
middle-class L.A., where
he comes from. Beauty.
We might some
day shower
together, wash
each other's back.
Traveling share a bed.
Flesh on flesh,
a head pillowed
on an arm. Touch.
Running from a cab to
the deli, the energy

(grace) of youth.
Thomas Paul Carey of
Sherman Oaks, California,
who writes and sings
his own rock songs, the
son and grandson of two
great movie actors, the
two Harry Careys. Love
is only and always beautiful.

JAMES SCHUYLER
in *A Few Days* (1985)

**James Schuyler** at the
Chelsea Hotel, New York, NY, 1989

## Wings of a Wild Goose

A hen, one who could have brought more geese, a female, a wild one
dead   Shot by an excited ignorant young blond boy, his first
His mother threw the wings in the garbage   I rinsed them
brought them home, hung them spread wide on my studio wall
A reminder of so much, saving what I can't bear to be wasted
Wings
I dream of wings which carry me far above human bitterness
human walls   A goose who will have no more tiny pale fluttering
goslings to bring alive   to shelter   to feed   to watch fly
off on new wings   different winds
He has a lawn this boy   A pretty face which was recently paid
thousands of dollars to be in a television commercial   I clean
their house every Wednesday morning
2 dogs which no one brushes   flying hair everywhere
A black rabbit who is almost always out of
water   usually in a filthy cage   I've cleaned the cage
out of sympathy a few times although it is not part of what
are called my duties   I check the water as soon as I arrive
This rabbit & those dogs are the boy's pets   He is very lazy
He watches television constantly leaving the sofa in the den
littered with food wrappers, soda cans, empty cereal bowls
If I'm still there when he comes home, he is rude to me   If he
has his friends with him, he makes fun of me behind my back
I muse on how he will always think of the woods
as an exciting place to kill   This family of three lives
on a five acre farm   They raise no crops   not even their own
vegetables or animals for slaughter   His father is a
neurosurgeon
who longs to be a poet   His mother frantically searches
for christian enlightenment   I'm sad for her   though I don't like
her   because I know she won't find any   The boy does nothing
around the house to help without being paid   I'm 38 & still

haven't saved the amount of money he has in a passbook found
in the pillows of the couch under gum wrappers   That
dead goose
This boy will probably never understand that it is not right
to take without giving   He doesn't know how to give   His mother
who cleaned & cooked the goose says she doesn't really like
to do it but can't understand why she should feel any different
about the goose than a chicken or hamburger from the
supermarket
I bite my tongue & nod   I could explain to her that meat raised
for slaughter is very different than meat taken from the woods
where so few wild beings survive   That her ancestors are
responsible for the emptiness of this land   That lawns feed no
one   that fallow land lined with fences is sinful   That hungry
people need the food they could be growing   That spirituality
is not separate from food or wildness or respect or giving
But she already doesn't like me   because she suspects me
of reading her husband's poetry books when no one is around
& she's right   I do   I need the 32 dollars a week tolerating
them provides me   I wait for the wings on my wall to speak to me
guide my hungers   teach me winds I can't reach   I keep
these wings because walls are so hard   wildness so rare   because
ignorance must be remembered   because I am female   because I fly
only in my dreams   because I too
will have no young to let go

CHRYSTOS
in *Not Vanishing* (1988)

**Chrystos,** Bainbridge Island, WA, 1994

# Winkte*

*"He told me that if nature puts a burden on a man by making
him different, it also gives him a power . . ."*
John (Fire) Lame Deer, Sioux Medicine Man

We are special to the Sioux!
They gave us respect for strange powers
Of looking into the sun, the night.
They paid us with horses not derision.

To the Cheyenne we were no curiosity!
We were friends or wives of brave warriors
Who hunted for our cooking pots,
Who protected our tipis from Pawnee.

We went to the mountain for our puberty vision.
No horse or lance or thunderbird
Crossed the dreaming eye which would have sent us
Into war or the hunter's lonely woods.
To some song floated on mountain air,
To others colors and design appeared on clouds,
To a few words fell from the eagle's wind,
And they took to the medicine tent,
And in their holiness made power
For the people of the Cheyenne Nation.
There was space for us in the village.

The Crow and Ponca offered deerskin
When the decision to avoid the warpath was made,
And we were accepted into the fur robes
Of a young warrier, and lay by his flesh
And knew his mouth and warm groin;
Or we married (a second wife) to the chief,
And if we fulfilled our duties, he smiled
And gave us his grandchildren to care for.

We were special to the Sioux, Cheyenne, Ponca
And the Crow who valued our worth and did not spit
Names at our lifted skirts nor kicked our nakedness.
We had power with the people!

And if we cared to carry the lance, or dance
Over enemy scalps and take buffalo
Then that, too, was good for the Nation,
And contrary to our stand we walked backwards.

MAURICE KENNY
in *Only As Far As Brooklyn* (1979) and *Between Two Rivers:
Selected Poems 1956–1984* (1987)

*Sioux word for male homosexual

**Maurice Kenny,** Saranac Lake, NY, 1992

*Etlekhe verter oyf mame-loshn/*
A few words in the mother tongue
עטלעכע ווערטער אויף מאַמע-לשון

*lemoshl:* for example

*di kurve*   the whore
a woman who acknowledges her passions

*di yidene*   the Jewess   the Jewish woman
ignorant   overbearing
let's face it: every woman is one

*di yente*   the gossip   the busybody
who knows what's what
and is never caught off guard

*di lezbianke*   the one with
a roommate   though we never used
the word

*dos vaybl*   the wife
or the little woman

*in der heym*   at home
where she does everything to keep
*yidishkayt* alive

*yidishkayt* a way of being
Jewish   always arguable

*in mark*   where she buys
*di kartofl un khalah*
(yes, potatoes and challah)

*di kartofl*   the material counterpart of *yidishkayt*

*mit tsibeles*   with onions
that bring *trern tsu di oygn*
tears to her eyes   when she sees

how little it all is
*veyniker un veyniker*
less and less

*di khalah*   braided
*vi ihr hor far der khasene*
like her hair before the wedding
when she was *aza sheyn meydl*
such a pretty girl

*di lange shvartse hor*
the long black hair
*di lange shvartse hor*

*a froy kholmt*   a woman
dreams *ihr ort oyf der velt*
her place in this world
*un zi hot moyre* and she is afraid
so afraid of the words
*kurve*
*yidene*
*yente*
*lezbianke*
*vaybl*

*zi kholmt*   she dreams
*un zi hot moyre* and she is afraid
*ihr ort*
*di velt*
*di heym*
*der mark*

*a meydl kholmt*
*a kurve kholmt*
*a yidene kholmt*
*a yente kholmt*
*a lezbianke kholmt*

*a vaybl kholmt*
*di kartofl*
*di khalah*

*yidishkayt*

*zi kholmt*
*di hor*
*di lange shvartse hor*

*zi kholmt*
*zi kholmt*
*zi kholmt*

די קורווע
די יידענע
די יענטע
די לעזביאַנקע
דאָס ווײַבל
אַ מיידל
אַ פֿרוי

זי חלומט
זי חלומט
זי חלומט

IRENA KLEPFISZ
in *A Few Words in the Mother Tongue:*
*Poems Selected and New, 1971–1990* (1990)

**Irena Klepfisz,** Brooklyn, NY, 1987

Mr. Rosenthal raised the silver kiddush cup, brimming with wine, and we went on with dinner.

We talked without stop; that is, Bonnie and Daniel did, about their trips to Israel, their youth groups. Daniel seemed almost to be competing with his sister to be more interesting—but since I was an only child, I found that fascinating to watch. And I was glad that he wasn't cold to me anymore. Almost like a little kid pulling at your shirt, he kept grinning at me, trying to top his sister's stories. His eyes were wide and bright.

I felt drunk with *yiddishkeit*, Jewishness, as if I were in a Jewish Disneyland; they all knew so much about history, tradition, customs, religion, books, and legends. I felt the way I imagined Hindus were supposed to feel when they bathed in the Ganges—purified and whole.

They were so relaxed, so beautiful and kind to me.

"*Gotenyu!*" Mr. Rosenthal said when Bonnie brought me a third cup of coffee. "It's so late there won't be any buses."

"I can walk home. It's not far."

Bonnie frowned. "It isn't so safe anymore."

"I can call my folks for a ride."

Mr. Rosenthal shook his head. "You will stay with us."

"Sure," Daniel said. "I've got a double bed, or you could use my sleeping bag. Whichever."

After I called my parents, we talked some more in the quiet living room dominated by the Krakauer baby grand that Daniel's mother had taught him to play. But the thought of sleep had made me tired, and a little anxious. Bonnie bustled around getting me towels, linens, and a pillow, and in a chorus of good nights I found myself alone with Daniel in his bedroom beyond the kitchen, converted from the original maid's room and pantry.

His walls were painted a glossy dark blue and lined with Velvet Underground posters, as loud in that silent apartment as a car radio heard in a discordant flash on some still summer night.

"So," Daniel said, "bed or sleeping bag? The bed's really more comfortable."

I nodded as he stripped off his clothes, dropping them on his desk. He padded out to the little maid's bathroom.

He came back and slipped into bed. I turned away as I undressed, because I thought he was watching me, with the same disturbing look he'd had at the pizza place.

"You're not circumcised," he said. "Because your parents are survivors?"

I nodded.

Then he said good night and rolled closer to the wall, clicking off the bed lamp. When I was finished washing up, I hit the wall switch, turning off the overhead fixture with four bulbs just like the one in my room, and moved slowly to the bed across the darkened floor.

LEV RAPHAEL
in *Dancing on Tisha B'av* (1990)

**Lev Raphael,** Okemos, MI, 1993

In the beginning was the fire, *ha esh*, which burned in my sister Nadine Pagan's eyes, then lit up like a burning bush around her head and took with it most of her hair. It spoke to us like God spoke unto Moses. In a high thin voice it sputtered, *Your sister is a lunatic, your middle child has gone mad.* For who else but a crazy person would steal the *Shabbes* candles from off the kitchen table and with them light her own head on fire? Who else would run as she ran through our house, shrieking like a blue jay until my mother caught her by the arm. "You *dybbuk!*" she screamed at the top of her mother lungs, and shook my sister as if she could put her out like some match.

Around in circles my father spun, first in one direction, then another, pulling at his chin as if he wore a beard. "What to do what to do what to do," he muttered, and still Nadine burned from the hair down until I myself came running and screaming, and poured water on her head, dumped it out of a waste basket until she was quiet and the fire in her head went out.

We all of us stopped and stared. The house smelled like someone had burned at the stake. Nadine's eyes were huge and hot. She did not cry, neither did she shout. We stared at her, and she stared back. For the first time since I could remember, the house was absolutely quiet.

Suddenly my mother took matters into her own hands. "You want something to cry about, how's this?" she shouted. She slapped Nadine first on one cheek and then the other. "It's not enough to set yourself on fire like a Buddhist nun, you had to do it with my grandmother's candlesticks, and on *Shabbes!* Whoever heard of such a thing?"

My father looked deep into Nadine's hot face. "See how you've upset your mother!"

I couldn't stand it any longer. "Nadine just tried to burn herself up! Call a doctor! Get an ambulance!" The words stuck in my throat like mud.

My father spun toward the telephone.

"Sure, call a doctor," my mother spat. "Call the hospital and a million psychiatrists. While you're at it, call the fire department, too. This is your older sister Nadine, Jane. Take a good look at her. She's a real beaut."

It wasn't the first time Nadine ever exploded, but it certainly was the most graphic.

JUDITH KATZ
in *Running Fiercely Toward a High Thin Sound* (1992)

**Judith Katz,** Minneapolis, MN, 1993

(When the audience enters, they see a huge, three-dimensional "1981" on stage. Two huge flashlights—the kind used to land planes at airports—are seen at the back of the stage behind the numbers. We cannot see who is manipulating them, but the lights are slowly prescribing the dimensions of the stage. Then the flashlights are turned into the eyes of the audience.)

## Opening

**Mendel** (*acting as our tour guide*)    Homosexuals.

(*He searches the audience for them.*)

Women with children.

(*Ditto.*)

Short insomniacs.

(*He shines the lights on his face.*)

And a teeny tiny band.

(*He shines them on the band upstage. The band area lights up and the band waves.*)

Come back in,
The welcome mat is on the floor.
Let's begin.
This story need an ending.

**(Marvin** *enters.*)

Homosexual.

(*Light on* **Marvin.**)

Father with children.

(**Jason** *enters.*).

One bar mitzvah that
Is scrupulously planned.

(**Whizzer** and **Trina** *enter, followed by everyone else.*)

**All:**
Lovers come and lovers go.
Lovers fight and sing fortissimo.
Give these handsome boys a hand.
Welcome to Falsetto—

**Men:**
—land!

WILLIAM FINN
in *Falsettoland* (1989)

**William Finn,** New York, NY, 1993

**Evelyn Torton Beck,** Washington, DC, 1993
Beck edited *Nice Jewish Girls: A Lesbian Anthology* (1982)
including the work of Irena Klepfisz, Melanie Kaye/Kantrowitz,
Adrienne Rich, Savina Teubal, Andrea Freud Lowenstein, Martha
Shelley, and JEB (Joan E. Biren) among others.

**Richard Plant** with a photograph of himself, New York, NY, 1989
Plant wrote *The Pink Triangle* (1986), an account of the treatment
of homosexuals in Nazi Germany.

A clutch of little bells rang as I pushed the heavy door open. Warmth came mingling out into the cool evening air to greet me. I stepped inside and stood still for a moment, bathing in it, the sweet decaying smell, old musty books, the hard wooden shelves, an acrid smoky trace of cigars. From off my coat, the freshness of a December storm, the tiny flakes melting, their dampness evaporating into the shop's still interior. There seemed to be no one else there. "Hello," I called, singing the word softly. "Hello?" Nothing. No one. "Hello," I whispered once more. Sweet silence. It would be simple enough to just listen for the tram. I slipped my shoes off, setting them by the radiator, and made my way in to the books.

I could trace, perhaps, the history of this pleasure. Find its contours and depth, the echoes and sympathies, the shifting repetitions of this moment for me: once, with my father, on a day when the winter cold lay thick in my woolen jacket, my soft and tiny fingers held tight in his hard, smooth hand; and I, watching the motion of his long legs, the gabardine trousers moving softly with each step forward along the frozen walk (the empty blue winter sky), could imagine the warm, close air behind his working knees, the small hollow where the trousers hung loosely, holding the heat and odor of his strong legs; and he, looking down at me asking what it was I was thinking then, and would I like to stop for a moment, the small bells ringing as he pushed the heavy door open, the sweet smell of books mingling out into the cold air to greet me. The moment inside the door, the pause upon entering. I feel it closing behind me, its slow progress back, the slip of the latch, and the silent puff of air, the door fit neatly back in its frame.

I had a little list in my pocket, a scribbled note. Titles I might never find. Boyish fantasies of the intellectual:

Bruno, Causabon, Fludd. Older now, too big to be led around by my father. And the hours that passed, my list lost on the floor unnoticed. The drift of my attentions through the windowless interior rooms—the simple etchings of flowers, pistil and stamen enlarged, names of tropical birds, stones of the glacial plateau, the English manor house, methods of instruction in the time of Charlemagne, a chart I once saw and could never again find chronicling bridge disasters, the mint, its history and manufacture, disorders of the brain, furtively and for several hours Welsh bundling (fearing that any practice with so intimate and blowsy a name must be obscene), maps, of course, islands and river deltas, a boat, once, that sailed over the Angel Falls, a woman's death by fire, fleeing Paris and the plague, the comparative sweetness of regional waters, the tongue and teeth, a sensitivity to cold, its touch upon the heart, the impossibility of Maxwell's demon, meaning and song, speech impediments. My legs asleep, the book upon my lap.

Impossible to judge the time, all light of day lost among the twisting walls of books. My sudden fear that time had come unhinged, whole lives drifted past, my mind having fallen so far. I rose too quickly, older still, a terrible ache in my knees. Difficult to find my balance. The muscles of my legs were still unwinding. A pile of books stood beside me, an accusation. I rubbed the backs of my knees through the warm gabardine and sat down, thinking to select one or two titles with which to appease the owner.

MATTHEW STADLER
in The *Dissolution of Nicholas Dee* (1993)

**Matthew Stadler,** Seattle, WA, 1994

I gradually made my way to the bookshelves, once or twice lifting an object from a table to inspect it, but less out of interest than out of a feeling of obligation. I was more comfortable at the bookshelves, my eyes scanning the titles quickly, zooming in on the interesting ones. I was always looking for the same thing, and every now and then I found it. Once I located an old copy of Radclyffe Hall's *The Well of Loneliness;* in another store with shelves of old paperbacks, I found several lesbian pulp novels from the fifties, including Vin Packer's famous *Spring Fire.* It had been inscribed on the title page, "To my Charlotte, you set me on fire, Yours forever, Jeannie."

I had a small shelf in my apartment for these books. It wasn't really a hobby yet, maybe just a passing phase that I would someday look back on and say, "Oh, yes, that's when I was buying old books about lesbians." I never read them, I just stacked them on the shelf. More than being interested in the books, I was fascinated by trying to imagine the women who had owned them, who read and reread them, who dog-eared the pages, who dusted them every week, whose fingerprints oiled the pages and whose tears made circles on the paper. When I held the books, it was almost like holding the women, protecting them from the silence of time.

Because it wasn't a real hobby yet, I didn't know exactly what to look for. I didn't know the titles I should be hunting, beyond the most obvious ones, and I must have passed over a lot of valuable books because the titles were vague. I tended to look at anything with the word "woman" in it, which was usually not very fruitful. I had a few authors' names, like Helen Hull and Jo Sinclair, but I almost never found anything written by them.

So mostly it was luck. And that day I remember I had almost turned away from the bookshelves. I was thinking of looking at the pins, because I needed a present for Catherine's birthday. I thought I had spent a reasonable amount of time shopping, so that leaving wouldn't be rude. And just as I was turning, my eye caught an oversized green Moroccan leather book on the table next to the bookshelves, which looked as if it had just been tossed there. On the cover in gold leaf was stamped the word "Scrapbook."

PAULA MARTINAC
in *Out of Time* (1990)

**Paula Martinac,** New York, NY, 1991

**Salley Gearhart,** Willits, CA, 1996
In 1978 Gearhart published *The Wanderground,* a lesbian
utopian novel, with Persephone Press.

**Joseph Hansen,** Los Angeles, CA, 1994
Novelist Hansen is the author of the David Brandstetter detective
series.

*Opposite:* **Marion Zimmer Bradley,** Oakland, CA, 1994
Author of science fiction and fantasy, Bradley also compiled
several early bibliographies of lesbian writing.

Climbing the stairs now two at a time, Amos smiled and talked aloud as if to prepare himself for the joy of seeing his beloved's face.

The odd thing about Daniel Haws was not his dark coloring, but the striking difference in his character awake and asleep. Awake, he not only never made a single pass at Amos Ratcliffe but seemed to keep a gulf between them all the time. He once said of a newspaper scandal story about two men who had killed themselves over their love that he was opposed to physical relations between members of the male sex, and they ought to electrocute faggots.

The very night Amos moved into the rooming house, the mystery of Daniel was revealed—he turned out to be an incurable sleepwalker. There were no locks or bolts on any of the roomers' doors (Daniel had explained that he must have access to quarters at any time, otherwise they would all be burned to death some fine day on account of the careless habits of his transients), and at two o'clock in the morning of his first night Amos was awakened by the squeak of the opening door. In the feeble hallway light, he saw someone standing on his threshold. The man advanced toward Amos with his eyes open, but the expression in their pupils was so changed that Amos did not at once recognize his landlord. Daniel came directly to Amos's cot, sat down in the manner of a regular visitor, lifted the boy's head casually, touched his hair and, leaning over him close enough for Amos to feel the warmth of his breath, said, without expression or feeling: "Promise me you'll want to stay." A few seconds after saying this, he rose and returned to his own room, having closed the shell of a door behind him.

That had been two months ago. Hardly a night now went by that Daniel did not return, with words and actions nearly identical to those of his first night's visit. Amos knew that his nighttime caller was as different from the daytime Daniel Haws as a dream is from everyday reality. Amos also remembered a description Cousin Ida had given of sleepwalkers: "People who walk in their sleep don't remember a thing, especially where they have walked."

JAMES PURDY
in *Eustace Chisholm and the Works* (1967)

**Jerome**  (*Looking at Malcolm carefully.*) Yup, you're just as Mr. Cox described you. Yup. (*Nods several times.*) Would you like some wine, Malcolm?

**Malcolm**  (*As a glass is being poured for him.*) I usually don't drink.

**Jerome**  (*Hands Malcolm a glass, takes one himself.*) Do have some.

**Malcolm**  You're so . . . very polite.

**Jerome**  (*Returning the compliment.*) You're much nicer than I even thought you would be for a boy of your class. My name, by the way, is Jerome. (*They shake hands. Hope and enthusiasm in his voice now.*) I don't suppose you've heard of me. I'm an ex-con, a burglar. You're not drinking up. (*Pours Malcolm more wine.*)

**Malcolm**  (*Rather drunk, vague.*) But you see . . . I don't drink. Jerome, what is an ex-con?

**Jerome**  A man's who's been in prison. An ex-convict.

**Malcolm**  Ah; I see!

**Jerome**  I wrote a book about it.

**Malcolm**  How *difficult* that must have been!

**Jerome**  (*Going to get a copy.*) Would you like to read my book?

**Malcolm**  Well, I . . . I don't know; I've . . . I've never read a complete book—all the way through.

**Jerome**  (*Leering some.*) You'll read this one. (*Hands it to Malcolm.*) It's called *They Could Have Me Back.*

**Malcolm**  (*Looking the book over.*) What a nice title. Is that you naked on the cover? (*Jerome smiles, touches Malcolm lightly on the ear.*) I . . . I don't read very much.

**Jerome**  (*Touches Malcolm gently on the ear again.*) Do you dig that music, kid?

**Malcolm**  (*Touching his ear where Jerome had touched it.*) What did you do that for?

**Jerome**  (*Pouring Malcolm more wine.*) Look, Malcolm, I know you make a point of being dumb, but you're not *that* dumb. (*Jerome sits at Malcolm's feet, his arm around his leg, his head against his knee.*) I *do* want you to read my book; I want you to, well, because, because I guess you don't seem to have any prejudgments about anything. Your eyes are completely open. (*Malcolm jumps a little as Jerome starts stroking his thigh.*) Look, Malcolm, I'm not a queer or anything, so don't jump like that.

**Malcolm**  (*Drink, vague.*) I see.

**Jerome**  Will you be a good friend, then?

**Malcolm**  (*From far away.*) Of course, Jerome.

**Jerome**  Thank you, Malcolm. It's going to be a wonderful friendship. (*Strokes some more.*) But I think you better give up Girard Girard and Mr. Cox and all those people, because they don't believe in what you and I believe in . . .

**Malcolm**  (*Very dizzy.*) But what do we believe in, Jerome?

**Jerome**  What do we believe in, Malc? What a lovely question, and you said we; I'll appreciate that for one hell of a long time. One hell of a long time from now I'll think of that question of yours, Malc: What do *we* believe in? You carry me right back to something. . . .

**Malcolm**  (*The jazz music is louder, Malcolm's head spins.*) But you see, I don't know what I believe in, or any . . .

**Jerome**  Don't spoil it, Malc! Don't say another word!

**Malcolm**  (*A tiny voice, he is about to pass out.*) Jerome . . .

**Jerome**  Don't say a word, now. Shhhh . . . (*At this moment the glass falls out of Malcolm's hand, and he topples from the chair, head first, across Jerome's lap.*) Jesus Christ! Malc? (*Shakes Malcolm, but he has passed out.*) Malc? (*Lights fade on the tableau.*)

EDWARD ALBEE
in *Malcolm* (1966), adapted to the stage from the 1959 novel by James Purdy

**Bob**  I went to the baths last night.

**Denise**  You usually have fun at the baths.

**Bob**  Mixed reviews—I knew before I went it was going to be difficult. The last time was really awful—I couldn't get an erection.

**Denise**  Then why did you go?

**Bob**  I needed sex.

**Denise**  Needed?

**Bob**  If I don't have sex every week or so I feel out of kilter and hysterical. Don't you?

**Denise**  No. Are you ruled by your body?

**Bob**  Well, yesss . . . I hope so. What else?

(Pause)

**Denise**  Your mind.

**Bob**  My mind. Are you?

(Pause)

**Denise**  Yes.
(Both backtrack.)

**Denise**  Your mind's in your body.

**Bob (musically)**  Nooooooooo. It's about half way between my body and the world.

**Denise**  So your body rules?

**Bob**  Let's say it's a constitutional monarchy.

ROBERT GLÜCK
in *Jack the Modernist* (1985)

**Robert Glück,** New York, NY, 1985

What I told Sylvia was that I wanted to be ravished. After I explained everything—that I wanted the encounter to be anonymous, that it had to be in a public place, that I wanted to resist, and that I never wanted to see the other woman again—she told me I was confused.

"You want to be raped," she said, disgusted. "You can't want to be raped."

"I don't want to be *raped*," I said. "I want to be taken."

"Against your will?"

"Well, a little against my will," I admitted.

"That's like being a little pregnant," she said, clearly frustrated.

"It's a fantasy, Syl," I said. "The same rules don't apply."

"I'm worried about you," she said, then turned on her side with her back to me.

We stayed like that in the dark for a few minutes until, finally, I molded my body around hers. She was a little stiff at first, but eventually relaxed and pushed back against me so that the fabric of her slip rubbed lazily against my bare stomach. She groped behind her, meaning, I think, to stroke me with her free hand, but instead of feathers her nails felt like little claws this time. I wanted to get a glass of water and to pee, but I didn't want to move either, afraid whatever I did would have meaning well beyond my actual gestures.

"I can't rape you," she said in a whisper that sounded both frightened and wistful.

I pulled her closer. "I don't want you to rape me."

"I can't *ravish* you either," she said. "I can't do anything like that. It's completely beyond me."

I sighed. "Honey, relax, it's a fantasy," I said. "It's not about you." Then I felt her stiffen again, and her body peeled away from me in an instant, as if her slip were a layer of skin, blistering.

ACHY OBEJAS
in *We Came All the Way from Cuba So You Could Dress Like This?* (1994)

It is a very strange thing but the lesbian community is a community of liars. Liars and believers, tops and bottoms, butches and femmes, doers and wannabes, yuppies and deadbeats, mommies and daddies, enemies and friends. It is all so dynamic.

"Troy?" I asked.

"Yeah?"

"Troy? When did you first realize that you were in love with me?"

"It was in New Jersey," she said. "In January. Rolling industrial tundra where cancer is king. Where every day of your life is 1962 and the dairy truck still rattles down a hard-working run-down street. Kentucky Fried Chicken looks so old fashioned in the graying dusk from a passing bus. Ho-Hum, New Jersey. Even the countryside is dreary. Stomping ground for traveling oldies revivals. The Marvelettes are sixty. Still singing *Mister Postman, please. Please bring me my social security check. I'm an aging Marvelette pass-ing through New Jersey.* There's not one person who I envy in that entire state."

"And that's when you fell in love with me?"

She was so handsome, beautiful. My boy, my sailor. Dirty, sexy blue eyes. Soft lips sink ships. It was strange what was happening. All the while I kept pretending I was really just some woman living in a ball of confusion pretending to be a lady-killer, but being very usual instead. Then, one day, as Troy was loving me, I realized that I was exceptional. I realized that I will never be alone for very long. I will never be bored and I will always be loved. I had to come to terms with the fact that I am sexy and I am easy to love.

"Honey," she said. "I'm going to the corner to get a cup of coffee."

SARAH SCHULMAN
in *Rat Bohemia* (1995)

Walking back—the water is higher up the beach. She has to pass closer to the figure that is still sprawled in the sand. Sees it's a woman. Stops. Before the morning is out, the ocean will claim this place. Is she asleep? Is something wrong? Gabriel steps just close enough to be heard.

"Hey! The tide's coming in!"

The woman rouses, turns over, sits up. Rubs hands across eyes and pushes clumsy fingers through sandy hair, squinting up into Gabriel's face. It's Curlytop.

"What'd you say?"

"I said the tide's coming in." She tosses the words across the stretch of sand like a ring of keys. "I just thought you'd better know."

There seems to be no need to say more. She turns a quarter turn, moving the pail to her other hand and Piper says, "Wait a minute."

Gabriel waits.

"C'mere," says Piper.

She would love to. It's the way the woman says it that holds her back. She shifts the shells to her left hand again, and her eyes travel down the beach in the direction she was headed.

"I've seen you before—at the bar. Haven't I?"

The words draw Gabriel back to meet the recognition in the woman's eyes, head-on. If she answers, her voice will give everything away. She nods her head.

"So, what about the tide? How high does it come?"

Gabriel points to the mark on the concrete breakwater.

Piper feels suddenly foolish, fragile. She can think of no suitable answer. Her eyes drop. Gabriel sees it, hears it in the voice that says, "Well, thanks."

Piper is out of her element; the snap, the authoritativeness are lost on this black woman who wears a dress and carries a bucket on the beach at some unthinkable hour of morning. It occurs to Piper that this is someone from a world she knows nothing about. Yet there has always been a crossing, a place where their two worlds intersected. Now there are two, morning and night.

BECKY BIRTHA
in *Lovers' Choice* (1987)

Miss Tom was not a pretty woman, she was handsome like a man. Tall, broad-shouldered, big-boned, lean and lanky like a man. Her soft silver hair was cut short and curled tight round her narrow face that was smooth and honey brown. She had silver sideburns, thick eyebrows that almost met across the top of her face, dark black eyes that could see through almost anything, and a silver mustache, like a man. Kids, and some grownfolks, who didn't know Miss Tom was always asking her if she be man or woman. Miss Tom was patient with small children and strangers, so she would say in a deep, husky voice, "Don't judge a book by looking at the cover." Her chest was flat as a man's, her hands was big, thick, and calloused. But she had a woman's eyes, dark black eyes that held woman secrets, eyes that had seen miracles and reflected love like only a woman can. Her walk was slow and deliberate—like she had somewhere to go but wasn't in no hurry to get there.

Me and Miss Tom was friends, good friends. She taught me how to fish, throw a knife, tie knots, tame birds, and believe in a world of impossibilities. She lived in a big white house next door to Miss Rosa. It was a nice old house with long porches that wrapped round the sides, with green shutters behind where lace curtains whipped in the breeze. She had lived there with Miss Lily for as long as I can remember.

SHAY YOUNGBLOOD
in *The Big Mama Stories* (1989)

**Shay Youngblood,** Providence, RI, 1993

After Luisa left, Anita began sobbing. "How could you do this to me?" she kept repeating.

"I told you I was attracted to her," I said. The degree of her upset was surprising, and interesting—perhaps the most interesting thing I had noticed so far about her.

"Why? Just because of her phony hair. That is so silly, when she is such a horrible person."

"She introduced us," I said. "And in many ways she is a very good friend."

"Good friends don't betray you," she said. "I suppose now you will want to sleep with her instead of me."

"I want to sleep with you too," I said, though at the moment I couldn't have cared less.

"She won't sleep with you again. She always does this to people. How much did she make you pay her?" I thought of lying. "Don't lie, because she will tell me the truth—not because she is honest, but just to torture me." I tried not to laugh at the melodrama of her language.

"Ten dollars," I admitted.

"Then you must give me eleven dollars," she said.

"No."

"Why not?"

I told the easy part of the truth. "Because you've been doing it for free."

"*No más,*" she said. "And you must also buy me dinner."

"No."

"Yes."

"No."

"Why not?"

Usually I would have lied, but I was tired and relaxed. "To be honest," I said. "It's not worth it to me."

We stared at each other. She slapped my face. I could hardly blame her. She pulled back her arm as if to do it again, but I grabbed her hand. Our faces were close to each other, and so I kissed her, for the first time with passion. Then we began clawing at each other.

"Luisa was right. You do like me," I said, several hours later. The bed was wet with sweat and other body fluids, but for once I didn't mind it. I felt almost tender toward her.

"Idiot. It was because you smelled like Luisa."

"You're in love with her?" I asked. Once I heard my astonished voice, I couldn't believe I hadn't figured this out before.

"Isn't everyone?" she said, rather bitterly.

JANE DELYNN
in *Don Juan in the Village* (1990)

She laughs.

"Tell me a secret," he says.

"What kind of secret?"

"You know."

"The next morning in the Hôtel Rivoli we drank pamplemousse juice."

He laughs. "Tell me another one."

I tell him I have been with women who love men.

"You mean women who are not lesbians?"

"Oui."

"How many?"

"Beaucoup. I meet them. They are everywhere. I tell them how I will make them feel. And exactly how I will do it."

"And then?"

"And then they resist. But not for long."

"And then?"

"And then I make them feel that way."

"There are many women like that?"

"Oui."

He laughs again. It's nervous laughter.

"Women are so beautiful in their curiosity," I say, "their openness to everything. They are not like men."

He turns away.

It is a mistake to think that because our vocabularies are not large that we cannot hurt each other.

I have gotten my hair cut a little so that now Lucien's and mine are the same length. He pulls my cheveux longs. "I like it when you do that," I say.

"What else do you like?"

"Many things."

"Like what?"

"I like it when you pull my arms back, comme ça, like wings."

"Tell me the names of the women."

"What women?"

"The names of the women you have loved."

I look at him. He is blurry with pleasure.

CAROLE MASO
in *The American Woman in the Chinese Hat* (1994)

**Carole Maso,** New York, NY, 1994

192

Leaning in the doorway, waiting to be called downstairs for movietime, still wearing my business clothes, I suddenly felt a bit uneasy, worried by a famous thought: What are you *doing* here, Dave?

Well, Barker brought me home with him, is what. And, as far back as my memory made it, I'd only wanted just such guys to ask me over. Only they held my interest, my full sympathy.

The kid with the terrible slouch but (for me) an excellent smile, the kid who kept pencils in a plastic see-through satchel that clamped into his looseleaf notebook. The boy whose Mom—even when the guy'd turned fourteen—*made* him use his second-grade Roy Rogers/Dale Evans lunchbox showing them astride their horses, Trigger and Buttermilk. He was the kid other kids didn't bother mocking because—through twelve years of schooling side by side—they'd never noticed him.

Of course I could tell, there were other boys, like me, studying the other boys. But they all looked toward the pink and blond Stephens and Andrews: big-jawed athletic office holders, guys with shoulders like baby couches, kids whose legs looked turned on lathes, solid newels—calves that summer sports stained mahogany brown, hair coiling over them, bleached by overly chlorinated pools and an admiring sun: yellow-white-gold. But while others' eyes stayed locked on them, I was off admiring finer qualities of some clubfooted Wendell, a kindly bespectacled Theodore. I longed to stoop and tie their dragging shoestrings, ones unfastened so long that the plastic tips had worn to frayed cotton tufts. Math geniuses who forgot to zip up: I wanted to give them dating hints. I'd help them find the right bar-

ber. I dreamed of assisting their undressing—me, bathing them with stern brotherly care, me, putting them to bed (poor guys hadn't yet guessed that my interest went past buddyhood). While they slept (I didn't want to cost them any shut-eye), I'd just reach under their covers (always blue) and find that though the world considered these fellows minor minor, they oftentimes proved more major than the muscled boys who frolicked, unashamed, well-known, pink-and-white in gym showers.

What was I *doing* here? Well, my major was art history. I was busy being a collector, is what. And not just someone who can spot (in a museum with a guide to lead him) any old famous masterpiece. No, I was a detective off in the odd corner of a side street thrift shop. I was uncovering (on sale for the price of the frame!) a little etching by Wyndham Lewis—futuristic dwarves, or a golden cow by Cuyp, one of Vuillard's shuttered parlors painted on a shirt cardboard.

Maybe this very collector's zeal had drawn me to Carol, had led me to fatherhood, to the underrated joys of community. See, I wanted everything—even to be legit. Nothing was so obvious or subtle that I wouldn't try it once. I prided myself on knowing what I liked, and going shamelessly after it. Everybody notices grace. But appreciating perfect clumsiness, that requires the real skill.

"Won't be long now!" I heard Barker call.

"All *right*," I hollered, exactly as my sons would.

ALLAN GURGANUS
in *White People* (1991)

Doug has a passion for pornography. It's both a world he can think very clearly about and the purely aesthetic experience he feels most comfortable with. He has a row of magazines twelve inches long on his closet shelf. He's dipping into them this afternoon. He's been collecting since high school, when they had titles like *Lust-in* and featured overweight long hairs waddling out of bell bottoms. Gay tastes were less refined then, but Doug maintains the affection for those prototypes one does for one's first lovers. Ten years back he longed to writhe like an epileptic at the tips of their flicking, black and white tongues. Now the guys he was so rabid for might just as well be silent film stars they're so outdistanced. They've become representatives of what Doug perceives as a sweeter, easier time, waving from fuzzy photographs like Presidential candidates from the backs of trains.

DENNIS COOPER
IN *Safe* (1984)

"But as far as Rhyonon is concerned—the *world* of Rhyonon, the complex of information that was that world; well, as you have already heard, Rhyonon no longer exists." Japril stood up, stepped from her chair, and turned away from me. She joined her hands behind her back. "I said I was going to tell you about your relation to our survivor." She spoke to the window.

"That *is* what you said."

"The relation's very simple." (Listening to someone speaking towards someplace you're both facing has always been hard for me. But people have stranger customs than that with which to decorate what they consider important statements.) "Besides being the single survivor of Rhyonon, Korga happens to be your perfect erotic object—out to about seven decimal places."

"What—?"

While I frowned, behind her back Japril moved the fingers of one hand into a little bud of four with the thumb about an inch away—a sign, I suddenly remembered, on her world for something highly amusing. "More to the point," she went on, voice perfectly deadpan, "out to about nine decimal places, you happen to be Rat's." Hadn't she once told me folks on her world frequently make that sign of amusement without even being conscious of it? Oh, a diplomat's life is not an easy one.

As Japril turned back, I thought: What a strange thing to hear on an afternoon's library research session ten thousand light years away from anywhere—maybe seven hundred thousand k's if you happen to think Batria is someplace; and I'm sure the odd three-quarters of a billion do. "How do you *know* what . . . ?" but stopped at the memory: dozens of times in an ID's life fairly complete synaptic maps are made of the brain; and such things as Japril spoke of can as easily be read from my maps as from Korga's—though admittedly mostly no one cares to. While I sat there, I actually recalled Japril, once when I'd told her I found males who bit their nails sexually exciting, asking me just what my ideal sexual type was. Go look it up in your files, I had said most curtly.

She had.

"It occurs to me, Japril," I said, wondering why, on top of that anger, I felt so strangely disoriented, "that in one version or another, I've been hearing references to this Rat Korga over half a galaxy now. Sex is no longer the mystified subject it once was. What you are saying, in a word, is: Rat and myself are sexually attracted to men. Also: Rat and myself both fulfill a number of tricks and turns of physical build, bodily carriage, and behavioral deployment that would make making love with each other not only fun but . . . well, rewarding. Now that's part of the simple truth—"

"The truth is not simple. I am saying a great deal more. And you know it."

SAMUEL R. DELANY
in *Stars in My Pocket Like Grains of Sand* (1984)

*All the protagonists are blond; all the Blacks are criminal and negligible.* By mid-1983 I had grown weary of reading literature by white gay men who fell, quite easily, into three camps: the incestuous literati of Manhattan and Fire Island, the San Francisco cropped-moustache-clones, and the Boston-to-Cambridge politically correct radical faggots. None of them spoke to me as a Black gay man. Their words offered the reflection of a sidewalk; their characters cast ominous shadows for my footfalls. I called a personal moratorium on the writing by white gay men, and read, exclusively, work by lesbians and Black women. At the very least, their Black characters were credible and I caught glimpses of my reality in their worlds.

I was fed by Audre Lorde's *Zami*, Barbara Smith's *Home Girls*, Cherríe Moraga's *Loving in the War Years*, Barbara Deming's *We Cannot Live Without Our Lives*, June Jordan's *Civil Wars*, and Michelle Cliff's *Claiming an Identity I Was Taught to Despise*. Their courage told me that I, too, could be courageous. I, too, could not only live with what I feel, but could draw succor from it, nurture it, and make it visible.

More and more each day, as I looked around the well-stocked shelves of Giovanni's Room, Philadelphia's gay, lesbian, and feminist bookstore where I worked, I wondered where was the work of Black gay men. I devoured *Blacklight* and *Habari-Daftari*; welcomed *Yemonja* (which later became *Blackheart*); located and copied issues of the defunct newspaper *Moja: Black and Gay*—but they simply weren't enough. How many times could I read Baldwin's *Just Above My Head* or Yulisa Amadu Maddy's *No Past, No Present, No Future?* . . .

That fall I wrote in the Philadelphia *Gay News* (10/25/84):

Visibility is survival.

JOSEPH BEAM
in the Introduction to *In the Life* (1986)

This anthology included work by Samuel R. Delany, Essex Hemphill, Assotto Saint, Melvin Dixon, Donald Woods, Reginald Shepherd, and other black gay writers.

Five members of **Other Countries,** New York, NY, 1987
Other Countries is a large group of black gay writers who have published two anthologies and perform their own work. *From left to right:* Ronald Dildy, David Frechette, Colin Robinson, Carlos Segura, and Donald Woods.

## In the Life

Mother, do you know
I roam alone at night?
I wear colognes,
tight pants, and
chains of gold,
as I search
for men willing
to come back
to candlelight.

I'm not scared of these men
though some are killers
of sons like me. I learned
there is no tender mercy
for men of color,
for sons who love men
like me.

Do not feel shame for how I live.
I chose this tribe

of warriors and outlaws.
Do not feel you failed
some test of motherhood.
My life has borne fruit
no woman could have given me
anyway.

If one of these thick-lipped,
wet, black nights
while I'm out walking,
I find freedom in this village.
If I can take it with my tribe
I'll bring you here.
And you will never notice
the absence of rice
and bridesmaids.

ESSEX HEMPHILL
in *Ceremonies* (1992)

**Sapphire,** author of fiction and poetry, New York, NY, 1988

**Larry Duplechan,** novelist, Santa Monica, CA, 1988

Worshipping Callas, am I behaving like a vulture? . . .

. . . Callas, an icon already circulating through culture, was not placed on the market at gay men's instigation. Worshipping her, I don't affect the woman sleeping inside the image's shell: my love can't harm dead Callas. And yet homophobic society wants me to abandon my fantasies. To demand that I renounce my veneration is to suggest the desirability of erasing what makes me gay. Gays are considered a dispensable population. Listening to Callas, we become less dispensable: we find a use, a reflection, an elevation.

Imagine that one has a soul or an interior. Imagine that one tries to name the sensations of exhaustion or elation buried there. I call my expansions "gay." (Is the word "gay" an armor, a disguise, a uniform: a trait of the moment, resonant today, useless tomorrow?) You may feel similar exaltations and not be gay, or may not choose to call yourself gay, or may not choose to connect your Callas adoration and your sexuality. But for political, ethical, combative, and ineluctable reasons, I consider my interest in Callas to be a piece of my sexual and cultural identity.

WAYNE KOESTENBAUM
in *The Queen's Throat* (1993)

**Wayne Koestenbaum,** New Haven, CT, 1992

Callas is my favorite singer, but I've only
seen her once—;

I've never forgotten that night . . .

—It was in *Tosca*, she had long before
lost weight, her voice
had been, for years,
                    deteriorating, half itself . . .

When her career began, of course, she was fat,

enormous—; in the early photographs,
sometimes I almost don't recognize her . . .

The voice too then was enormous—
healthy; robust; subtle; but capable of
crude effects, even vulgar,
                    almost out of
high spirits, too much health . . .

But soon she felt that she must lose weight,—
that all she was trying to express

was obliterated by her body,
buried in flesh—;
                    abruptly, within
four months, she lost at least sixty pounds . . .

—The gossip in Milan was that Callas
had swallowed a tapeworm.

But of course she hadn't.

                    The *tapeworm*
was her *soul* . . .

—How her soul, uncompromising,
insatiable,
                    must have loved eating the flesh from her
    bones,

revealing this extraordinarily
mercurial; fragile, masterly creature . . .
—But irresistibly, nothing
*stopped* there; the huge voice

also began to change: at first, it simply diminished
in volume, in size,

                    then the top notes became
shrill, unreliable—at last,
usually not there at all . . .

—No one knows *why*. Perhaps her mind,
ravenous, still insatiable, sensed

that to struggle with the *shreds* of a voice

must make her artistry subtler, more refined,
more capable of expressing humiliation,
rage, betrayal . . .

—Perhaps the opposite. Perhaps her spirit
loathed the unending struggle

to *embody* itself, to *manifest* itself, on a stage whose

mechanics, and suffocating customs,
seemed expressly designed to annihilate spirit . . .

—I know that in *Tosca*, in the second act,
when, humiliated, hounded by Scarpia,
she sang *Vissi d'arte*
                    —"I lived for art"—

and in torment, bewilderment, at the end she asks,
with a voice reaching
                    harrowingly for the notes,

"Art has *repaid* me LIKE THIS?"
                    I felt I was watching
autobiography—

FRANK BIDART
in *The Book of the Body* (1977)

**Galas**   (*Stricken, assumes the postures of Greek tragedy*) Tell them I'm not at home. I don't even want to speak to them. (*Looks about the room as though she does not recognize the place*) Well, it seems I must find my joy in my music again. To live is to suffer, to endure pain. Anyone who says differently is a liar. People should tell their children that! (*Exits behind screen, laughing wildly*) Oh well, I was never really popular. I really wanted to be a dentist. What difference would it have made? Life is the same for every human being on this earth. The only difference is the weapons used against one and the weapons one uses in turn. What you want and what you're willing to do to get it, that is personality. Personality plus circumstance equals fate. (**La Galas** *reenters in a kimoni. The pose and gestures suggest Madame Butterfly.* **Bruna** *ties the obi*) Bruna, do you know where I put the fan that was given to me by the female impersonator of the Kabuki theater?

(**Bruna** *goes to fetch the fan.* **La Galas** *enters more fully into the character of Butterfly.* **Bruna** *reenters, looks on horrified at* **Galas's** *mad behavior.*)

**Bruna**   Here it is, madam.

**Galas**   You see, the fan (*Snaps open the fan*) conceals a knife (*Draws knife from fan*)—the perfect weapon for a female impersonator. Bruna?

**Bruna**   Yes, madam?

**Galas**   Would you sing the "Vissi d'arte" to me? (*She blindfolds* Bruna *with a glove.* Bruna *moves her lips hesitatingly and sings the "Vissi d'arte." We hear the full orchestra. La Galas kneels in prayer*) What do I do from morning to night if I don't have my career? I have no family, I have no husband, I have no babies, I have no lover, I have no dog, I have no voice, and there's nothing good on television tonight. What do I do, what do I do from morning to night? I can't just sit around and play cards or gossip—I'm not the type. (*Suddenly her gaze falls on the fan. She looks to heaven as if for permission, smiles, takes fan, rises, opens fan, and exits toward the screen. Before she disappears behind the screen, she looks back at* **Bruna** *and smiles in affirmation. She throws a scarf over the screen, then raises her hand with the dagger*) Grazie, Bruna.

(*Her hand comes down with great force. As the last notes of the "Vissi d'arte" fade away, the scarf is dragged down behind the screen. Pounding on the door is heard, and the door being broken down.* **Mercanteggini** *rushes onto the stage, sees* **Bruna** *blindfolded, looks behind the screen, and cries out.*)

**Mercanteggini**   Magdalena? What has happened here?

(*Tableau vivant as the lights fade alowly.*)
   *Curtain*

CHARLES LUDLAM
in *Galas: A Modern Tragedy* (1983)

**Homage to Charles Ludlam**, 1989

**Jay**   There's a question I've always wanted to ask someone.

**Frank**   What is it?

**Jay**   I hope you won't be offended.

**Frank**   Well, what? No, of course not. What?

**Jay**   Well—you're heterosexual, aren't you?

**Frank**   Sure!

**Jay**   Now, don't get angry, I'm only satisfying my curiosity—or perhaps I should say I'm satisfying only my curiosity—

**Frank**   Oh, come on—

**Jay**   Tell me, Frank, how long have you *been* heterosexual?

**Frank**   What do you mean? I've *always* been heterosexual!

**Jay**   Started as a kid, huh? Tsk-tsk. Tell me, do you think one of your teachers, or possibly even one of your parents might have been heterosexual? Do you think that might have been the reason you—

**Frank**   (*Interrupting*) All right, all right, just shut up, okay?

**Jay**   Okay, Frank. Gee, I didn't think you'd be so touchy about it. Wow. (*Brief pause*) Tell me, is your play heterosexual?

**Frank**   (*Snappy*) You mean does it sleep with plays of the opposite sex?

**Jay**   (*Delighted to have drawn wit*) Oooo. Getting off, ain't-cha? Well, you know, you people *do* tend to let heterosexuality *creep* into all your work.

ROBERT PATRICK
in *The Haunted Host* (1964)

**Robert Patrick** (*left*) with **Bette Bourne** (*right*) of the performance group Bloolips, New York, NY, 1988

**Emma**   We should do a rehearsal in costume. What color should each wear? It matters. Do you know what you're wearing?

**Paula**   I haven't thought about it. What color should I wear?

**Emma**   Red.

**Paula**   Red!

**Emma**   Cherry red or white.

**Sue**   And I?

**Emma**   Dark green.

**Cindy**   The treasurer should wear green.

**Emma**   It suits her too. Who else wants to know? (*Fefu raises her hand.*) For you, all the gold in Persia.

**Fefu**   There is no gold in Persia.

**Emma**   In Peru.

**Fefu**   O.K.

**Emma**   I brought my costume. I'll put it on later.

**Fefu**   You're not in costume?

**Emma**   No. This is just a dress. My costume is . . . dramatic. I won't tell you any more about it. You'll see it.

**Sue**   I had no idea we were going to do theatre.

**Emma**   Life is theatre. Theatre is life. If we're showing what life is, can be, we must do theatre.

**Sue**   Will I have to act?

**Emma**   It's not acting. It's being. It's springing forth with the powers of the spirit. It's breathing.

MARIA IRENE FORNES
in *Fefu and Her Friends* (1977)

*Top left:* **Lisa Kron,** performance artist, New York, NY, 1993

*Opposite:* **Ana Maria Simo,** New York, NY, 1990
This stage set was designed by Fornes who also directed the play by Simo.

*Top right:* **Eric Bentley,** playwright, critic, and translator of Brecht, New York, NY, 1986

*Bottom left:* **Craig Lucas,** playwright, New York, NY, 1989

*Bottom right:* **Victor Bumbalo,** playwright, New York, NY, 1987

**Stephen**   What ever happened to you and that curator at the Modern anyway?

**Mendy**   I took him to PELLÉAS ET MÉLISANDE and he fell asleep in the first scene. I had to wake him for intermission.

**Stephen**   PELLÉAS? Give the guy a break. Take him to TOSCA, TROVATORE. Something with balls.

**Mendy**   Debussy has balls. He just doesn't wear them on his sleeve.

**Stephen**   You're going to die with your secret, Mendy.

**Mendy**   I don't even know what it is.

**Stephen**   That's why it's your secret. I think you'd rather listen to opera than fuck.

**Mendy**   Opera doesn't reject me. The real world does. I don't understand love. *Non capisco amore.*

**Stephen**   I don't think I understand anything but.

**Mendy**   I don't understand agreements either. I never thought the two of you would last. And when it did, I was a little envious. No, a lot envious. And now that it's sort of over . . .

**Stephen**   It's not over.

**Mendy**   I feel a little sad.

**Stephen**   I said, it's not over.

**Mendy**   The part I was jealous of is. The passion.

**Stephen**   Our passion is just fine. Thank you. It's just a little different.

**Mendy**   That's for sure. If he's with someone else, it sounds like the first act of CARMEN is turning into the last. The final duet. Only in your production, who's Carmen and who's Don Jose?

**Stephen**   Wouldn't you like to know? (*Spoken*) *Frappe-moi donc ou laisse-moi passer!*

**Mendy**   You need more chest. Maria does it with more chest. *Frappe-moi donc ou laisse-moi passer!* (Stephen *"stabs" him and* Mendy *falls dramatically. "Death" convulsions*) Can I ask you a personal question?

TERRENCE MCNALLY
in *The Lisbon Traviata* (1990)

(*Whitesnake's "Bad Boys" plays as a young Black gay enters dressed in the style of the Queer Nation kids: leather jacket, white T-shirt, babushka on his head, chains around his neck. He dances like a nerdy rocker and sings along, strumming an air guitar*)

**Kid**   (*singing*) "I'm the black sheep in my family!" (*He cuts the music off*) Whitesnake. Cool, huh? They're racist. Sexist. If you could actually decode the lyrics, they're probably homophobic, but they are so cool! Do you think if you're Black and you're queer and a bit of a metalhead, that's a truly transgressive act? Huh? Huh, I'm trying to be a rebel, but I'm having trouble finding a cause. I used to hang out with the Lesbian/Gay/Bisexual/Transgender/Queer Student Alliance. There aren't actually any transgender persons in the Lesbian/Gay/Bisexual/Transgender/Queer Student Alliance, but if one shows up, they're covered! The kids in the Alliance, they swear they are the last transgressives, but you know what? They bother me, they really bother me.

Last meeting, we're having a discourse on the efficacy of staging a direct action at Toys "Я" Us. We break into subgroups, and start dialoguing our way through our various isms and schisms, and the facilitator comes in with his four different colored Magic Markers and big pieces of paper and we write down all our issues and tape them up to the wall and this is going on for hours, as you might imagine, and I'm thinking if some little six-year-old future homophobe wants to buy a Mr. Potato Head, let him. I finally stand up and say, "Yo, dudes. Dykes. I mean, dykes, dudes. I am beginning to feel oppressed by all this clonedom here. I don't want to put stickers on the back of my leather jacket, that reminds me of my parents' Volvo!" Then Joey, this white dude from my Foucault seminar, thinks he is so hip, says, "Oppressed? Your parents make more dough than the Huxtables. When they found out you were gay, they threw a coming-out party. You've never felt oppression in your life." I say, "Yo, dude. You know what you can do? Deconstruct this (*He flips the finger*), dude!"

BRIAN FREEMAN
in *Fierce Love* (1995), performed by Pomo Afro Homos.

**Pomo Afro Homos,** performance artists, San Francisco, CA, 1994
*From left to right:* Bernard Djola Branner, Brian Freeman, and Eric Gupton.

*Top left:* **Jeff Hagedorn,** Los Angeles, CA, 1994
In 1983 the Lionheart Theatre in Chicago staged Hagedorn's *One,*
probably the earliest known performance of a play about AIDS.

*Top right:* **Lawrence Bommer,** Chicago, IL, 1993
Bommer's work, such as *The Tyrannicides* (1980), was performed
by the Lionheart Theatre.

*Bottom left:* **Rick Paul,** Wilmette, IL, 1993
In 1979 stage designer and playwright Paul founded the Lionheart
Theatre, a gay company in Chicago.

*Bottom right:* **Rebecca Ranson,** Atlanta, GA, 1992

Hospital. Charles Enters Warren's Room.

**Charles**   Warren.

**Warren**   Yes?

**Charles**   I'm your nurse for the day, darling. Let me look at your face. You have a good face, good eyes. I like catering to the needs of the pretty. (Kisses Warren's Forehead) Don't get me wrong. I like catering to needs. I figured as long as I was a faggot, I might as well be a nurse, get paid for what I like to do anyhow. I also like to talk. You could tell me to stop though. Sometimes it helps.

**Warren**   Don't stop talking.

**Charles**   I knew I would like you, Warren. I've been off-duty since you checked into this hotel. 17B has the best patients on the ward. It's a magic room. I work nights most of the time and I usually spend about half the night in this room talking. I've got a bottle of champagne. You want a glass? It is, after all, the holiday season.

**Warren**   Should I drink champagne?

**Charles**   If you want champagne, you should drink champagne. I even brought a couple glasses. I detest drinking out of the wrong kind of glass, don't you?

**Warren**   Absolutely.

**Charles**   How are you feeling?

**Warren**   Not too bad.

**Charles**   Bore me to tears, Warren. I asked you how you felt.

**Warren**   Okay but you asked for it. I feel rotten, scared, mad as hell, like I'm getting cheated out of my life.

**Charles**   I thought that was probably how you were feeling. If it's all the same to you, let's just talk straight about these things.

REBECCA RANSON
in *Warren* (1984)

One of the earliest plays about AIDS, *Warren* was first produced at Seven Stages in Atlanta, Georgia, in August 1984 and directed by the playwright.

Albert, I think I loved him best of all, and he went so fast. His mother wanted him back in Phoenix before he died, this was last week when it was obvious, so I get permission from Emma and bundle him all up and take him to the plane in an ambulance. The pilot wouldn't take off and I refused to leave the plane—you would have been proud of me—so finally they get another pilot. Then, after we take off, Albert loses his mind, not recognizing me, not knowing where he is or that he's going home, and then, right there, on the plane, he becomes . . . incontinent. He starts doing it in his pants and all over the seat; shit, piss, everything. I pulled down my suitcase and yanked out whatever clothes were in there and I start mopping him up as best I can, and all these people are staring at us and moving away in droves and . . . I ram all these clothes back in the suitcase and I sit there holding his hand, saying, "Albert, please, no more, hold it in, man, I beg you, just for us, for Bruce and Albert." And when we got to Phoenix, there's a police van waiting for us and all the police are in complete protective rubber clothing, and looked like fucking astronauts, and by the time we got to the hospital where his mother had fixed up his room real nice, Albert was dead. (Ned starts toward him.) Wait. It gets worse. The hospital doctors refused to examine him to put a cause of death on the death certificate, and without a death certificate the undertakers wouldn't take him away, and neither would the police. Finally, some orderly comes in and stuffs Albert in a heavy-duty Glad Bag and motions us with his finger to follow and he puts him out in the back alley with the garbage. He says, "Hey, man. See what a big favor I've done for you, got him out, I want fifty bucks." I paid him and then his mother and I carried the bag to her car . . .

LARRY KRAMER
in *The Normal Heart* (1985)

By October 2, 1985, the morning Rock Hudson died, the word was familiar to almost every household in the Western world.

AIDS.

Acquired Immune Deficiency Syndrome had seemed a comfortably distant threat to most of those who had heard of it before, the misfortune of people who fit into rather distinct classes of outcasts and social pariahs. But suddenly, in the summer of 1985, when a movie star was diagnosed with the disease and the newspapers couldn't stop talking about it, the AIDS epidemic became palpable and the threat loomed everywhere.

Suddenly there were children with AIDS who wanted to go to school, laborers with AIDS who wanted to work, and researchers who wanted funding, and there was a threat to the nation's public health that could no longer be ignored. Most significantly, there were the first glimmers of awareness that the future would always contain this strange new word. AIDS would become a part of American culture and indelibly change the course of our lives.

The implications would not be fleshed out for another few years, but on that October day in 1985 the first awareness existed just the same. Rock Hudson riveted America's attention upon this deadly new threat for the first time, and his diagnosis became a demarcation that would separate the history of America before AIDS from the history that came after.

The timing of this awareness, however, reflected the unalterable tragedy at the heart of the AIDS epidemic: By the time America paid attention to the disease, it was too late to do anything about it. The virus was already pandemic in the nation, having spread to every corner of the North American continent. The tide of death that would later sweep America could, perhaps, be slowed, but it could not be stopped.

The AIDS epidemic, of course, did not arise full grown from the biological landscape; the problem had been festering throughout the decade. The death tolls of the late 1980s are not startling new developments but an unfolding of events predicted for many years. There had been a time when much of this suffering could have been prevented, but by 1985 that time had passed. Indeed, on the day the world learned that Rock Hudson was stricken, some 12,000 Americans were already dead or dying of AIDS and hundreds of thousands more were infected with the virus that caused the disease. But few had paid any attention to this; nobody, it seemed, had cared about them.

The bitter truth was that AIDS did not just happen to America—it was allowed to happen by an array of institutions, all of which failed to perform their appropriate tasks to safeguard the public health. This failure of the system leaves a legacy of unnecessary suffering that will haunt the Western world for decades to come.

RANDY SHILTS
in *And the Band Played On* (1987)

**Randy Shilts,** San Francisco, CA, 1989

It was worse than I'd expected.

It was the worst five minutes of my life.

I casually palmed a tab of AZT and cleared my throat. We were in the kitchen. I had just eaten my last dish of fried matzo for the year. "Mom, I've been taking AZT for the past six months. Do you know what AZT is?"

"No." She stopped. She was at the sink, cleaning the frying pan.

"It's a drug that's supposed to inhibit the replication of the HIV virus. Do you know what HIV is?"

"No." She held the scrub brush in her left hand, the frying pan in her right. Soapy water dripped from the scrub brush. Behind her, through the window, the outside thermometer read 72 degrees. A red-winged blackbird whizzed by.

"It's the virus that people believe causes AIDS." I couldn't believe I was phrasing it in *New York Native* terms. Sure. And spermatozoa were the organisms that people believed caused pregnancy.

She knew what AIDS was.

"I found out I was HIV-positive about two and a half years ago. This doesn't necessarily mean I'm going to get sick."

She didn't look at me, as if I were a monster.

"But you tested positive for it," she spat out.

I looked back at her. She looked away.

"They're coming up with a lot of advances. They're making a lot a progress scientifically. Eventually, HIV infection will be a chronic manageable disease, like diabetes." In ten, fifteen, maybe twenty years. I'd believe it when I saw it in the pages of the *Journal of the American Medical Association*.

She sighed heavily, a sigh that took her sixty-two years to perfect. With harsh sadness, my long-suffering mother said, "It's a wonderful life." I realized that this was where I had learned irony.

DAVID B. FEINBERG
in *Spontaneous Combustion* (1991)

**David B. Feinberg,** New York, NY, 1989

". . . I'm pretty sure it was death calling me. But I'll be damned if I go before I'm ready. I wanted to be conscious once more, so I could see Joel and even you, if you can believe that. Seriously now," he went on, "I had a good life. I sure got away from Barranquilla. I remember how I used to despair thinking I would never get away from that dreadful macho town. I knew I had to get away from there and become the gorgeous queen I was meant to be."

"You sure did," I said.

"And I had a good time with Joel these past five years so actually I don't give a flying fuck about all the other stuff. And you know, I'm glad that it's been such a long illness. This has been the first time since childhood that I've had time to think about spiritual matters. I became so wrapped up in making money that I thought only money and success could make me happy, but secretly I've always envied your freedom."

"Sure. Come on, Bobby. Get real. You wouldn't have liked Eighth Avenue all these years," I said referring to my place of residence.

"You'll be able to move now that you're marrying Claudia. Lucy told me all about it the last time she was here. Now you'll live in mansions for the rest of your life."

"Bobby, I can't believe you're talking such nonsense!"

"Hey, why not? Many of my fag friends are marrying women. And look at all the famous queens who've gone back into the closet. Besides, it might save your life. Although, since you never have sex, you must be HIV nega-tive. Tell the truth, have you had any in the last ten years since you came out?"

The uneventfulness of my sex life had always been a source of great amusement to Bobby. The truth is that other than the occasional vertical sex, I had practiced a single-handed celibacy for many years. Only recently had I realized that it wasn't so much AIDS I was afraid of, but of being sexually intimate with another person.

"Anyway," Bobby went on, "we were crazy about Claudia when we were kids; we had such great times. And she adores you. Plus she's rich. What more do you want? A true match made in heaven. A fag who's afraid of sex and a dyke who won't ask you for any! If she asked me to marry her—fat chance—I'd marry her in a second."

"Bullshit. You wouldn't. Just because you think you're dying I'm not going to let you take advantage of me. Is that your idea of having the last laugh?"

"No, it's not, *cariño*. I always said we were like Miriam Hopkins and Bette Davis in *Old Acquaintance*. You know me, a drama queen to the last. I really believe we were their modern-day incarnation. But the movie is over, Sammy. You've won the bet. This queen is dead."

JAIME MANRIQUE
in *Latin Moon in Manhattan* (1992)

**Jaime Manrique,** Sag Harbor, NY, 1992

When I went back in, Carlos's eyes were closed. His mouth was slightly open and his breath was jerky. His hand was still above the sheet.

I went to the bathroom and washed my hands and put on some gloves. I found a white plastic pan and took it to the living room. I put it under the urine bag and closed off the tube and opened the bottom valve and the urine drained into the pan. The urine was orange. I closed the valve and made sure the bag was still hooked securely and took the pan to the bathroom and emptied it into the toilet. I cleaned and bleached it and put the pan back. I took off my gloves and tossed them in the trash and washed my hands.

I don't know how I could hear his voice over the water, but I did.

"Marty!" he was trying to shout, "Marty!"

I ran to the living room.

"Marty?" he said. His eyes were fluttering.

I took his hand. "Marty's at work. He'll be back later."

He squinted at me. "Who are you?"

I told him my name. He looked completely blank.

"I'm from Urban Community Services. I'm gonna be with you for a while until the nurse comes. Marty won't be back till after work."

He kept looking. After several seconds he said, "Oh." Then, "We met earlier?"

"A few minutes ago," I said.

He thought about that for a while. "Where were you now?"

"In the bathroom. I was washing my hands." I held my hands out, palms up, and flipped them over like a kid for inspection. "I didn't have time to wash behind my ears," I said.

That took him a few seconds, then he got it and laughed and said, "Very good."

His laugh was rusty. It was great to hear it. I laughed too.

He took my left hand in his right. "Your skin feels so clean," he said. He pulled his other arm out from the sheet and took my other hand. "Your skin feels so clean."

REBECCA BROWN
in *The Gifts of the Body* (1994)

Get out on the Expressway, a living lit-up belt that slid, as if through the loops on an old faded cherished sexy pair of jeans, under bridges and skyways all the way across Long Island.

Then stop the car. Sure! These woods were dark and deep. Sure! And the night simmered with dozens of strangers, my "meat," like an iron pot steaming with a tantalizing stew.

All these strangers, young, old, younger, older; some dressed, some undressed; some dressed for bathhouse life, complete with towels and spray cans of bug repellent. But this forest of course was no bathhouse, and took from the open air the pine and pain of Long Island's great North Shore. I felt immensely cheered at once; someone gave me another beer. For a bit I leaned against a shadowy chainlink fence—just to soak up some atmosphere. I wasn't wearing a hell of a lot myself. In the dark I couldn't see what I was or wasn't wearing, but I felt the chain links bite blue squares into my back, friendly fish in a Club Med vacation lagoon.

I stood in the midst of a spiky friendly forest. *Heterosexuals have orgasms*, I thought, *too, but they have to make dates first*. Poor things . . . out on the Expressway police-car lights ("cherries" I remembered calling them once, on the corner, in the twilight, a kid, then as now with a beer foaming in one hand) cruised by half a mile away or more. Everything and everyone, it seemed, was into cruising tonight. I couldn't be too descriptive of the scene, I preferred to be vague and to bask in glamor, in moonlight, in follies. Hands grasped my waist; with hands on your waist, with this particular pair of hands, you don't remember til later it may be bad luck. Anyway one's luck usually held out and out until, I thought, the end of time. Bewitched luck: *for this, from stiller seats we came*, wearing the face of Oberon, or wearing the face of an ass, across one's own face or ass. Now that we live in the era of AIDS, this story makes me nervous, it seems like a romance, but it seemed one then. It can never happen again. But I felt that then too.

KEVIN KILLIAN
in *Shy* (1989)

**Kevin Killian** (*left*) and **Dodie Bellamy** (*right*), San Francisco, CA, 1989

When the time came I wasn't waiting for him to die. I didn't wait. I wasn't really able to think about what was happening. I didn't think. I was just there. I got used to the sight of the tubes that sucked at his arms like hungry little snakes, trying to put the life back in. And I got used to hearing my nice, soft, furry tranquilizer talked about like some kind of textbook experiment. It was sometimes hard to trust that I was awake, that what was happening was what was happening. When I went in to see him for the last time it didn't seem like a last anything. At least not at the time. Later those moments, what happened in them and what didn't, would always stand out.

I don't remember driving home. I unlocked the door and closed all the windows. I took a bath. I sat. I listened to the phone ring. I went to bed. It was day again and then it wasn't. This happened several times. I was born, I died, and slowly the night would seep back in. Sometimes I'd reach out as if to touch his face in the dark so I'd know I wasn't alone.

Later I made the calls. I tried not to listen to the people on the other end. I'd already said all of the things anyone else could say. After a while I just dialed the numbers, said my lines, and hung up. "He had to go. He's gone. I'm sorry. Goodbye."

When it happens it's like the film broke in mid-reel, you don't expect it and you're still expecting everything you were before. Everything in my life except me was suddenly different. Eventually that would make me different too, but it takes a while to catch up. Someone said the pain would go away, but I'm not sure that's where I want it to go. It's how I feel him most sharply. Without it, every move I make echoes because he's not here to absorb me. I don't like bouncing back at myself. A dead lover wants your soul, wants your life, and then your death too. And you give it, it's the only way to feel anything again. Take the death as a lover and sleep with it and eat it and purge it and suck it back in quick. And finally it's no event, it's nothing that happened, it's just you: an anger and a beauty that never really goes away. Not something you can wait out as it disappears, nothing ever really just disappears.

Everything's OK now. I'm not waiting for anything. I shave and comb my hair every morning. I look fine. Nothing about me looks different. I change the sheets. I do the dishes. I pay the bills. Just like before.

Everything's OK. I spelled out his name with trash on the beach, poured the gasoline and lit it up. Pretty, but he didn't come back.

I'm OK. I was thinking: we were fine—some usual things happened, some unusual. That's normal. I wonder if there was a moment when he decided to let go and fall into it, or if he didn't notice when such a moment could have occurred because he was already falling. We can't take responsibility for everything that happens to us. After all, there is such a thing as the tyranny of fate. I had wanted to be comfortable with not seeking comfort. I had wanted to be challenged but not in pain. I guess a lot of things seem to carry connotations other than those most obvious.

I went to the grocery store and bought everything frozen. Except for the freezer the refrigerator's empty. So I've been keeping the film for his next project in there. It looks really clean with just the yellow and black boxes against the white.

SAM D'ALLESANDRO
in *The Zombie Pit*, published posthumously in 1989

**Sam D'Allesandro,** San Francisco, CA, 1988

. . . I pick up the gray envelope from Amagansett DO NOT BEND in it are 2 1/4 contact sheets of your photo session with Robert Giard the month before you died—Giard's never shown these pictures to anyone. . . . I rip open the envelope. You're gaunt, yes, but these days I see men on the street who are more so, thin men meeting friends for coffee and pastries thinner men getting out of cars with canes—it's your eyes that shock, Sam, eyes too large for their sockets eyes round as globes and large enough to swallow the world eyes that seem to be pinned open with details rushing in like locomotives. You look exhausted. I pull out your boxcar glamor shot (BEFORE) your face looks chubby, vicious with youth *horizontal bedroom eyes heating up the frame with a careless sexual nature that slightly threatens and promises nothing* I clip Giard's contacts on my copystand (AFTER) so that as I write I can stare back at you, and keep staring until this new Sam no longer startles but IS. You collected dusty vomit-encrusted *things* I could only imagine held at arm's length between the tips of finger and thumb, your lover's scarred face was like a map X's and lines curved around the cheekbones in a constant motion of intersections and near-misses you pushed him against the wall and licked and probed every little trench and ridge and rent *sucking out the invisible poison* your eyes will remain unreadable to me, will never "reveal"—but that's not the point, is it—the point is to look, not in horror not in pity or even in compassion, but to look as precisely as possible at the ever-wavering presence right in front of one—this is the closest beings as imperfect as we can come to love.

DODIE BELLAMY
in *Real: The Letters of Mina Harker and Sam D'Allesandro*
(1994)

Stone, Short Mountain Sanctuary, TN, 1991
This is one of a number of memorial stones carved by Michael Mason and others. These stones are assembled on a ridge at the commune which currently publishes the journal *RFD*.

## Aunt Ida Pieces a Quilt

They brought me some of his clothes. The hospital gown,
those too-tight dungarees, his blue choir robe
with the gold sash. How that boy could sing!
His favorite color in a necktie. A Sunday shirt.
What I'm gonna do with all this stuff?
I can remember Junie without this business.
My niece Fancine say they quilting all over the country.
So many good boys like her boy, gone.

At my age I ain't studying no needle and thread.
My eyes ain't so good now and my fingers lock in a fist,
they so eaten up with arthritis. This old back
don't take kindly to bending over a frame no more.
Francine say ain't I a mess carrying on like this.
I could make two quilts the time I spend running my
     mouth.

Just cut his name out the cloths, stitch something nice
about him. Something to bring him back. You can do it,
Francine say. Best sewing our family ever had.
Quilting ain't that easy, I say. Never was easy.
Y'all got to help me remember him good.

Most of my quilts was made down South. My mama
and my mama's mama taught me. Popped me on the tail
if I missed a stitch or threw the pattern out of line.
I did "Bright Star" and "Lonesome Square" and "Rally
     Round,"
what many folks don't bother with nowadays. Then Elmo
     and me
married and came North where the cold in Connecticut
cuts you like a knife. We was warm, though.
We had sackcloth and calico and cotton, 100% pure.
What they got now but polyester rayon. Factory made.

Let me tell you something. In all my quilts there's a secret
nobody knows. Every last one of them got my name Ida
stitched on the back side in red thread.
That's where Junie got his flair. Don't let nobody fool you.
When he got the Youth Choir standing up and singing
the whole church would rock. He'd throw up his hands
from them wide blue sleeves and the church would hush

right down to the funeral parlor fans whisking the air.
He'd toss his head back and holler and we'd all cry holy.

And nevermind his too-tight dungarees.
I caught him switching down the street one Saturday night,
and I seen him more than once. I said, Junie,
you ain't got to let the world know all your business.
Who cared where he went when he wanted to have fun.
He'd be singing his heart out come Sunday morning.

When Francine say she gonna hang this quilt in the church
I like to fall out. A quilt ain't no showpiece,
it's to keep you warm. Francine say it can do both.
Now I ain't so old-fashioned I can't change,
but I made Francine come over and bring her daughter
Belinda. We cut and tacked his name, *JUNIE*.
Just plain and simple. "*JUNIE, our boy*."
Cut the *J* in blue, the *U* in gold. *N* in dungarees
just as tight as you please. The *I* from the hospital gown
and the white shirt he wore First Sunday. Belinda put the
     necktie *E* in the cross stitch I showed her.

Wouldn't you know we got to talking about Junie.
We could smell him in the cloth.
Underarm. Afro Sheen pomade. Gravy stains.
I forgot all about my arthritis.
When Francine left me to finish up, I swear
I heard Junie giggling right along with me
as I stitched Ida on the back side in red thread.

Francine say she gonna send this quilt to Washington
like folks doing from all 'cross the country,
so many good people gone. Babies, mothers, fathers
and boys like our Junie. Francine say
they gonna piece this quilt to another one,
another name and another patch
all in a larger quilt getting larger and larger.

Maybe we all like that, patches waiting to be pieced.
Well, I don't know about Washington.
We need Junie here with us. And Maxine,
she cousin May's husband's sister's people,
she having a baby and here comes winter already.
The cold cutting like knives. Now where did I put that
     needle?

**Melvin Dixon,** New York, NY, 1988

MELVIN DIXON

## The Missing

Now as I watch the progress of the plague,
The friends surrounding me fall sick, grow thin,
And drop away. Bared, is my shape less vague
—Sharply exposed and with a sculpted skin?

I do not like the statue's chill contour,
Not nowadays. The warmth investing me
Led outward through mind, limb, feeling, and more
In an involved increasing family.

Contact of friend led to another friend,
Supple entwinement through the living mass
Which for all that I knew might have no end,
Image of an unlimited embrace.

I did not just feel ease, though comfortable:
Aggressive as in some ideal of sport,
With ceaseless movement thrilling through the whole,
Their push kept me as firm as their support.

But death—Their deaths have left me less defined:
It was their pulsing presence made me clear.
I borrowed from it, I was unconfined,
Who tonight balance unsupported here,

Eyes glaring from raw marble, in a pose
Langorously part-buried in the block,
Shins perfect and no calves, as if I froze
Between potential and a finished work.

—Abandoned incomplete, shape of a shape,
In which exact detail shows the more strange,
Trapped in unwholeness, I find no escape
Back to the play of constant give and change.

August 1987

THOM GUNN
in *The Man with Night Sweats* (1992)

from "Cancer Winter"

I woke up, and the surgeon said, "You're cured."
Strapped to the gurney, in the cotton gown
and pants I was wearing when they slid me down
onto the table, made new straps secure
while I stared at the hydra-headed O.R.
lamp, I took in the tall, confident, brown-
skinned man, and the ache I couldn't quite call pain
from where my right breast wasn't anymore
to my armpit. A not-yet-talking head,
I bit dry lips. What else could he have said?
And then my love was there in a hospital coat;
then my old love, still young and very scared.
Then I, alone, graphed clock hands' asymptote
to noon, when I would be wheeled back upstairs.

. . . . . . . . . . . . . . . . . . . . . .

The hand that held the cup next was my daughter's
—who would be holding shirts for me to wear,
sleeve out, for my bum arm. She'd wash my hair
(not falling yet), strew teenager's disorder
in the kitchen, help me out of the bathwater.
A dozen times, she looked at the long scar
studded with staples, where I'd suckled her,
and didn't turn. She took me/I brought her
to the surgeon's office, where she'd hold
my hand, while his sure hand, with its neat tool, snipped
the steel, as on a revised manuscript
radically rewritten since my star
turn nursing her without a "nursing bra"
from small, firm breasts, a twenty-five-year-old's.

. . . . . . . . . . . . . . . . . . . . . .

Should I tattoo my scar? What would it say?
It could say "K.J.'s Truck Stop" in plain English, highlighted with a nipple ring
(the French version: Chez K. J./Les Routiers).
I won't be wearing falsies, and one day
I'll bake my chest again at Juan-les-Pins,
round side and flat, gynandre/androgyne,
close by my love's warm flanks (though she's sun-shy
as I should be: it's a carcinogen
like smoked fish, caffeine, butterfat and wine).
O let me have my life and live it too!
She kissed my breasts, and now one breast she kissed
is dead meat, with its pickled blight on view.
She'll kiss the scar, and then the living breast.

. . . . . . . . . . . . . . . . . . . . . .

Friends, you died young. These numbers do not sing
your requiems, your elegies, our war
cry: at last, not "Why me?" but "No more
one-in-nine, one-in-three, rogue cells killing
women." You're my companions, traveling
from work to home to the home I left for
work, and the plague, and the poison which might cure.
The late sunlight, the morning rain, will bring
me back to where I started, whole, alone,
with fragrant coffee into which I've poured
steamed milk, book open on the scarred pine table.
I almost forget how close to the bone
my chest's right side is. Unremarkable,
I woke up, still alive. Does that mean "cured"?

MARILYN HACKER
in *Winter Numbers* (1994)

**Marilyn Hacker** (*left*) and **Karyn London** (*right*), New York, NY, 1995
Hacker is a poet. In 1974 London was one of the founders of
Womanbooks, a bookstore in New York City.

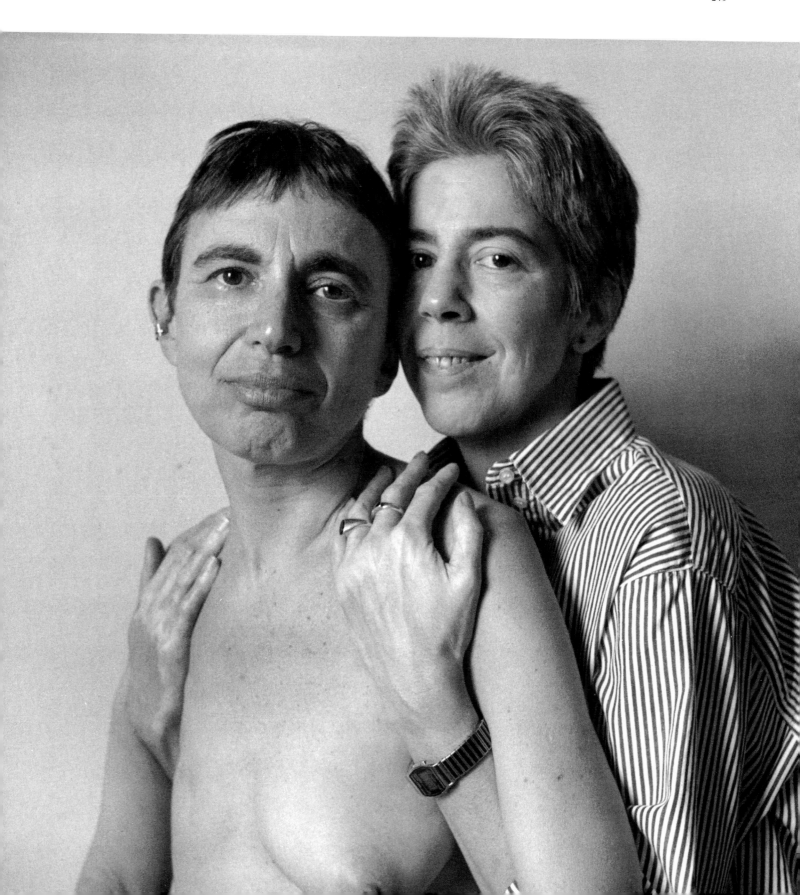

244

So I guess it's appropriate, since I was born at County General and live on an avenue and not an *avenida*, that I should be arrested at Her Majesty's, The Federal Building.

We have a long history together, this *ruca** and I. She has watched me grow up and play on her steps. Watched me low ride in front of her. Watched me spit at her face at an Immigration demonstration that I don't understand but comprehend enough to know that my dad can go back anytime, just never when he wants to.

I attended *Gabacho*† civil disobedience training in Santa Monica, and it sounded like we were going to war.

"That nasty ole dirty downtown is going to get a good look at us, uh-huh. We are going to run up and down her streets and when we get to Miss Federal Building we are going to spit in the old bitch's face." And we shout like a CBS news break in the sixties. "Freedom of Speech"— "AIDS funding now"—"Alto a la censura"—"Stop AIDS, ACT UP, Fight Back"—"We're here, We're queer, Get used to it."

A man in a helmet and plastic gloves puts handcuffs on me while hundreds of people blow whistles and yell shame, shame, shame.

"You are trespassing on government property. If you do not leave the premises, you will be arrested. Do you understand?"

"Yes."

"Are you going to leave the premises?"

"No."

"Are you going to resist arrest?"

"No."

"Then you have the right to remain silent . . ." and it all trails off like an "Adam Twelve" rerun on Channel 13.

And all I can think about is a fourth grade field trip to City Hall where I met the Mayor, Sam Yorty, got his picture and a lesson in becoming a model citizen of this great city of ours.

And I want to run my hand along her marble curves, play with her buttons, stare up at her long tall walls and admire her beauty. But these handcuffs lead me to a cell in her basement. So it isn't distant Mexican relatives from *ranchos* in *Jalisco* that get to share intimate moments with Justice deep in her bowels. It's one of her own.

Beautiful buildings like big *chingona** sharp women have secrets that can scare the shit out of you. Their looks call to you, but the hardness and coldness of her gaze can crush the little you, caught deep in the stare. The Federal Building was once a woman with long arms who reached down and touched you.

I didn't get arrested because my government wants to control the content of art money, or because a Republican from Orange County thinks that all AIDS activists are a "dying breed," or because a black-and-white can stop you anytime, anywhere, for whatever reason.

I got arrested because Mayor Sam Yorty told me we were all the Mayor. Because big beautiful buildings stare down at you with a *chale* stare. Because I've lived here all my life and I've never owned anything, much less this city.

LUIS ALFARO
in *Pico-Union* (1992)

*Tough "broad."

†Caucasian.

*Female gangster.

**Luis Alfaro,** Los Angeles, CA, 1994

"I'm sorry, but I still don't get why we're wasting out time with this man," said Glick, a conventionally bright student who already had law school and a career in politics written all over him. "It's not history. It's just one man complaining about business and family."

"History is only the big public events, Mr. Glick?" Meg tried not to spar sarcastically with her students, but this exchange might lead somewhere.

"Well, yeah. The ones that affect us. *History* history. The stuff in our outside reading never has anything to do with what's in the textbook." The textbook was a standard narrative. The supplemental readings chosen by Meg were all bits of social history.

"Anybody else?" she asked. "Agree or disagree? Mr. Glick's made a good point. Why read about Rufus Flagg? Why waste our time with social history?"

Somebody offered a commonplace about getting the flavor of the past. When another student observed that Rufus Flagg made the past more real for her, "like it is in novels," Glick came back with the argument that novels were trivia and stories like Rufus Flagg's were just distractions from the real story, interruptions. "What does this guy's worrying about marrying off his daughter have to do with the debates on the Constitution?"

"It's the kitchen and the moon," Meg declared.

Everyone looked baffled.

"Social history and what Mr. Glick called *history* history. How *do* they connect?" She began to laugh at herself; the class was going well enough that she could afford to goof. "I'm sorry. The kitchen and the moon is my private language for this, the two opposite poles of human experience. At one end you have the kitchen: personal life, domestic life, absolutely indifferent to the world outside. And then there's the moon, distant and abstract, the spectacle of public life. It's not a female moon, but a lunatic moon, an abstract moon." She almost described it as a male moon, but calling the images male and female would take her from the point she wanted to make. "This is derived from Rebecca West, but you don't need to know who I'm stealing from. Years ago, the study of history was all moon. Now we're trying to work the kitchen in, and they do seem like different realities. It's difficult to understand how to connect the two, just as it's hard to connect them in real life."

Alice, the calf-eyed, short-haired freshman, raised her hand. "How do *you* connect them?"

"Well, as a historian I look for episodes where the two interact, the public and private, so I can see how they affect each other."

"No, what I meant was—how do you connect them in real life?"

CHRISTOPHER BRAM
in *Almost History* (1992)

It is the same year, and Heinz, who is certain now that he is a homosexual, has decided to end the silence which he feels to be a burden to him. From the earliest years of his childhood he has trusted his mother with all of his secrets. Now he will tell her another secret, the secret of whom he loves. *My dear child*, she tells him, *it is your life and you must live it.*

It is 1936. Though he does not know it, Himmler is moving into the sphere of Heinz's life now. He has organized a special section of the Gestapo to deal with homosexuality and abortion. On October 11, he declares in a public speech, *Germany's forebears knew what to do with homosexuals. They drowned them in bogs.* This was not punishment, he argues, but *the extermination of unnatural existence.*

As I read these words from Himmler's speech, they call to mind an image from a more recent past, an event I nearly witnessed. On my return from Berlin and after my search for my grandmother, I spent a few days in Maine, close to the city of Bangor. This is a quiet town, not much used to violence. But just days before I arrived a young man had been murdered there. He was a homosexual. He wore an earring in one ear. While he walked home one evening with another man, three boys stopped him on the street. They threw him to the ground and began to kick him. He had trouble catching his breath. He was asthmatic. They picked him up and carried him to a railing of a nearby bridge. He told them he could not swim. Yet still, they threw him over the railing of the bridge into the stream, and he drowned. I saw a picture of him printed in the newspaper. That kind of beauty only very graceful children possess shined through his adult features. It was said

that he had come to New England to live with his lover. But the love had failed, and before he died he was piecing his life back together.

When Himmler heard that one of his heroes, Frederick the Great, was a homosexual, he refused to believe his ears. I remember the year when my sister announced to my family that she was a lesbian. I can still recall the chill of fear that went up my spine at the sound of the word "queer." We came of age in the fifties; this was a decade of conformity, awash with mood both public and private, bearing on the life of the body and the body politic. Day after day my grandfather would sit in front of the television set watching as Joseph McCarthy interrogated witnesses about their loyalty to the flag. At the same time, a strict definition of what a woman or a man is had returned to capture the shared imagination. In school I was taught sewing and cooking, and I learned to carry my books in front of my chest to strengthen the muscles which held up my breasts.

I was not happy to hear that my sister was a homosexual. Moved from one member of my family to another, I did not feel secure in the love of others. As the child of divorce I was already different. *Where are your mother and father? Why don't you live with them?* I dreaded these questions. Now my sister, whom I adored and in many ways had patterned myself after, had become an outcast, moved even further out of the circle than I.

SUSAN GRIFFIN
in *A Chorus of Stones* (1992)

## "Where Will You Be?"

Boots are being polished
Trumpeters clean their horns
Chains and locks forged
The crusade has begun.

Once again flags of Christ
are unfurled in the dawn
and cries of soul saviors
sing apocalpytic on air waves

Citizens, good citizens all
parade into voting booths
and in self-righteous sanctity
X away our right to life.

I do not believe as some
that the vote is an end,
I fear even more
It is just a beginning.

So I must make assessment
Look to you and ask:
Where will you be
when they come?

They will not come
a mob rolling
through the streets,
but quickly and quietly
move into our homes
and remove the evil,
the queerness,
the faggotry,
the perverseness
from their midst.

They will not come
clothed in brown,
and swastikas, or
bearing chest heavy with
gleaming crosses.
The time and need
for ruses are over.
They will come
in business suits
to buy your homes
and bring bodies to
fill your jobs.
They will come in robes
to rehabilitate
and white coats
to subjugate
and where will you be
when they come?

Where will we *all* be
when they come?
And they will come—

they will come
because we are
defined as opposite—
perverse
and we are perverse.

Every time we watched
a queer hassled in the
streets and said nothing—
It was an act of perversion.

Everytime we lied about
the boyfriend or girlfriend
at coffee break—
It was an act of perversion.

Everytime we heard,
"I don't mind gays
but why must they
be blatant?" and said nothing—
It was an act of perversion.

Everytime we let a lesbian mother
lose her child and did not fill
the courtrooms—
It was an act of perversion.

Everytime we let straights
make out in our bars while
we couldn't touch because
of laws—
It was an act of perversion.

Everytime we put on the proper
clothes to go to a family
wedding and left our lovers
at home—
It was an act of perversion.

Everytime we heard
"Who I go to bed with
is my personal choice—
It's personal not political"
and said nothing—
It was an act of perversion.

Everytime we let straight relatives
bury our dead and push our
lovers away—
It was an act of perversion.

And they will come.
They will come for
the perverts
& it won't matter
if you're
    homosexual, not a faggot
    lesbian, not a dyke
    gay, not queer
It won't matter
if you
    own your business
    have a good job
    or are on S.S.I.
It won't matter
if you're

Black
Chicano
Native American
Asian
or White

It won't matter
if you're from
    New York
    or Los Angeles
    Galveston
    or Sioux Falls
It won't matter
if you're
    Butch, or Fem
    Not into roles
    Monogamous
    Non Monogamous
It won't matter
if you're
    Catholic
    Baptist
    Atheist
    Jewish
    or M.C.C.

They will come
They will come
to the cities
and to the land
to your front rooms
and in *your* closets.

They will come for
the perverts
and where will
you be
When they come?

PAT PARKER
in *Jonestown and Other Madness* (1985)

**Pat Parker,** Pleasant Hill, CA, 1989

from "Crime Against Nature"

The upraised arm, fist clenched, ready to hit,
fist clenched and cocked, ready to throw a brick,
a rock, a Coke bottle. When you see this on TV,

robbers and cops, or people in some foreign alley,
is the rock in your hand? Do you shift and dodge?
Do you watch the story twitch in five kinds of color

while you eat Doritos, drink beer; the day's paper
sprawled at your feet, supplies bought at the 7-11
where no one bothered you? Or maybe he did. All

depends on what you look like, or if you can smile,
crawl, keep your mouth shut. Outside the store,
I, as usual, could not believe threat meant me, hated

by four men making up the story of their satiated
hot Saturday night and what they said at any woman
to emerge brash as a goddess from behind smoky glass,

how they won, if she would not bend her eyes or laugh,
by one thrusting question, broke her in half,
a bitch in heat, a devil with teeth for a cunt.

*What's wrong with you, girl?* the grin, gibe, chant.
*What's the matter?* (Split the concrete under her feet,
send her straight to hell, the prison pit fire,

blast her nasty self.) *You some kind of dyke?*
Sweating, damned if I'd give them the last say,
hissing into the mouth of the nearest face, *Yesss,*

hand jumped to car door, metal slam of escape
as he raised his hand, green bomb of a bottle,
I flinched, arm over my face, split-second

wait for the crash and shards of glass. His nod
instead, satisfied he'd frightened me back down
into whatever place I'd slid from. Laughter

quaked the other men. At me, a she-dog, queer
enough to talk? At him, tricked by a stone-face
drag woman stealing his punch line, astonished

as if a rock'd come to life in his hand and slashed
him? He dropped his hand, nodded like he'd won.
Slammed into my car, I drove away, mad, ashamed.

All night I seethed, helpless, the scene replayed,
slow-motion film, until I heard my *Yes,* and the dream
violence cracked with laughter. I was shaken out

on the street where my voice reared up her snout,
unlikely as a blacksnake racing from a drain, fire-
spitting, whistling like a siren, one word, *yes,*

and the men, balanced between terror and surprise,
laugh as the voice rolls like a hoopsnake, tail
in her mouth, obscure spinning blur, quiet howl,

a mouth like a conjuring trick, a black hole
that swallows their story and turns it inside out.

For a split second we are all clenched, suspended:
upraised fist, approving hoots, my inverted ending.

MINNIE BRUCE PRATT
in *Crime Against Nature* (1990)

Nothing happened when I stopped taking hormones. For months I got up every morning and raced to the mirror, breathless with anticipation. Nothing changed. It was sort of anticlimactic. It took many of hours of electrolysis before I began to feel the softness of my cheeks again. One morning I got up and found menstrual blood on my BVD's. I threw them out rather than risk anyone at the laundry seeing the apparent contradiction. But the real motion was taking place inside of me. I had to be honest with myself, it was as urgent as breathing. When I sat alone and asked what it was I really wanted, the answer was *change*.

I didn't regret the decision to take hormones. I wouldn't have survived much longer without passing. And the surgery was a gift to myself, a coming home to my body. But I wanted more than to just barely exist, a stranger always trying not to get involved. I wanted to find out who I was, to define myself. Whoever I was, I wanted to deal with it, I wanted to live it again. I wanted to be able to explain my life, how the world looked from behind my eyes.

Yet I was so afraid to come out and face the world again. I wondered why I had to choose the opening years of the Reagan administration and the rise of the Moral Majority to demand the right to be myself. Would they arm villagers with torches and stakes and stalk me through the countryside? Would I stand alone, handcuffed in a precinct cell, with no one to turn to if I survived the nightmare? But then I acknowledged that no matter who had been in the White House, it had always been hard to be me. Between a rock and a hard place—something told me this lifetime wasn't going to get any easier. I'd already been through a lot though, and it didn't seem to me it could get much worse.

Once again I couldn't see the road ahead. I was still steering my own course through uncharted waters, relying on constellations that were not fixed. I wished there was someone, somewhere I could ask: *What should I do?* But no such person existed in my world. I was the only expert on living my own life, the only person I could turn to for answers. I knew I was changing when people began to gawk at me again. It had taken a year. My hips strained the seams of men's pants. My beard grew wispy and fine from electrolysis. My face looked softer. Once my voice was hormone-lowered, however, it stayed there. And my chest was still flat. My body was blending gender characteristics, and I wasn't the only one who noticed.

I remembered what it was like to walk a gauntlet of strangers who stare—their eyes angry, confused, intrigued. Woman or man: they are outraged that I confuse them. The punishment will follow. The only recognition I can find in their eyes is that I am "other." I am different. I will always be different. I will never be able to nestle my skin against the comfort of sameness.

"How the hell should I know what it is?" the man behind the counter remarked to a customer as I walked away. The pronoun echoed in my ears. I had gone back to being an *it*.

Before, strangers had raged at me for being a woman who crossed a forbidden boundary. Now they really didn't know what my sex was, and that was unimaginable, terrifying to them. Woman or man—the bedrock crumbled beneath their feet as I passed by. *How the hell should I know what it is?* I had forgotten how hard this was to endure.

LESLIE FEINBERG
in *Stone Butch Blues* (1993)

# Husband

The man sitting next to me on the grass at the March on Washington asks, "Is he your husband?" as I return from kissing you, as you step down from the microphone. On stage, a drag queen in beaded white chiffon is ferociously lip-synching and tail-switching an answer to the introduction you have given her, praise from a drag king resplendent in your black-on-black suit. In the audience, I hesitate over my answer. Do I change the pronoun *and* the designation of *husband?* Finally I reply, "Yes, she is." He hesitates in his turn: "He hasn't gone through the operation?" The complexity of your history crowds around me as I mentally juggle your female birth sex, male gender expression. I say, "She's transgendered, not transsexual." Up on stage Miss Liberty is reading, with sexy histrionics and flourishes of her enormous torch, a proclamation from a woman who is a U.S. senator, a speech that trumpets and drums with the cadences of civil rights. The man blinks his eyelashes flirtatiously, leans toward me, whiskey on his breath, waves his hand at his companions, "We're up from North Carolina." Then, femme to femme, he begins to talk of your beauty: "He is perfect. If I ever wanted a woman it would be someone just like her." With innuendo and arch look he gives truthful ambiguity to what he sees in me, in you, something not simply about "gay rights." The queen whispers in my ear with his sharp steaming breath, "Don't let her get away. Hang *on* to him."

MINNIE BRUCE PRATT
IN *S/HE* (1995)

Leslie Feinberg (*left*) and Minnie Bruce Pratt (*right*), Jersey City, NJ, 1994

In many ways from a contemporary point of view, the most pressing question addressed by this work is probably whether the Christian ceremony of same-sex union functioned in the past as a "gay marriage ceremony." It is clear that it did, although, as has been demonstrated at length, the nature and purposes of every sort of marriage have varied widely over time. In almost every age and place the ceremony fulfilled what most people today regard as the essence of marriage: a permanent romantic commitment between two people, witnessed and recognized by the community. Beyond this, it might or might not fulfill specific legal or canonical expectations predicated on the experience of the heterosexual majority (procreative purpose, transfer of property, dowry), but the extent to which particular heterosexual unions matched such niceties did not usually determine whether the neighbors regarded the couple (same-sex or heterosexual) as married. Indeed, in all times and places in its history (including the present) the official teaching of the Roman Catholic church (one of the two bodies in which the ceremony developed) has been that the two parties *marry each other*; the priest merely acts as a witness. If the couple intend to be married, they are. By contrast, in the Eastern Orthodox church the priest *does* perform the ceremony, and in all known cases priests performed the same-sex union.

Such are the historical facts. Their social, moral, and political significance is arguable, but considerable. Even persons who argue that same-sex couples should *now* have the right to contract marriage like anyone else are apt to view such unions as an exotic indulgence of our time, a novel experiment in a liberal society. And many people—both homosexual and heterosexual—argue that same-sex couples should not undertake traditional relationships similar to heterosexual matrimony. While I was preparing this study, I received a visit from a well-known prelate, who remarked to me that heterosexual matrimony had become such a ragged institution in the second half of the twentieth century that it hardly constituted a useful model for same-sex couples, who might better devise something entirely new.

I replied that I had not composed the same-sex union ceremony that seems to parallel heterosexual marriage, but only discovered it, and felt it my duty as a historian to share it. In this connection I offer as a concluding observation that whatever significance the ceremony might (or might not) have for persons living at this juncture of history, its greatest importance lies, along with all the other forms of same-sex union known in premodern Europe, in its role in European history. It is not the province of the historian to direct the actions of future human beings, but only to reflect accurately on those of the past. "Humanity does not pass through phases as a train passes through stations: being alive, it has the privilege of always moving yet never leaving anything behind. Whatever we have been, in some sort we are still," observed C. S. Lewis in a related context. Recognizing that many—probably most—earlier Western societies institutionalized some form of romantic same-sex union gives us a much more accurate view of the immense variety of human romantic relationships and social responses to them than does the prudish pretense that such "unmentionable" things never happened.

JOHN BOSWELL
in *Same-Sex Unions in Premodern Europe* (1994)

Around this time the front door flew open and there stood two sky-blue grooms. They were surrounded by their ushers, the ruffians who were expressly forbidden to attend but, look at them, they'd really made an attempt at playing their parts. They'd unearthed their fathers' (or grandfathers') wedding costumes and stood pridefully erect in twisted cummerbunds, elephant bell-bottoms, and pleated shirts in apricot, lime, banana, and, of course, shocking pink.

The room fell utterly silent for longer than a moment, and then someone shouted either "Hurray!" or "Hurry!," I don't know which.

And then a big boom of music began. It took some time to adjust the volume, but in the interim the jolly drunken priest danced down an aisle he created himself by making high kicks, clicking his heels in the air, and swinging his arms above his red head.

Now I knew why everyone was so cooperative working all day in this house. They would be given the honor of dancing in a madhouse. It was worth the longish drive, the cutting-up of little things with scissors you were instructed to carry from home, the skinning of grapefruit sections, the hooking-up of light and sound systems, the endless destemming of the tarragon leaves for the minced chicken salad.

When the party seemed the least "real," a woman who'd hired a van to fill with out-of-season flowers at 8:30 a.m. in the Manhattan flower district and now stood with her residue—violets, tea roses, lilies of the valley laced around her like a perfumer's web—shouted, "THIS IS REAL!"

HARRY KONDOLEON
in *Diary of a Lost Boy* (1993)

**John Albert Manzon-Santos** (*left*), activist and writer, and
**B. Michael Hunter** (*right*), author and editor of *Sojourner: Black
Gay Voices in the Age of AIDS* (1993), New York, NY, 1994

**Blanche Wiesen Cook** (*left*), author, and **Clare Coss** (*right*), poet
and playwright, East Hampton, NY, 1987

**Mariana Romo-Carmona** (*left*), author, and **June Chan** (*right*),
activist, New York, NY, 1988

**James Broughton** (*left*) and **Joel Singer** (*right*), both poets and
filmmakers, New York, NY, 1988

## Shuffle Along

hooked up
to the same pole
i.v. garlands
of cytovene & pentamidine
unravel queer patterns
of a survival ritual
that strings us
thread-thin yet tight
as life-partners
trapped in this marathon
of disintegration

the rhythm mutates
like the noxious virus
inside collapsing veins
& atrophied muscles
blurry eyes swirl
round the dying room
dizzily we drag on
carry each other
through the 11th hour
clinging desperately
while time ticks

ASSOTTO SAINT
in *Wishing for Wings* (1994)

**Assotto Saint,** New York, NY, 1987

## Star Trek III

The fantasy spaceman
returning from death
greets his captain
gingerly: "Jim?"

Spock's Vulcan father explains
that only time will tell
if the priestess' magic
will bring him totally back.
Instead of "the end"
the film's last frames promise,
"the adventure continues."

I want to cry a little:
I grew up on these heroes—
to be as good as Kirk . . .

But life is a little closer now.
We watch the film together
and I explain the plot
the way one would talk to someone
trapped under ice. My manuals say
I mustn't convey anxiety.

I remember the day after
weeks at your beside when
you said my name finally.
You were IN there,
KNEW me.

The same shock the cardiac nurse
felt the year before when she
randomly took the tape from
your sweet eyes and they flew open
as she called your name.

We've been in a few
tight spots lately.

All these months.
My loneliness deepens.
I cry in private
when you forget my name.

Still, you love me clearly,
whoever I am.

The adventure continues.

RICHARD HARTEIS
in *Internal Geography* (1987)

## The Seasons' Difference

Here on the warm strand, where a turquoise light
without horizon combs and breaks, menacing
only as love or morning menace
the man-made errors of the world,
I receive a contrary vision:
For an instant I seem to stand alone
under a lead sky, in late afternoon,
in winter. The grey will thicken soon
to snow, and I desire this vision
as one desires his own smell and person.
The mind waiting for snow is the true mind.
Numb tongue and lips speak for it clumsily
but turquoise baubles cannot distract it for long.

Before the thick-lipped winter-thinker
in me can explain, you explain. *Both*,
you call from where the sheer ocean
shelves off from a man's height, *Both*,
with the impatience of summer
and whatever is always between us.
As if to show me how to take a season
on its own terms, you ride a glass sea-slide
into the foamy shallows where I stand,
grey and stubborn as a snow-man.

WILLIAM MEREDITH
in *Partial Accounts* (1987)

**William Meredith** (*left*) and **Richard Harteis** (*right*),
Uncasville, CT, 1993

## Translation

The words are these: queer, homo, *maricón*
In certain neighborhoods; in others, fag
Or faggot, fairy—queen when wearing drag—
Not to mention pansy, pussy, baton-
Twirler, and girl-in-your-dreams. Creative names,
But none describe us as we really are.
Take me, for instance. Married, in my heart;
A father, to my sister half my age
(But by imagination only). One
Forever unimaginable man,
A Catholic son to parents who are sad,
Or not, to see what cannot be undone:
Those pines we planted in their yard. They grow
Because they grow. My sister waters them.
The water seems like crying, now and then.
The water is our lives. It overflows.

## Sonnet for Our Son

Pretending fatherhood was simply sperm,
Biological concatenation,
And men and children holding hands, we hastened
To the task. Perhaps we wanted to ensure
That someone loved us at the end. Perhaps
We wanted children simply to defend
Whichever complicated arguments
They'd make to shock the world. Perhaps,
My son, we wanted naming privileges
Just once—to name you Jorge, Rafael,
The way we never really named ourselves.
We aren't ashamed. I can't explain the edge
Of people's understanding, why it stops
Where we begin. I can't explain the cliff
My dad once was, the razor Grandpa left.
Forgive us, but we love you very much.

RAFAEL CAMPO
in *The Other Man Was Me: A Voyage to the New World* (1994)

**Ruthann Robson,** Nyack, NY, 1992

When I was learning to read, it was that same smell of free-dom that intensified my hunger. Sitting on my mother's lap, I learned the skills which would make it possible for me to have a life different from hers. It was in a book where I first found out about women who loved each other. I like to imagine I was reading those books at the same time Cecile was sprawled in a windowseat reading *National Geographic* articles about women with dogsled teams.

For Cecile and me, learning to read allowed our world to be different from our mothers'. But now that Cecile and I are mothers, I find myself not wanting Colby's world to be different from ours.

I want to protect Colby from the *F*-word: father. I want to censor all those books with their perfect Daddy and Mommy dyads. I want to forbid all the fairy tales and leg-ends and myths full of insipid women who are either bad or beautiful, and boys who are either handsomely virtuous or stupidly ugly. Since he was born, Cecile has been reading to Colby and changing the words. Now we are teaching him to read. Soon, he is going to figure out that MOM cannot be spelled both M-O-M and D-A-D.

Our phone rings.

"Who is it?" Cecile asks.

"The school," I say, without moving. My ability to know who is on the phone without answering it used to spook Cecile. After all these years, she now merely thinks it is convenient.

"Should I answer it?" she asks.

"Go ahead."

The poor mother (it is never a darling daddy) unlucky enough to be on our branch of the phone tree soliciting items for the Co-op Free School garage sale finishes her spiel to Cecile.

"If we aren't good enough to be represented in family month, then I doubt our white elephants are good enough for the garage sale." Cecile slams down the phone.

"I hate the whole idea of families," I tell Cecile.

"We've had that discussion a thousand times," Cecile estimates.

In less than an hour, the phone rings again.

"It's the school," I say.

"Even *I* know that," Cecile says, picking up the receiver.

"We *did* tell you how upset we are." Cecile is telling the director.

"No, I don't expect you to read our minds. We told you this morning." Cecile is raising her voice.

"Another bulletin board sounds like a pretty token ges-ture." Cecile is pretending to be even-tempered.

"Well, we'll talk it over." Cecile hangs up.

"Talk what over?" I ask Cecile.

"Oh, that jerk thinks she can fix everything with a bulle-tin board filled with photographs from the kids' families. We should send a picture with him on Wednesday. The teacher will do a collage."

While Colby is in the bathtub, Cecile and I talk about victory and compromise, about consensus and politics, about when we were kids. About being different from other mothers because we are dykes, and being different from other dykes because we are mothers, and about being differ-ent from other dyke mothers because we are who we are and who we are means we are different even from each other.

After Cecile's anger has subsided and Colby is clean, she wants to compromise by sending an outrageous photograph of the three of us.

After Cecile's anger has subsided and Colby is clean, I want to pull Colby out of school for Family Month.

RUTHANN ROBSON
in *Cecile* (1991)

It was still early. I went out on the landing to watch the cars pass by, people from the nearby housing development on their way out to the new discount grocery, a few trucks with men coming home late from work, a bus from Bushy Creek Baptist with flat-faced children pressed against the windows staring at me hatefully. I glared back at them. Anger was like a steady drip of poison into my soul, teaching me to hate the ones that hated me. Who do they think they are? I whispered to myself. They piss honey? Shit morning-glory blossoms? Sit on their porches every Sunday morning and look down on the world with contempt?

"I hate them," I told Aunt Raylene when she came up behind me, waving at the bus as it passed. "Looking at us like we're something nasty."

Aunt Raylene was picking blackberry seeds out of her teeth, looking off into the distance, and she surprised me when she reached over and slapped my shoulder. "They look at you the way you look at them," she told me bluntly. "You don't know who those children are. Maybe they're nasty and silly and hateful. Maybe not. You don't know what happens to them when they go home. You don't know their daddies or mamas, who their people are, why they do things, or what they're scared of. You think because they wear different clothes than you and go by so fast, they're rich and cruel and thinking terrible things about you. Could be they're looking at you sitting up here eating blackberries and looking at them like they're spit on a stove— could be they're jealous of you, hungry for what you got, afraid of what you would do if they ever stepped in the yard."

She reached down and pulled her string bag from her pocket and began to roll a cigarette. "You're making up stories about those people. Make up a story where you have to live in their house, be one of their family, and pass by this road. Look at it from the other side for a while. Maybe you won't be glaring at people so much."

DOROTHY ALLISON
in *Bastard out of Carolina* (1992)

**Dorothy Allison** (*standing*) with Alix Layman and their son Wolf
Michael, Guerneville, CA, 1994

After taking a morning off work to see my lawyer, I come home, not caring if I call in. Not caring, for once, at the loss in pay. Not caring. My lawyer says there is nothing more we can do. I must wait. As if there has been something other than waiting. He has custody and calls the shots. We must wait and see how long it takes for him to get tired of being a mommy and a daddy. So, I wait.

I open the door to Patricia's room. Ellen and I keep it dusted and cleaned in case my baby will be allowed to visit us. The yellow and blue walls feel like a mockery. I walk to the windows, begin to systematically tear down the curtains. I slowly start to rip the cloth apart. I enjoy hearing the sounds of destruction. Faster, I tear the material into strips. What won't come apart with my hands, I pull at with my teeth. Looking for more to destroy, I gather the sheets and bedspread in my arms and wildly shred them to pieces. Grunting and sweating, I am pushed by rage and the searing wound in my soul. Like a wolf, caught in a trap, gnawing at her own leg to set herself free, I begin to beat my breasts to deaden the pain inside. A noise gathers in my throat and finds the way out. I begin a scream that turns to howling, then becomes hoarse choking. I want to take my fists, my strong fists, my brown fists, and smash the world until it bleeds. Bleeds! And all the judges in their flapping robes, and the fathers who look for revenge, are ground, ground into dust and disappear with the wind.

The word *lesbian*. Lesbian. The word that makes them panic, makes them afraid, makes them destroy children. The word that dares them. Lesbian. *I am one.* Even for Patricia, even for her, *I will not cease to be!* As I kneel amidst the colorful scraps, Raggedy Anns smiling up at me, my chest gives a sign. My heart slows to its normal speech. I feel the blood pumping outward to my veins, carrying nourishment and life. I strip the room naked. I close the door.

BETH BRANT (DEGONWADONTI)
IN *Mohawk Trail* (1985)

Settling for my left side, I curl into the configuration of Debra's back. She is twenty-four. I am forty. I know her only from my affinity group, but I like the independence of her ideas and the way her hair springs out frizzy from her head. Yesterday she was still undecided about doing civil disobedience. Her reasons: the job interview she had to get home for, fear of violence, and, after a pause, she confessed—her period. I wonder if the onlookers, who were here when two hundred fifty women went over the fence, realize that some of us have our periods, and worry that we will be arrested, detained for a long time, and handcuffed and without supplies, will begin to bleed through.

I think of the faces of the children who returned with their parents to watch us after the storm, the deep curiosity they displayed. I see the boy with sharp green eyes. Holding his father's hand, he shifted his glance from his father to me, then stayed with my eyes. I remembered myself, watching the civil rights movement on T.V.—mostly black kids not much older than I, sitting in at lunch counters and being dragged away, sometimes clubbed. My father, snorting, said, "Dumb kids, don't know enough to move when they're about to be clobbered." I said, "No, they know. They're choosing." I wanted to see the close ups. They kept showing the violence, the blood, but I wanted to see the faces, I wanted to see inside them. *How they knew who they were when others told them no.*

My dad, lurching drunk at the county fair, told us, "Come with me, the car's down here," as he pulled against the knowledge of three children, hands in a chain, all pulling the opposite direction, where we *knew* the car was parked. I tried to think it out—is it possible to believe him even though I am ninety-nine percent positive he is wrong? Who am I to stay with the ninety-nine? Maybe, for no good reason, he had someone move the car to the other end of the fairgrounds. And if I go along with him without believing, how will I be able to *be* when he finds out he's wrong? He'll say, "Get lost, scram, I'll meet you back at the car." Pretend it's a joke. I'll pick up the cue and make my disappearance.

Lies have always been deadening to me. When Suzanna was drinking too much, she wanted me to agree with her that she wasn't alcoholic, or at least to shut up about it, but the more I was silent, the less I was able to *be*. The less I was able to be, the more she was able to lie.

I remember the boy's eyes holding true on mine, his small hand enfolded by his father. He wanted to see inside me. He wanted to know how we knew who we were when others told us no.

MAUREEN BRADY
in *The Question She Put to Herself* (1987)

I stood on the sidewalk in front of City Hall in downtown Los Angeles on a warm April morning thinking of my father, who had been dead for a long time, and "Dragnet," his favorite TV series. City Hall was engraved on the badge that Sergeant Friday flashed weekly in his dour pursuit of law and order, and my father never missed a single episode. He was a big believer in law and order. "Dragnet" fueled his black-and-white vision of the world as consisting of humorless machos like Sergeant Friday and himself battling the forces of evil. In my father's expansive view this included most Anglos, all blacks, many Mexicans, priests, Jews, lawyers, doctors, people on welfare, the rich, and everyone under forty. He was a great and impartial hater; anyone different from him became an object of his contempt. Homosexuals, had he allowed that such creatures existed, would certainly have qualified.

As I started up the steps to City Hall I wondered whether my father would have hated me more because I was homosexual or a lawyer. Then I reminded myself that he had never needed a reason to hate me. It was enough that I was not him. For my own part, I no longer hated my father, though, admittedly, this had become easier after his death. Forgiveness was still a problem.

I took the steps too fast and stopped to catch my breath when I reached the top. I was forty, and I found myself thinking of my father more often now than in all the years since his death. He was ferociously alive in my memory where all the old battles still raged on. Sometimes I had to remind myself not only that he was dead, but that I had been there. He had died in a brightly lit hospital room, slapping away my consoling hand and screaming at my mother, "*Mas luz, mas luz.*" It had never been clear to me whether he was asking for more light, or crying out in fear at a light he perceived that the rest of us could not see. He had died with that mystery, as with so many others.

I entered the rotunda of City Hall, a grave, shadowy place, its walls made of great blocks of limestone. Three limp flags hung high above a circular floor of inlaid marble that depicted a Spanish galleon. Around the domed ceiling were eight figures in tile representing the attributes of municipal government: Public Service, Health, Trust, Art, Protection, Education, Law, and Government. I searched in vain for the other four: Expedience, Incompetence, Corruption, and Avarice. Undoubtedly I would encounter them in the hearing I was there to attend.

MICHAEL NAVA
in *The Hidden Law* (1992)

**Michael Nava,** Los Angeles, CA, 1988

## Our American Way of Life

Chapter Fifteen Our Flag What is this
This is the American Flag
As a new citizen you have a new country
You must pledge allegiance to a new Flag
Every American loves the Flag
There are thirteen stripes in red and white
Next to the staff is a blue field or union
filled with fifty five-pointed white stars
The stars represent a new constellation
Never allow them to touch the ground
Fly the Flag only from sunrise to sunset
Do not use it on handkerchiefs
or paper napkins Pledging Allegiance
Face the Flag Stand at attention
Put your right hand over your heart
A man should hold his hat in his right hand
Answer completely the questions below
Do you know these words Abjure Absolutely
Allegiance Fidelity Potentate Oath
Have you belonged to the Communist Party
Are you a gambler a polygamist
a foreign agent a criminal
Whom do you kiss Have you removed your hat
Fill in the blanks A _____ is a promise
One nation with liberty and _____ for all

SUZANNE GARDINIER
in *The New World* (1993)

**Suzanne Gardinier,** Sag Harbor, NY, 1994

Bicycling together through a midwestern midsummer's night to our village's only gay watering hole, Bob and I are stopped at a red light. A jalopy pulls alongside us in this deserted commercial district. The driver shouts, "Faggots!" He and his partner riding shotgun have all the traits of the classic queerbasher's profile. They are teenaged, bored, white, and male. As a death chill runs my spine, I think "This is it." But then, almost under his breath, the sidekick queries, "Are you motherfuckers gay?" A vertigo of relief doesn't stop a humorous defense from forming. I shape my lips to say, "Just exactly to the extent that we were motherfuckers, we wouldn't be gay, now, would we?" But the light changes—the car lurches, screeches, and rockets into the dark.

Although I have had scarier encounters with toughs, this one is the most haunting. America is at a loss for words when it comes to gays. As I have often recalled that encounter, I wonder what the real question was which lay behind the sidekick's stated one. For surely he wasn't asking for a confirmation of what his friend had had no problem perceiving—that we were in fact gay. I would like to think that the clarity of our love was the giveaway, but my hunch is that it was the leather vests. I now optimistically think that the sidekick in his own stumbling way was asking something like: "What is this gay stuff anyway? Fill me in." Or: "What is the social significance of being gay?" Or: "How am I to act toward you? Here is an opportunity for you to define

yourselves to me." If this reading is right, this book is written for him, his parents, his friends, and their relations. . . .

. . . perhaps paradoxically, in extending to gays the rights and benefits it has reserved for its dominant culture, America would confirm its deeply held vision of itself as a morally progressing nation, a nation itself advancing and serving as a beacon for others—especially with regard to human rights. The words with which our national pledge ends—"with liberty and justice for all"—are not a description of the present, but a call for the future. America is a nation given to a prophetic political rhetoric which acknowledges that morality is not arbitrary and that justice is not merely the expression of the current collective will. It is this vision that led the black civil rights movement to its successes. Those senators and representatives who opposed that movement and its centerpiece, the 1964 Civil Rights Act, on obscurantist grounds, but who lived long enough and were noble enough, came in time to express their heartfelt regret and shame at what they had done. It is to be hoped and someday to be expected that those who now grasp at anything to oppose the extension of that which is best about America to gays will one day feel the same.

RICHARD D. MOHR

in *A More Perfect Union: Why Straight America Must Stand Up for Gay Rights* (1994)

**Richard D. Mohr,** Urbana, IL, 1993

from *An Atlas of the Difficult World*

xi

A patriot is not a weapon. A patriot is one who wrestles for
      the soul of her country
as she wrestles for her own being, for the soul of his
      country
(gazing through the great circle at Window Rock into the
      sheen of the Viet Nam Wall)
as he wrestles for his own being. A patriot is a citizen
      trying to wake
from the burnt-out dream of innocence, the nightmare
of the white general and the Black general posed in their
      camouflage,
to remember her true country, remember his suffering
      land: remember
that blessing and cursing are born as twins and separated at
      birth to meet again in mourning
that the internal emigrant is the most homesick of all
      women and of all men
that every flag that flies today is a cry of pain.
         Where are we moored?
         What are the bindings?
         What behooves us?

xii

What homage will be paid to a beauty built to last
from inside out, executing the blueprints of resistance and
      mercy
drawn up in childhood, in that little girl, round-faced with
      clenched fists, already acquainted with
      mourning
in the creased snapshot you gave me? What homage will be
      paid to beauty
that insists on speaking truth, knows the two are not always
      the same,
beauty that won't deny, is itself an eye, will not rest under
      contemplation?
Those low long clouds we were driving under a month ago
      in New Mexico, clouds an arm's reach away
were beautiful and we spoke of it but I didn't speak then
of your beauty at the wheel beside me, dark head steady,
      eyes drinking the spaces
of crimson, indigo, Indian distance, Indian presence,
your spirit's gaze informing your body, impatient to mark
      what's possible, impatient to mark
what's lost, deliberately destroyed, can never any way be
      returned,
your back arched against all icons, simulations, dead letters
your woman's hands turning the wheel or working with
      shears, torque wrench, knives, with salt
      pork, onions, ink and fire
your providing sensate hands, your hands of oak and silk,
      of blackberry juice and drums
—I speak of them now.

(FOR M.)

ADRIENNE RICH
in *An Atlas of the Difficult World* (1991)

**Adrienne Rich,** Santa Cruz, CA, 1989

During the '90s and early part of the new century, queers, people of color, women made enormous advances until finally the U.S. elected the first black lesbian president of the U.S. This is where I need your help. We are no longer in this glamorous theatre. We are now at the Kennedy Center in Washington, D.C. It is the inaugural gala for the first black lesbian president of the U.S. She has appointed me performance art laureate of the nation. As you might imagine, I have accepted. But she has given me a very serious challenge. She has commissioned me to create a symphonic homoerotic performance art cantata that will exorcise homophobia and bigotry from our land. Basically she wants me to create a work that will, via a global satellite TV hookup, explain to the planet how fabulous it is when two men have sex together. The lesbian a capella group from Portland, Maine, will be doing the same for dyke/dyke sex during the second half of the program. I have been working with the L.A. Philharmonic for about two months in California and now here in Washington. There is tremendous excitement here tonight. AIDS activists from all over the country are here and both houses of Congress. I'm going to go put on my evening clothes. The lights in the Kennedy Center dim.

There is a buzz of anticipation in the hall. I step out onto the stage. There is immediately thunderous applause . . .

My conductor, Zubin Mehta, steps to the platform. We exchange a meaningful gesture. And I begin.

Good evening. As your performance art laureate, I welcome you to the inauguration of the first black lesbian president of the U.S. I offer this piece in memory of all our friends who have died of AIDS and in honor of the breath and pleasure that exists in everybody here tonight.

Music, Maestro Zubin. (*The music comes up. Yes. It's the BOLERO . . .* )

TIM MILLER
in *My Queer Body*, a performance work (1994)

**Tim Miller** (*right*) and novelist **Douglas Sadownick** (*left*), Venice, CA, 1994

**Prior**   This angel. She's my favorite angel.

I like them best when they're statuary. They commemorate death but they suggest a world without dying. They are made of the heaviest things on earth, stone and iron, they weigh tons but they're winged, they are engines and instruments of flight.

This is the angel Bethesda. Louis will tell you her story.

**Louis**   Oh. Um, well, she was this angel, she landed in the Temple square in Jerusalem, in the days of the Second Temple, right in the middle of a working day she descended and just her foot touched earth. And where it did, a fountain shot up from the ground.

When the Romans destroyed the Temple, the fountain of Bethesda ran dry.

**Prior**   And Belize will tell you about the nature of the fountain, before its flowing stopped.

**Belize**   If anyone who was suffering, in the body or the spirit, walked through the waters of the fountain of Bethesda, they would be healed, washed clean of pain.

**Prior**   They know this because I've told them, many times. Hannah here told it to me. She also told me this:

**Hannah**   When the Millennium comes . . .

**Prior**   Not the year two thousand, but the Capital M Millennium . . .

**Hannah**   Right. The fountain of Bethesda will flow again. And I told him I would personally take him there to bathe. We will all bathe ourselves clean.

**Louis**   Not literally in Jerusalem, I mean we don't want this to have sort of Zionist implications.

**Belize**   Right on.

**Louis**   But on the other hand we *do* recognize the right of the state of Israel to exist.

**Belize**   But the West Bank should be a homeland for the Palestinians, and the Gaza Strip . . .

**Louis**   Well not *both* the Gaza Strip and the West Bank, I mean no one supports Palestinian rights more than I do but . . .

**Belize**   Oh yeah right, Louis, like not even the Palestinians are more devoted than . . .

**Prior**   I'm almost done.

The fountain's not flowing now, they turn it off in the winter, ice in the pipes. But in the summer it's a sight to see. I want to be around to see it. I plan to be. I hope to be.

This disease will be the end of many of us, but not nearly all, and the dead will be commemorated and will struggle on with the living, and we are not going away. We won't die secret deaths anymore. The world only spins forward. We will be citizens. The time has come.

Bye now.

You are fabulous creatures, each and every one.

And I bless you: *More Life*.

The Great Work Begins.

TONY KUSHNER

in *Angels in America: A Gay Fantasia on National Themes, Part Two: Perestroika* (1992)

"Whereupon the Virgin, Daisy, begins to twirl the balls on her fingertips, faster and faster. And the sun is now her nimbus, and now all we see are three furious balls of red, their center a cone of blue. Then the balls fly from her hands. Over the falls, down into water, weightless, buoyed up by the spume."

"Rose and Rose-lima, by now, have drowned in their own blood. I didn't expect that," said Flynn.

"No! Listen to me, Flynn—you are looking for more than you're given to see. All you see is light, water, blood."

"They crash against the rocks. Glass flies like glitter in all directions. There is no difference now between glass and water; and water has become a river of blood. Those on shore leap—they dive like the famous Esther Williams—and swim to Rose and Rose-lima. Using all their arms, they lift us up."

"Everyone ascends into Heaven then."

"There are a few details to be ironed out."

"But the ending?" Flynn asked. Since Lydia Somerleyton there was nothing more interesting to her than endings. But the brain, she recalled, was sometimes the heaviest part of the body. If you lay unconscious—perhaps dead drunk—perhaps hit on the back of the skull with a hammer—and someone came along to pick you up, that person would have to lift the head first. Take care of the brain, and the rest takes care of itself—flesh, the ball-and-chain comes tumbling after. Isn't that what she had done?

"It ends with Justice being done," said Rose.

"Isn't that nice?" said Rose-lima.

But Flynn was silent, half-asleep in the cold. As her eyelids closed, the stage beyond the open doors narrowed, darkened; lights burned out, the farce complete; mistaken identity unmasked; true lovers united. Pure and simple Justice accomplished, as if she had every right to expect such a thing.

BERTHA HARRIS
in *Lover* (1976)

**Bertha Harris** (*left*), **Franklin Philip** (*center*) , and **Harlan Lane** (*right*), Boston, MA, 1993

My name is Laurent Clerc. I am eighty-three years old. My hair is white, my skin wrinkled and scarred, my posture crooked; I shuffle when I walk. Undoubtedly my life will soon end in this time and place: 1869, Hartford, Connecticut. I spend most of my day sitting alone at my dining room window, looking at my orchard and remembering. I also read the paper and occasionally friends come to visit. I know what's going on. Important people, distinguished gentlemen, are repudiating the cause to which I have devoted my life. Endowed with the sacred trust of my people's welfare, they seek, without consulting us, to prevent our worship, marriage, and procreation, to stultify our education, and to banish our mother tongue simply because our way and our language are different from theirs. As I write, America licks its nearly fatal wounds; the enslavement of colored people has been ended, and the Union has begun the Reconstruction. Yet how should we rejoice who remain imperiled? The disease of intolerance itself is unchecked and threatens to invade other limbs of the body politic.

Every creature, every work of God, is admirably made; perhaps what we find faulty in its kind turns to our advantage without our knowing it. One day the sun shines on my orchard, another it does not. The orchard has fruitful trees and unfruitful; even in the same species there are different varieties—everything is variable and inconstant. And we ourselves: we vary in our forms and functions, in our hearts and minds. I do not know, as you do not know, why this should be so. We can only thank God for the rich diversity of His creation and hope that in the future world the reason for it may be explained to us all.

Meanwhile—language must come once again to my aid. It has always been my weapon to fight evil, my vessel to fill minds thirsting for knowledge, my lure to solicit relief.* It must serve me grandly one last time and cast such a brilliant light on the history of present injustices that their perpetrators will cringe and their victims rally.

I am impelled by the present threat to the well-being, dignity, and freedom of my people to tell our story.

HARLAN LANE
in *When the Mind Hears: A History of the Deaf* (1984)

Censorship has always been more problem than solution. It purges society of books, movies, and music, leaving hate, racism, sexism, drug abuse, poverty, and violence flourishing as they did before the printing press and movie camera. It flatters the nation into thinking it has done something to better life while it ignores what might be done.

MARCIA PALLY
in *Sex and Sensibility: Reflections on Forbidden Mirrors and the Will to Censor* (1994)

*Aid for the deaf.

**Marcia Pally,** New York, NY, 1988

The walls of the closet—cultural invisibility and erasure—have tended to dull the resonances between works of lesbian literature: to obscure the tradition. As Eliot remarked, "No poet, no artist of any art, has [her] complete meaning alone." Any literary tradition grows in subtlety and complexity as text answers and elaborates on text, author on author, generation after generation, over time. By this process writers give their people back a deepened sense of reality, a survival tool if there ever was one. In a tradition, the individual author feels less desperate and responsible for saying it all, getting it right. As Gates quotes Ralph Ellison on the work of Richard Wright, "I had no need to attack what I considered the limitations of Wright's vision, because I was quite impressed by what he had achieved. . . . Still, I would write my own books."

"Who will find me buried under the days?" Angelina Weld Grimké had asked. A tradition unburies people, provides context, so no author or work ends up lonesome with the lonesomeness of McCullers' Frankie Addams sitting in her kitchen miserable all summer, longing to be straight and so denying the importance of the company she already had—her little faggot cousin and her Black woman friend, both of whom gave her love and support—"that we of her and John Henry and Berenice . . . the last we in the world she wanted." Here at the end, I have to believe in the irony of McCullers' words, in their signifying to me over the years that there is company for people who grow up and decide to be themselves, there is a tradition that does not escape from eccentricity. An eccentricity of traditions—of freaks and queers and survivors, of Black people and white trash and Jews—fugitives making themselves a home; their traditions as their *we* of *me.*

MAB SEGREST
in *My Mama's Dead Squirrel: Lesbian Essays in Southern Culture* (1985)

**Mab Segrest** (*right*) and family, North Carolina, 1991

## The Winners and the Losers

I stood before them
and told them of my life,
the sorrows and the losses—
in short, the human condition.

I could see them all, so young,
hair shiny, with their lives before them—
they were looking on me as a loser,

and had no pity,
so determined were they
to make it big, to be winners.

Even the clerk in the social security office
looked at me with wonder and asked:
Have you always earned so little?

I had never thought of it that way—
to her too I was a loser
with bad luck written all over my tax records.

What happened to the beautiful losers of my youth
who let the world destroy them
but stayed true to their dream,

scoffed at materialism, conventions,
a small, beleagured band
who kept their integrity against the world
and devoted their lives
to Art, Sex, and Revolution?

Youth once believed in them,
the madmen who burned themselves out with drugs and
    drink,
disappeared into the desert
or battered society with their shaggy heads.

There was one period even
when everybody was rushing off
in search of the underground man.

But now that winners are in fashion,
disappearing are the last of the bohemians
left over from the old days of the Village,

and I am of another era, like the grizzled poet
who slept in Village doorways
and showed up at the Poetry Society
with his life work in a shopping bag

and read his poem "Crows":
Caw, caw, he cried, as he jumped
off a table, flapping his arms.

EDWARD FIELD
in *Counting Myself Lucky: Selected Poems 1963–1992* (1992)

**Edward Field**, New York, NY, 1987

# Some Like Indians Endure

i have it in my mind that
dykes are indians

they're a lot like indians
they used to live as tribes
they owned tribal land
it was called the earth

they were massacred
lots of times
they always came back
like the grass
like the clouds
they got massacred again

they thought caringsharing
about the earth and each other
was a good thing
they rode horses
and sang to the moon

but i don't know
about what was so longago
and it's now that dykes
make me think i'm with indians
when i'm with dykes
because they bear
witness bitterly
because they reach
and hold
because they live every day
with despair laughing
in cities and country places
because earth hides them
because they know
the moon

because they gather together
enclosing
and spit in the eye of death

indian is an idea
some people have
of themselves
dyke is an idea some women
have of themselves
the place where we live now
is idea
because whiteman took
all the rest
because father
took all the rest
but the idea which
once you have it
you can't be taken
for somebody else
and have nowhere to go
like indians you can be
stubborn

the idea might move you on,
ponydrag behind
taking all your loves and
children maybe downstream
maybe beyond the cliffs
but it hangs in there
an idea
like indians
endures

it might even take your
whole village with it
stone by stone
or leave the stones
and find more

to build another village
someplace else

like indians
dykes have fewer and fewer
someplace elses to go
so it gets important
to know
about ideas and
to remember or uncover
the past
and how the people
traveled
all the while remembering
the idea they had
about who they were
indians, like dykes
do it all the time

dykes know all about dying
and that everything belongs
to the wind
like indians
they do terrible things
to each other
out of sheer cussedness
out of forgetting
out of despair

so dykes
are like indians
because everybody is related
to everybody
in pain
in terror
in guilt
in blood
in shame

in disappearance
that never quite manages
to be disappeared
we never go away
even if we're always
leaving

because the only home
is each other
they've occupied all
the rest
colonized it; an
idea about ourselves is all
we own
and dykes remind me of indians
like indians dykes
are supposed to die out
or forget
or drink all the time
or shatter
go away
to nowhere
to remember what will happen
if they don't

they don't anyway—even
though the worst happens
they remember and they
stay
because the moon remembers
because so does the sun
because the stars
remember
and the persistent stubborn grass
of the earth

PAULA GUNN ALLEN
(Laguna Pueblo/Sioux)

**Paula Gunn Allen,** Oakland, CA, 1988

We stepped into the water together while Bobby was getting out of his jeans. The first impression was of warmth—an inch of temperate water floated on the surface. But when we penetrated that, the water beneath was numbingly cold.

"Oh," Erich exclaimed as it lapped his ankles.

"Maybe this isn't a very good idea after all," I said. "I mean, it can't be good for you."

"No," he said. "Let's just go a little ways in. I want to—well, I just want to."

"All right," I said. I was still holding his hand. For the first time I felt intimate with him, though we had known one another for years and had made love hundreds of times. We shuffled ahead, taking tiny steps on the sandy bottom. Each new quarter-inch of flesh exposed to water was agony. The sand itself felt like granular ice under our feet.

Bobby splashed out to us. "Crazy," he said. "Goddamn crazy. Erich, you got two minutes in here, and then I'm taking you out."

He meant it. He would lift Erich bodily and carry him to shore if necessary. Since he and I were boys together, he had made it his business to rescue fools from icy water.

Still, we had two minutes, and we advanced. The water was clear—nets of light fluttered across our bare feet, and minnows darted away from us, visible only by their shadows skimming along the bottom. I glanced at Bobby, who was grave and steady as a steamship. He was a reverse image of Erich; time had thickened him. His belly was broad and protuberant now, and his little copper-colored medallion of pectoral hair had darkened and spread, sending tendrils up onto his shoulders and down along his back. I myself was losing hair—my hairline was at least two inches higher than it had been ten years ago. I could feel with my fingertips a rough circle at the back of my head where the growth was thinner.

"This is good," Erich said. "I mean, well, it feels very good."

It didn't feel good. It was torture. But I thought I understood—it was a strong sensation, one that came from the outer world rather than the inner. He was saying goodbye to a certain kind of pain.

"You're shivering," Bobby said.

"One more minute. Then we'll go in."

"Right. One more minute, exactly."

We stood in the water together, watching the unbroken line of trees on the opposite bank. That was all that happened. Bobby and I took Erich for what would in fact turn out to be his last swim, and waded in only to our knees. But as I stood in the water, something happened to me. I don't know if I can explain this. Something cracked. I had lived until then for the future, in a state of continuing expectation, and the process came suddenly to a stop while I stood nude with Bobby and Erich in a shallow platter of freezing water. My father was dead and I myself might very well be dying. My mother had a new haircut, a business and a young lover; a new life that suited her better than her old one had. I had not fathered a child but I loved one as if I was her father—I knew what that was like. I wouldn't say I was happy. I was nothing so simple as happy. I was merely present, perhaps for the first time in my adult life. The moment was unextraordinary. But I had the moment, I had it completely. It inhabited me. I realized that if I died soon I would have known this, a connection with my life, its errors and cockeyed successes. The chance to be one of three naked men standing in a small body of clear water. I would not die unfulfilled because I'd been here, right here and nowhere else. I didn't speak. Bobby announced that the minute was up, and we took Erich back to shore.

MICHAEL CUNNINGHAM

in *A Home at the End of the World* (1990)

**Michael Cunningham**, New York, NY, 1991

# I Met My Solitude

I met my Solitude. We two stood glaring.
I had to tremble, meeting her face to face.
Then she saying, and I with bent head hearing:
"You sent me forth to exile and disgrace,

"Most faithful of your friends, then most forsaken,
Forgotten in breast, in bath, in books, in bed.
To someone else you gave the gifts I gave you,
And you embraced another in my stead.

"Though we meet now, it is not of your choosing.
I am not fooled. And I do not forgive.
I am less kind, but did you treat me kindly?
In armored peace from now on let us live."

So did my poor hurt Solitude accuse me.
Little was left of good between us two.

And I drew back: "How can we stay together,
You jealous of me, and I laid waste by you?

"By you, who used to be my good provider,
My secret nourisher, and mine alone.
The strength you taught me I must use against you,
And now with all my strength I wish you gone."

Then she, my enemy, and still my angel,
Said in that harsh voice that once was sweet:
"I will come back, and every time less handsome,
And I will look like Death when last we meet."

NAOMI REPLANSKY
in *The Dangerous World: New and Selected Poems, 1934–1994*
(1994)

**Naomi Replansky,** New York, NY, 1995

## Becoming a Meadow

A bookstore in a seaside town,
the beginning of February, off season,
and snow outside the book-filled glass hurries down

and turns in whorls above the frozen
street, blurring the boarded storefronts (taffy, souvenirs),
tattooing the water with the storm's million

fingerprints. Gusts billow over the empty pier.
Someone comes in and the bell on the shop door rings;
then the words I hear in my head, from nowhere,

are *becoming a meadow*. Why does that jangling
shopkeeper's music translate itself to that phrase?
Yesterday morning we walked a beach where the tide
    angled

and broke in beautiful loops, the waves'
endless rows of bold cursive
one atop the other, scrawling an exercise page

of *O*s in a copybook the world's never tired of.
A place called Head of the Meadow.
I don't know how to say how perfect it was,

though it was only a short walk; the morning was cold,
we hadn't brought enough to wear.
For weeks I've been turning over and over

one barely articulated question; here,
among the cultivated disorder of the book-rows,
the words present themselves as a sort of answer:

a meadow accepts itself as various, allows
some parts of itself to always be going away,
because whatever happens in that blown,

ragged field of grass and sway
*is* the meadow, and threading the frost
of its unlikely brilliance yesterday

we also were the meadow. In the bookstore
while you are reading and I am allowing myself
simply to be comforted by the presence of stories,

the bound, steady presences on the shelves,
fixed as nothing else is, I am thinking of my terror
of decay, the little hell opening in every violated cell,

the virus tearing
away—is it?—and we are still a part of the meadow
because I am thinking of it, hearing

the bell-phrase of it: Head of the Meadow
in my head. The titles of the books,
the letters of the writers' names blow

like grasses, become individual stalks,
seedheads, burrs, rimed swell
of dune on which the beachgrass is writing its book

in characters unreadable or read:
the meadow-book
you are writing, and which you read.

And then the whole place, the narrow aisles and stacks,
is one undulant, salt-swollen meadow of water,
one filling and emptying wave, spilling and pulling back,

and everything waves are: dissolving, faster,
only to swell again, like the baskets of bread
and fish in the story, the miracle baskets.

And if one wave breaking says
*You're dying*, then the rhythm and shift of the whole
says nothing about endings, and half the shawling head

of each wave's spume pours into the trough
of the one before,
and half blows away in spray, backward, toward the
    open sea.

**MARK DOTY**
in *My Alexandria* (1993)

**Mark Doty,** Provincetown, MA, 1992

I begin to have intimations, now, of a return to some deep self that has been too absorbed and too battered to function for a long time. That self tells me that I was meant to live alone, meant to write the poems for others—poems that seldom in my life have reached the one person for whom they were intended.

Yesterday I got the manuscript of *A Durable Fire* off to Norton. When I began writing those poems I had had the dream that I would celebrate my sixtieth birthday with a book of joys, a book speaking of fulfillment and happiness. But on the final re-reading I saw clearly that it is an elegiac book and that the seeds of parting were in it from the beginning. This is where poetry is so mysterious, the work more mature than the writer of it, always the messenger of growth. So perhaps we write toward what we will become from where we are. The book is less and more than I had imagined it might be. But it could not have been written without all that X gave me, nor, for that matter, without what was lacking between us.

This is the first "Nelson day" for weeks, a day when I can stay home, work at my desk in peace, no appointment looming ahead, a day when I can rest after work, and garden in the afternoon. Once more the house and I are alone.

MAY SARTON
in *Journal of a Solitude* (1977)

**May Sarton,** York, ME, 1994

I am the storyteller now.

I spread open my hands, to tell them to sit. Larry, the smartest of them, the widest-eyed, grins. "Tell us that Keller story again. The Death of Donna-May Dean."

But I defer. Because Keller was right about this, as about so much else: the best stories, the ones we always want to hear, are bad for us. "No," I say to Larry. "Listen . . ." Then I shut my eyes, and am quiet for a long time. But smiling, like a man who knew a joke once, but does not remember the punch line: he waits. It will come. "I want us to make up a new story to tell," I whisper. "Where nobody has to die at the end."

My minions giggle, but they do not leave me. We sit here. We are waiting. It will come.

JOEY MANLEY
in the Epilogue to *The Death of Donna-May Dean* (1991)

Narratives chronicle the passing of time. They are built on the tensions between stasis and change, sameness and difference, tensions that we learn in our bodies long before language becomes a primary way of knowing. Narrative is the final transformation of rhythms that have their origin in body time. It is a writing out of the body, a writing into life. I want to be assured that those whom I have loved and cared for are inscribed in the book of life.

JONATHAN G. SILIN
in *Sex, Death, and the Education of Children* (1995)

## Acknowledgments

I wish to express my indebtedness to three public libraries.

The first is the Hartford Public Library of my childhood, both the preternaturally musty main building that was joined to the Wadsworth Atheneum and the more modestly scaled Broad Street Branch. It was at this latter, circa 1954, that the librarian found himself amused, affected, and a bit incredulous when a ninth-grader came to his desk to check out *The Turn of the Screw* and a book of Faulkner short stories. After some conversation and with cautious enthusiasm, he suggested that I might find *Women in Love* and Edmund Wilson's *The Wound and the Bow* of interest. I don't think he got to recommend those titles to young readers very often.

Second, I am grateful to the New York Public Library and, most particularly, to photography curator Julia Van-Haaften. It was her idea, when in 1990 I first approached the Library about exhibiting my work, that the Wallach Division begin to collect this archive. I thank photographer Bruce Cratsley for suggesting that I contact her and all those donors who made it possible for the Library to acquire copies of many of these portraits.

Third, my thanks to the staff of the Amagansett Free Library in my present hometown for obtaining from the county-wide system the many books I needed to assemble the present volume.

I extend my appreciation to all those who at some critical juncture offered practical, moral, or financial encouragement for this undertaking. Among these I should like to single out the following: Gregory Kolovakos; Carlos Gutierrez-Solana; Sherry Cohen at the Fund for Human Dignity; fellow artists and writers Joyce Culver, Allen Ellenzweig, Muriel Dimen, James Haigney, John Haigney, Phyllis Hirschberg, Jane Kogan, and Toba Tucker; Diana Lindley; Christianne Drabbe-Mbou; Pat Tuccio and Diane

Vahradian; Irma Brownfield and Fredrik Rostock; Tim Williams; Vance Martin; George Stambolian and Michael Hampton and Carlos Sandoval; Michael Piore; Deborah Ann Light; Robert and Joyce Menschel and the Horace W. Goldsmith Foundation; Flavia Robinson and the Daniele Agostino Foundation; the Posner-Wallace Foundation; Jeff Hoone and the Light Work Endowment for Mid-Career Artists; the New York State Council on the Arts; and the New York Foundation for the Arts/East End Arts Council in Riverhead, New York for their Special Opportunity Stipends.

I should like to acknowledge as well the many good people who provided me with books, food, transportation, and a place to stay when I was on the road for this work and, most particularly, the repeated "artist's residencies" with Stephen Shirreffs and Ian Mackenzie in San Francisco, Vicki Goddard in Los Angeles, Michael Piore and Rodney Yoder in Boston, and Chris Soller in Washington, D.C. Indispensable too were those individuals who guided me across the gay/lesbian literary map of a particular place— John Mitzel and poet Rudy Kikel in Boston, Richard Labonté at Different Light Bookstore in Los Angeles, Rebecca Ranson at SAME (Southeastern Arts, Media, and Education Project) in Atlanta, Alan G. Robinson at Faubourg-Marigny Bookstore in New Orleans, and Phil Willkie at *The James White Review* in Minneapolis. Over the years, periodic conversations with Joan Nestle and Christopher Bram on the subjects of lesbian and gay writing have sustained and informed me. I thank author Dolores Klaich for presenting me with my first lesbian reading list and sitting for my first portrait of a lesbian writer.

I wish to single out as well author Patrick Merla for being the first to purchase a portrait from this series (that of critic David Kalstone, generously enough for a friend) and

artist Jennifer Cross for being the first to exhibit the work—in 1988 at The East Hampton Center for Contemporary Art.

Needless to say, there would be no record of this nature without the cooperation of the many writers whom I have photographed for the project, both those who appear in these pages and, since this is a selection from more than three times as many portraits, those who do not.

It was photographer and writer Carole Gallagher who so generously guided me to The MIT Press and to her own editor there, Roger Conover. I thank Roger for persistently prodding me to shape a part of my record into book form. I am indebted to him and his acquisitions assistants Daniele Levine and Julie Grimaldi for walking me through the necessary steps. Thanks too to Katherine Arnoldi for a careful reading of the manuscript and to Jean Wilcox for a highly effective design.

Deepest gratitude I reserve for close personal friends of long standing, especially Bill Burns, George Mitchell, Charles Phillips, and Arlene and Barry Klingman, who over the years have cheerfully tolerated and even encouraged my impractical decision to become an artist.

Finally, I dedicate this book to Jonathan Silin, my partner of a quarter century.

## Source Notes

**Jim Kepner**  From *Sex, Death, and the Education of Children: Our Passion for Ignorance in the Age of AIDS* by Jonathan G. Silin. New York: Teachers College Press, 1995. © 1995 by Teachers College, Columbia University. Reprinted by permission of Teachers College Press.

**Joan Nestle**  From *A Restricted Country* by Joan Nestle. Ithaca, NY: Firebrand Books, 1987. © 1987 by Joan Nestle. Reprinted by permission of Firebrand Books.

**Harry Hay with John Burnside**  From *Gay American History* by Jonathan Ned Katz. New York: Thomas Y. Crowell Company, 1976. New York: New American Library, 1992. © 1972 by Jonathan Ned Katz. Reprinted by permission of the author.

**Del Martin and Phyllis Lyon**  From *Lesbian/Woman* by Del Martin and Phyllis Lyon. Volcano, CA: The Volcano Press, 1991. © 1972, 1983, 1991 (updated) by Del Martin and Phyllis Lyon. Reprinted by permission of the authors and Volcano Press.

**Samuel M. Steward**  From *Chapters from an Autobiography* by Samuel M. Steward. San Francisco: Grey Fox Press, 1981. © 1980, 1981 by Samuel M. Steward. Reprinted by permission of Grey Fox Press.

**Barbara Grier and Donna McBride**  From the Afterword by Barbara Grier to *Sex Variant Women in Literature* by Jeannette H. Foster. Tallahassee, FL: The Naiad Press. © 1956 by Jeannette H. Foster. © 1975, 1985 by Barbara Grier. Reprinted by permission of The Naiad Press.

**Adrienne Rich** The lines from "An Atlas of the Difficult World," from *An Atlas of the Difficult World: Poems 1988–1991* by Adrienne Rich. New York: W.W. Norton, 1991. © 1991 by Adrienne Rich. Reprinted by permission of the author and W.W. Norton and Company, Inc.

**Tim Miller and Douglas Sadownick** From *My Queer Body* by Tim Miller, as published in *Sharing the Delerium: Second Generation AIDS Plays and Performances,* Therese Jones, editor. Portsmouth, NH: Heineman, 1994. © 1994 by Tim Miller. Reprinted by permission of the author.

**Tony Kushner** From *Angels in America, Part Two: Perestroika* by Tony Kushner. New York: Theatre Communications Group, 1994. © 1992 and 1994 by Tony Kushner. Reprinted by permission of the author and Theatre Communications Group.

**Bertha Harris, Franklin Philip, and Harlan Lane** From *Lover* by Bertha Harris. New York: Daughters Publishing, 1976. New York: New York University Press, 1993. © 1976 and 1993 by Bertha Harris. Reprinted by permission of the author and New York University Press. From *When the Mind Hears: A History of the Deaf* by Harlan Lane. New York: Random House, 1984. © 1984 by Harlan Lane. Reprinted by permission of Random House, Inc.

**Marcia Pally** From *Sex and Sensibility: Reflections on Forbidden Mirrors and the Will to Censor* by Marcia Pally. Hopewell, NJ: The Ecco Press, 1994. © 1994 by Marcia Pally. Reprinted by permission of The Ecco Press.

**Mab Segrest and Family** From "Lines I Dare" in *My Mama's Dead Squirrel: Lesbian Essays in Southern Culture* by Mab Segrest. Ithaca, NY: Firebrand Books, 1985. © 1985 by Mab Segrest. Reprinted by permission of Firebrand Books.

**Edward Field** "The Winners and the Losers" from *Counting Myself Lucky: Selected Poems 1963–1992* by Edward Field. Santa Rosa, CA: Black Sparrow Press, 1992. © 1992 by Edward Field. Reprinted by permission of Black Sparrow Press.

**Paula Gunn Allen** "Some Like Indians Endure" by Paula Gunn Allen. Published in *Living the Spirit: A Gay American Indian Anthology,* Will Roscoe, editor (New York: St. Martin's Press, 1988). © 1988 by Paula Gunn Allen. Reprinted by permission of the author.

**Michael Cunningham** From *A Home at the End of the World* by Michael Cunningham. New York: Farrar, Straus and Giroux, 1990. © 1990 by Michael Cunningham. Reprinted by permission of Farrar, Straus and Giroux, Inc.

**Naomi Replansky** "I Met My Solitude" from *The Dangerous World: New and Selected Poems, 1934–1994* by Naomi Replansky. Chicago: Another Chicago Press, 1994. © 1994 by Naomi Replansky. Reprinted by permission of the author.

**Mark Doty** "Becoming a Meadow" from *My Alexandria* by Mark Doty. Champaign, IL: The University of Illinois Press, 1993. © 1993 by Mark Doty. Reprinted by permission of The University of Illinois Press.

**May Sarton** From *Journal of a Solitude* by May Sarton. New York: W.W. Norton, 1973. © 1973 by May Sarton. Reprinted by permission of W.W. Norton and Company, Inc.